Collective Action

Collective Action

Theory and Applications

Todd Sandler

Ann Arbor

THE UNIVERSITY OF MICHIGAN PRESS

2002   2001   2000   1999   6   5   4   3

Library of Congress Cataloging-in-Publication Data

Sandler, Todd.
    Collective action : theory and applications / Todd Sandler.
       p.   cm.
    Includes bibliographical references (p.   ) and index.
    ISBN 0-472-09501-3 (alk. paper). — ISBN 0-472-06501-7 (pa. alk.
paper)
    1. Public goods.   2. Social choice.   3. Pressure groups.
4. Decision-making.   I. Title.
HB846.5.S24   1992
338.9—dc20
                                                        92-18908
                                                        CIP

To Tristan Jon

Foreword

Mancur Olson

Though most scholarly and scientific publications are pertinent only to researchers in a single specialty, this book by Todd Sandler should be significant for economists in many different specialties, for serious students of the other social sciences, for applied game theorists, and for reading assignments in diverse courses. Perhaps I can, using the license usually allowed in a foreword, make the exceptionally wide relevance of this book apparent by setting out two "laws" or aphorisms that, in an evocative way, subsume a large part of economics and, indeed, all social sciences.

The first law is that "sometimes, when each individual considers only his or her interests, a collectively rational outcome emerges automatically"—the famous invisible hand coordinates the self-regarding efforts of the individuals involved and ensures an outcome that is socially efficient (in the familiar Paretian sense that no one could be made better off without someone else being made worse off). The second law is that "sometimes, the first law does not hold: no matter how intelligently each individual pursues his or her interest, no socially rational outcome can emerge spontaneously"—only a guiding hand or appropriate institution can bring about outcomes that are collectively efficient. These two aphorisms have a most serious and general purpose: almost all of economics and social science falls under one or the other of them.

Todd Sandler is not guilty of writing so brashly as I just have about "laws," but he has put forth what I call the second law in a most cautious and understated way: as he puts it in this book, "individual rationality is not sufficient for collective rationality." His book deals with the whole domain of this proposition—and that is why it is relevant, not only to economists in many different specialties, but also to serious readers in other social sciences and to many students of game theory and of environmental problems as well.

The author acknowledges the support of his project on Institutional Reform and the Informal Sector (IRIS), funded by the U.S. Agency for International Development, for his work on this foreword, but he is solely responsible for all of its shortcomings.

Since individual rationality is not sufficient for group rationality, there is no reason to suppose that a group of individuals will act in their common interest. The aggregate gains to a group from collective action could greatly exceed the total costs of that action, but it by no means follows from this that the collective action would occur, no matter how rational and intelligent the individuals in that group might be. Admittedly, there are groups whose size, circumstances, or institutional arrangements establish a presumption that they will normally act in their common interest. But there are many other cases— both important and commonplace—where we can be confident that groups will undertake little or no collective action even when the net gains to the group from doing so would be immense.

What keeps groups of rational individuals from acting rationally in their collective interest? The most notable thing that prevents this is that, in many situations, the benefits of any collective action go to every individual in some group, whether or not the individual made any contribution to the costs of collective action. In other words, the benefits of collective action are normally indivisible in the sense that, if they are made available to one person in a group they are thereby automatically also supplied to everyone in the group. As is by now widely known, nonpurchasers cannot be excluded from the consumption of the "collective goods" or "public goods" that collective action provides.

It is not only those services that governments have traditionally provided, such as pollution abatement, flood control, law and order, and defense, that are collective goods, but also the services provided by any nongovernmental or private association or informal group that seeks to achieve a common purpose. Whenever neighbors seek to beautify their neighborhood, or a trade association lobbies for a tariff to increase the profits of the firms in its industry, or a collusion or cartel seeks higher prices or wages in some market by restricting the supply, or a group of countries seeks to deal with a common enemy through a defense alliance or a transnational environmental problem through an international organization, it is a collective good that is being sought. Whether we are considering collective action that everyone agrees is needed for a socially rational outcome, such as flood control or the prevention of contagious disease, or whether we are thinking of a cartel or lobby that is seeking monopoly prices or special-interest legislation that is inconsistent with a rational allocation of resources for the larger society, it remains true that the benefits of any collective action go to everyone in the relevant group, industry, country, or category, whether or not they contributed to the cost of the collective action.

Since the benefits of any collective action go to every individual in a group whether or not that individual has borne any of the costs of the collective action, it follows that, unless the group is small or meets certain other special conditions, the collective good will *not* be provided through market mechanisms or other straightforward and voluntary arrangements. Just as governments require compulsory taxation to finance public goods, so large, nongovernmental organizations providing collective goods need special arrangements or "selective incentives" to support themselves. The "closed" or "union" shop commonly used by most labor organizations is only the most conspicuous and best-known example of a wide array of special (and subtle) arrangements that account for most of the membership of large organizations providing collective goods.

It is because collective action is the essence of many serious problems in many different areas and disciplines that this book is relevant for readers with the most diverse interests. Sandler considers an extraordinarily wide array of problems that some readers might at first suppose were unrelated, but all of the problems share a common structure. To put it briefly and evocatively again, they all deal with the second law and why it does—or does not—apply. Every logical deduction and empirical finding in this book is a part of, or a test of, a single general theory.

Thus, when Sandler moves from the problems of ozone depletion, global warming, and acid rain, on the one hand, to the problems an oppressed population has in overthrowing an oppressive tyrant, on the other, it is *not,* in fact, changing the subject. On the contrary, it sticks single-mindedly to the premise that, often, "individual rationality is not sufficient for collective rationality." As this book shows, this problem and the paradoxical logic that explains it are evident, for example, when many different workers must combine their efforts in a single firm to obtain the economies of scale and scope, when farmers and fishermen overuse common lands and waters, when charity is needed to alleviate the poverty in a community, and when we do not all obtain the gains from using a common set of weights and measures.

It is not appropriate to go into the many intriguing subtleties and technical issues that are presented here. Such issues are analyzed in a rigorous yet usually also intuitively understandable way. When Sandler's discussion becomes, as on occasion it must, modestly technical, I found it all the more interesting. (Those readers who are not economists will find brief sections that explain the main specialized concepts and also directions around a few technical sections that can be skipped without sacrificing comprehension of the rest of the book.)

There is one fundamental issue that, even though apparently difficult enough that many highly regarded technical analyses get it wrong, can nonetheless be handled with the simplicity and brevity appropriate to a foreword. The domain of the first law, under which the hidden hand automatically generates collectively rational outcomes, is naturally a domain of the private goods that analyses of markets have taken for granted since Adam Smith. With a sufficiently comprehensive definition of collective goods, the domain of the second law involves only such goods.

Now consider a small group of, say, two individuals who are in a situation in which the total cost of providing some amount of a collective good is definitely less than the aggregate value of the good to the two individuals, so that the collective good must be provided if there is to be group optimality. As we know, collective goods normally come under the second law, where the self-interest of the parties is *not* sufficient to obtain a collectively rational or group-optimal outcome.

But would it really be the second law, rather than the first, that applies when the group has only a few members? Would a sufficiently small group, even a group of only two members, be unable to obtain a collective good, even when the collective good was worth much more than it cost?

The conclusion usually drawn from the famous Prisoner's Dilemma model is that even groups of only two members normally fail to obtain a collective good. It is only when two individuals repeat the Prisoner's Dilemma game an indefinitely large number of times that they can achieve the gains from cooperation. In any single game (or in any set of games where the players know in advance how many games will be played), the dominant strategy for each player is to defect, and a collectively rational outcome will not be obtained. According to the Prisoner's Dilemma model, the number of individuals who would profit from the provision of a collective good does not affect the likelihood that it will be provided, since collective action will fail even for a group of two.

Why does the famous Prisoner's Dilemma metaphor illustrate the difficulties of obtaining the gains from social cooperation by focusing on outlaws concerned about the extent of their prison sentences? Obviously, societies work better when crime is deterred because criminals are likely to be punished. So why is the difficulty a pair of prisoners face in colluding on their alibi or strategy the standard game theory illustration of the barrier to mutually beneficial collective action generally? It is as though philosophers' only standard illustration of honor was honor among thieves.

I believe that the key to this strange situation is that the prisoners, already in the hands of the police and provably guilty of a lesser offense than the one with which the analysis is concerned, are purposely *isolated in separate cells* by the police, who have no other witnesses to the more serious crime. The prisoners are thereby denied communication with one another—and also the possibility of utilizing *any* of the manifold possibilities for making mutually advantageous deals that human ingenuity and social institutions normally supply.

Because the two prisoners are not allowed to communicate, they have no opportunity to make an agreement not to tell the authorities about their participation in the crime at issue and, therefore, no opportunity to serve their collective interest by making it impossible for the state to convict either of them of the more serious offense. Thus, a driving force in the two-person Prisoner's Dilemma is that an almost universal feature of any interaction of two individuals with a common problem—communication about how to obtain the outcome that is a collective good for both of them—is prevented by some exceptional circumstances: police officers who know that communication between the prisoners can stand in the way of inducing them to squeal on one another.

The hurried reader might object that the prohibition of communication does not matter, because the two individuals would still need to have a mutually credible agreement and this credibility may be lacking because of the difficulties of enforcing the deal. In fact, this objection does not alter the fact that the familiar two-person Prisoner's Dilemma applies only to wondrously special circumstances. Remember that, because their interest in evading punishment is itself illegal, the prisoners are, of course, also denied the device normally used for making mutually advantageous deals: a contract enforceable through the courts.

Thus, it is by no means an accident that it is criminals, of all people, who are used when there is an attempt to illustrate, with only two people, the difficulties societies face in obtaining social cooperation. In the overwhelming preponderance of cases with only two individuals, the dilemma blocking cooperation would simply not be there if the two parties were not criminals that the police keep from communicating with one another.

The *isolation* as well as absence of communication of the two prisoners is important in denying them a vast array of promising aids to credible agreements normally open even to criminals. They are, for example, denied the resource of using a third party acceptable to both of them as the arbitrator and enforcer of the deal, or the historically ancient device of each giving hostages to the other as assurance the deal is carried out. The array of arrangements that human ingenuity and communication can devise to make mutually advantageous deals credible is marvelously broad; I once heard of a movie in which two criminals insured the credibility of their illicit agreement by tearing a thousand dollar bill down the middle, so that it would be valueless until the parts were joined, with each of them keeping one of the halves until their agreement was fulfilled. But most enforcement mechanisms are incomparably simpler. The criminal who rats on agreements with his or her partner in crime also impairs his or her opportunities to obtain the gains from cooperation with others in future crimes—there are, after all, reasons why there is honor even among thieves. Finally, the ban on communication excludes the most familiar criminal device for enforcing agreements not to squeal to the police—the threat, made credible by standard criminal practice, to torture and kill any partner who welches on a criminal agreement.

If any further evidence about the decisive importance of the special circumstance of denying communication and enforcing isolation is needed, it is provided by the result, so well known it is often now described as a "folk theorem," of an indefinitely repeated number of two-person Prisoner's Dilemma games. The result of such games, evident from the logic of game theory, from careful experiments, and from observation of the real world, is cooperation rather than defection: the two parties, through strategies such as tit for tat, ultimately obtain the joint maximization outcome that is a collective good to the two of them.

Though this is not made explicit in many accounts, the essence of the matter is that the special circumstances of isolation and the prohibition of communication are *inherently* impossible to maintain in an indefinitely long sequence of two-person Prisoner's Dilemma games. Each party, by proffering instances of cooperation and then rewarding reciprocal cooperation with continued cooperation and punishing defection by defection, can implicitly communicate with the other and the two of them can thereby tacitly agree to cooperate to obtain the collective good. The ultimate result of this communication and nonisolation for two parties is that mutually beneficial collective action occurs.

The foregoing does not, of course, mean that it is inappropriate to put, in the familiar two-by-two matrix, the numbers that bear the ordinal relationships needed for the Prisoner's Dilemma result. The Prisoner's Dilemma example has generated a lot of fascinating research. When there is a real-world situation where rational players are isolated and unable to communicate with each other, and the other factors affecting the costs and benefits of the collective good are also consistent with a Prisoner's Dilemma, rational individuals playing a one-shot game will, indeed, find that the dominant strategy is to defect and the collective good for the two individuals will not be obtained. There is obviously nothing wrong with the arithmetic of the standard presentation of the one-shot Prisoner's Dilemma game. Rather, the problem is finding any significant number of real-world situations that correspond to this arithmetic.

As I see the world, groups of two, and typically even small groups that have somewhat more than two members, usually are able, through voluntary rational action, to obtain the gains from social cooperation even when collective goods are involved. Unless communication and interaction are prohibited, the group with only two members certainly cannot be in equilibrium if it has not obtained a collective good that is worth more than it costs; if the group has not provided itself with such a good, it is always possible for the members of the group to find at least one allocation of the costs of obtaining the good that leaves both of them better off than they are without the good, so they have an incentive to continue bargaining and interacting and, thus, cannot be in equilibrium. As I see it, it is only in the strangest cases that the second law applies to very small groups; they are characteristically covered by the first law.

Let us now be as general as possible and consider situations that can involve any number of people and in which there is no prohibition against communication and interaction. These situations are, however, like the Prisoner's Dilemma in that they involve an outcome or collective good such that, if the parties cooperate to provide it, they can all be made better off, but in which no individual acting unilaterally in furtherance of his or her individual interests would find it advantageous to supply any of the collective good, or at least not the amount that group optimality (i.e., collective rationality) would entail. That is, there is the "externality" that is inherent in all collective good situations, in that each individual's provision of any amount of a collective good would confer some benefit to others. We have just seen that there is a large likelihood that two individuals who can communicate and interact in the presence of a collective good will act to obtain it and that they certainly cannot be in equilibrium if they do not, but instead have an incentive to continue to seek the mutual gains that they have not yet obtained.

Now suppose that the situation, while in other respects retaining the same structure as before, involves a collective good that would, if provided, benefit three individuals rather than two. The three individuals would still have an incentive to communicate and interact with one another to provide the mutually advantageous collective good, just as the two individuals in the previous example did (though it is now conceivable that the "game" would not have a "core"), and there is no basis whatever for any general presumption that three rational and self-interested individuals would not voluntarily provide themselves with the collective good.

The switch to a three-person situation nonetheless entails a change, one that can be seen most simply if we temporarily suppose that all of the individuals at issue were identical in tastes and incomes and examine unilateral or unstrategic (Nash-Cournot) behavior. With two identical individuals, any individual engaging in unilateral action to provide the collective good would, while bearing all of the costs of whatever amount of the collective good he or she provided, obtain half of the benefit of the collective good—the "externality" also would be one-half. But if we have three identical individuals, each individual still bears the full cost of whatever amount of the collective good he or she provides, but gets only one-third of the benefit. So unilateral or

Nash-Cournot behavior must, other things being equal, fall farther short, with three identical individuals rather than two, of obtaining a group-optimal supply.

If other things remain equal and we continue on to groups of four persons, or to groups with arbitrarily large numbers of beneficiaries of a collective good, the "externality" inevitably becomes relatively more important—an individual in the group, while still bearing the full cost of whatever he or she contributes to the provision of the collective good, obtains a smaller part of the gains from the action he or she undertakes, so that the unilateral behavior of an individual falls farther and farther short of providing the amount of the collective good that would be consistent with collective rationality. Indeed, as numbers become very large, an individual's share of the gains from action in the interest of his or her group becomes minuscule and the level of provision (if there is any provision at all) becomes utterly insignificant in relation to the amount that it is in the collective interest of the group to obtain. In other words, when the group becomes sufficiently "large," for all practical purposes it ceases (in the absence of "selective incentives" or institutional arrangements to overcome the problem) to act in its collective interest.

This is true even if we add individuals to a group that receives a given, perfectly nonrival public good—one such that additional consumers do not at all subtract from or congest the consumption of others—so that the collective benefit arising from any given level of provision of the public good increases proportionately with the number in the group while the costs of provision are not increased in the slightest. As the number who enter such a group gets larger, the group falls further from achieving the level of provision consistent with group optimality. That is, the extent to which individual rationality falls short of obtaining the amount of the collective good needed for collective rationality becomes ever greater as the group becomes larger. (However, as Martin McGuire and others have shown, and as Sandler lucidly explains in this book, if the collective good is a normal good, in the sense that individuals will, other things equal, purchase more of it when their incomes are higher, then, in the case considered in this paragraph, the absolute level of provision must increase with the number in the group.)

The argument that has just been made assumes unstrategic behavior and is for this reason (among many others, most of which are explained in this book) too simple to do full justice to groups with only a small number of members. That is, the foregoing argument about how, as the number who would benefit from the provision of a collective good increases, the group falls farther short of obtaining an optimal amount of a collective good, ignores the possibility that individuals will interact strategically; it ignores, most notably, the possibility that one individual will say to another that he or she will contribute to the provision of the collective good if the other does, but not otherwise, thereby increasing the second individual's incentive to contribute.

We now get to what is probably the most important point of all: in a sufficiently large or "latent" group of individuals with no single member who gets more than a minuscule share of the benefits of a collective good, the incentive for strategic interaction—and even the incentive to bargain with other potential beneficiaries of the collective good—disappears. If no two members, or no other small subset of the members of the group of potential beneficiaries of a collective good, would, in the aggregate, gain from bearing the costs of providing some amount of the collective good, then there is no incentive for individuals to interact strategically or even to bear the costs of communicating and bargaining with each other about how to remedy the lack of the collective good.

This implies that the statements occasionally made by casual students of these matters, to the effect that only "transaction costs" or bargaining costs prevent collective action, or the internalization of all externalities, from taking place, are wrong. What is sometimes casually called the Coase theorem is extremely valuable in many contexts and analyses of transaction costs in many settings also make great contributions to understanding. But they are not applicable to sufficiently "large" or "latent" groups that would benefit from the provision of a collective good. They have brought only confusion when applied to such situations.

We are now in a position to see why one-shot Prisoner's Dilemma games, in spite of their exceptionally restricted assumptions about isolation and prohibition of communication, became so famous. Most people know viscerally, from their experience and observation, that the second law often applies—that socially rational outcomes by no means always come about automatically. Pollution, overfishing, and the anarchic international system, among many other collective action problems involving large numbers, are all around us. The one-shot, two-person Prisoner's Dilemma is a marvelously simple metaphor and it predicts that socially undesirable outcomes will occur. Because this fits practical experience in many situations where large numbers of people are involved, the Prisoner's Dilemma is taken, incorrectly, as a general explanation of the difficulties of collective action.

Admittedly, as the author of *The Logic of Collective Action,* I could hardly be expected to be impartial about the conclusions in that book, including the conclusion that the number of individuals in a group was a most important determinant of the likelihood that collective action would occur. In part for that reason, I want, above all, to emphasize the appeal and value of Sandler's emphasis on the point that reality is so complex that very simple general principles can almost never apply (without exception) to all cases. This point should be emphasized in using the theory in *The Logic of Collective Action* as in using any other model that claims broad explanatory power. It applies to all three of the main themes that Sandler so nicely abstracts from that book, including the theme that the size of a group is a major determinant of the likelihood of voluntary collective action.

As I have read this book, both where it involves the many totally new arguments that are offered, and also where it summarizes other work that has been done on collective action in the last quarter-century, I tend to see, in the remarkable variety of interesting and important cases considered, the underlying logical or theoretical unity of the diverse cases. But this is partly a function of my temperament and lack of detachment. There can be no question that, in any case of doubt, we should, until further analysis or evidence finally resolves the question, decide, with Todd Sandler, *against* the idea that a simple general principle adequately covers the whole range of cases.

This is a particularly important point to emphasize in a book of such remarkable richness and unity as this one. I learned a lot about many different subjects from reading this book. To some degree, this is due to prior gaps in my own thinking and reading. Even so, I do not see how capable economists or serious students of any of the several other fields that this book examines could fail to find that it brings into focus many important vistas that they had not seen before.

Preface

Collective action refers to activities that require the coordination of efforts by two or more individuals. As such, collective action involves group actions intended to further the interests or well-being of the members. Groups may be formal (e.g., a labor union or learned society) or informal (e.g., residents of a neighborhood). Whatever the nature of the group, a collective action problem arises when the actions of its members are interdependent: one person's reward (outcome) is dependent on the actions of others. To underscore the pervasiveness of collective action problems, consider the everyday act of driving a car on a two-lane highway with opposing traffic. A coordination problem requiring collective action arises every time two cars traveling in opposite directions approach one another. If both drivers coordinate and stay on their right-hand side of the road, then both will pass without mishap. In every country, collective action at the legislative or executive level has evolved a convention for which side of the road to drive on. Without these conventions, each vehicle must second guess oncoming traffic or else engage in a game of Chicken by driving in the middle of the road until one vehicle swerves. Collective action has also provided the road signs that warn, regulate, and inform drivers. Within the United States and throughout much of Europe, collective action has standardized road signs to facilitate interstate and international driving. The roadways' provision and maintenance are also the result of collective action at the county, state, or national level. Except for driveways, most people do not build and maintain their own roads. Snow removal, speed-limit enforcement, and some emergency services (e.g., ambulances) are also examples of collective action.

In some instances, collective action is voluntary, as in the case where the residents of a town pitch in to sandbag areas threatened by a rising river. In other instances, a government may have to provide the collective action, as in the case of highways and road signs. Whether collective action can be expected or not is a question of utmost importance.

In economics, the market is viewed as an impersonal mechanism to allow for the exchange of goods and services without the need for collective action. Individual pursuit of self-interest leads to the betterment of everyone when markets function perfectly. But the existence of a market economy depends on necessary conditions that are, themselves, collective actions. Among these conditions, property rights (or claims of ownership) must be defined and enforced. Enforcement requires the collective provision of a police force. Infrastructure (e.g., bridges, roadways, ports, and communication networks) is needed to facilitate trade and production. Collective action is often required to provide this infrastructure, which is then financed by taxes or user fees. In addition, collective action both within and between countries must eliminate trade distortions (e.g., quotas and tariffs) or refrain from imposing such barriers if markets are to function properly.

Collective action problems involve almost every aspect of an advanced economy. The institution of uniform standards of weights and measures is a collective action problem. The control of pollution both within and across national borders requires some form of collective action in terms of monitoring, control, and evaluation. Similarly, the provision of national defense to safeguard industry, territory, property, and lives is a collective action problem. Although individual action might provide an air raid shelter, the deployment of a nuclear deterrent must be done collectively (owing to cost). In recent times, the enactment of no smoking rules is also the result of collective action on the part of nonsmokers. Even the formation of a firm and its operation in an oligopolistic industry can be viewed as a collective action problem.

Given its pervasiveness, collective action must be studied to gain a better understanding of economic and political behavior. The purpose of this book is to synthesize what has been learned about collective action since the publication of Mancur Olson's seminal study, *The Logic of Collective Action*, in 1965. My intent is to analyze the factors that influence whether collective action will follow voluntarily or whether it needs to be fostered by government. My analysis is focused on those studies that have had the greatest impact on explaining what promotes collective action. In the real world, some forms of collective action come naturally (e.g., the pilots of a 747 coordinating their actions to land the plane or the provision of relief to disaster victims), while other forms (e.g., the control of toxic wastes) need government intervention.

Over the last two decades, sophisticated tools and techniques have been increasingly applied to the study of collective action. When Olson wrote *The Logic of Collective Action*, little preparation in economics was required for a reader to understand Olson's book. Some knowledge of economics is, however, necessary for any modern treatment of collective action. This book is intended for senior undergraduates in economics and political science as well as graduate students and researchers interested in an up-to-date view of collective action. For the most part, I assume a knowledge of the basic principles of intermediate microeconomics. Thus, the reader is assumed to be familiar with the standard economic representation of consumer behavior, as depicted with indifference curves. The reader is also assumed to understand the notion of the margin, average, and elasticity. To make the book more accessible and self-contained, I have included an appendix at the end of the book that summarizes and reviews some key concepts from intermediate microeconomics. The unprepared reader should study this appendix before starting the book. The informed reader need not consult this appendix. Throughout the book, more technically sophisticated subsections are marked by an asterisk to warn of a higher level of difficulty. Mathematical derivations are gathered in appendixes to the chapters.

A number of people have helped make this book possible. I have benefited greatly from the comments of Mancur Olson, John Tschirhart, Elinor Ostrom, John Conybeare, Colin Day, Martin McGuire, James Murdoch, Herman Quirmbach, Leigh Tesfatsion, and anonymous readers. Colin Day's comments were especially extensive and useful. I also owe a debt of gratitude to the many people I have worked with when developing my thinking on collective action. These people include Richard Cornes, John Conybeare, James Murdoch, John Posnett, Il-Dong Ko, Harvey Lapan, Frederic Sterbenz, Jyoti Khanna, Laurna Hansen, Jon Cauley, and John Tschirhart. I also appreciate the understanding and support of my wife, Jean Murdock, and my son, Tristan Jon, during the various stages of the book. I also owe a real debt of gratitude to Sue Streeter, Angela Jewett, and Eileen Mericle, who typed and retyped numerous drafts of the manuscript. Their care and accuracy, as well as their cheerfulness, are much appreciated. I also wish to thank the people at the University of Michigan Press, who transformed the manuscript into a book.

The research for this book was funded, in part, by a senior fellowship from the Institute for Policy Reform. The views expressed in this book, as well as any shortcomings, are solely the responsibility of the author.

Contents

CHAPTER 1
Collective Action: An Overview

> The rational individual in the economic system does not curtail his spending to prevent inflation (or increase it to prevent depressions) because he knows, first, that his own efforts would not have a noticeable effect, and second, that he would get the benefits of any price stability that others achieved in any case.
>
> —Mancur Olson (1965, 166)

Collective action arises when the efforts of two or more individuals are needed to accomplish an outcome. Activities that involve the furtherance of the interests or well-being of a group are often examples of collective action. From man's beginning, individuals have relied on the collective for their defense and safety. Collective action problems are typically characterized by an interdependency among the participants, so that the contributions or efforts of one individual influence the contributions or efforts of other individuals. The need for collective action abounds in any advanced society.

Are sufficient resources assigned to collective action? Must governments always intervene to accomplish collective action, or can individuals be expected to coordinate their actions without the need of governments? Will collective action achieve efficient results? What preconditions are conducive to successful collective action? These are questions of utmost importance that the study of collective action seeks to answer.

In the last quarter-century, few books in economics have achieved the wide-ranging, lasting, and profound impact of *The Logic of Collective Action* (hereafter called *Logic*) by Mancur Olson. The book's influence is noteworthy for at least four reasons. First, its analysis of collective action problems has transcended economics and has altered thinking about group behavior in sociology, anthropology, and political science (especially international relations). Prior to Olson's contribution, groups and political collectives were invariably viewed as furthering their members' and/or constituency's well-being. Olson showed that actions by group members may worsen, rather than enhance, collective or group well-being. That is, the pursuit of individual benefits might not augment the aggregate benefit of the group and, in a large number of reasonable scenarios, could lead to an inferior outcome. Second, the book has influenced thought on a variety of topics within economics, including the study of labor unions, local public goods, economic growth, macroeconomics, economic and military alliances, jurisdictional design, environmental questions (e.g., voluntary compliance, lobbying group activities), and public choice (e.g., voting behavior, rent-seeking behavior). Third, Olson's book contained the rudiments of the theory of clubs, which are voluntary groups deriving mutual benefits from sharing one or more of the following: production costs, the members' characteristics, or a good characterized by excludable benefits. Club theory has had a major impact on economics and related studies, and was cofounded and more formally developed by James Buchanan (1965). In essence, club analysis demonstrates that, in the presence of an exclusion mechanism (e.g., a turnstile, a toll booth, an electronic monitor), the provision of club goods (i.e., those whose benefits can be withheld at a reasonable cost)[1] can eliminate the need for government intervention. Fourth, many of the most-pressing problems confronting mankind today (e.g., the preservation of the environment) are of a collective action nature.

A glance at the world today indicates that collective action problems are no less important now than they were in 1965. In fact, advances in technology have made the world appear smaller and have added to the need for collective action both within and between nations. Extraterrestrial satellite networks link communication systems worldwide and open up new means for coordinating actions between agents in geographically separated countries. Supersonic airplanes (and, in the not-too-distant future, hypersonic airplanes capable of flying between Tokyo and New York in thirty minutes) facilitate high-speed travel. Engineering projects (e.g., the Chunnel under the English Channel) will join countries in ways never before possible.

Although technology opens up avenues for coordinating activities between nations, thereby facilitating collective action, it also creates collective action problems. For example, increased air travel means that plagues and diseases are transmitted more rapidly worldwide. The spread of AIDS and

---

1. By reasonable, I mean that the associated cost of the exclusion mechanism is less than the benefits gained from allocating the shared good within a club arrangement. Suppose that a club augments efficiency for a group of individuals by $2,000 per year by utilizing the exclusion mechanism to assign the proper per-visit tolls to the members. Without this exclusion mechanism, the good would be provided publicly, if at all, and its expenses paid through some form of taxation. Since the latter arrangement is likely to assign fees not truly based on marginal benefits received, efficiency losses result. In my example, these losses amount to $2,000 per year. Therefore, if the exclusion mechanism can be provided and operated for anything less than $2,000 per year, the costs are considered reasonable and the exclusion mechanism is justified.

antibiotic-resistant diseases are apt examples. Devising a cure for such diseases may require resource contributions and research efforts on a global scale. Technological advances also aid and abet transnational terrorism. In recent years, global communication linkages have given terrorists a worldwide audience to shock and intimidate with their acts of terror. Since 1968, international terrorism has increased from less than 125 incidents per year (Mickolus 1980, xxi) to more than 800 per year (U.S. Department of State 1990, 1). International terrorism threatens half of the world's nations and requires collective action by the international community in terms of deterrence, intelligence sharing, the elimination of safe havens, and the rigorous prosecution of captured terrorists.

Technological advances in weapons of mass destruction of a nuclear, chemical, or biological kind have put the world at risk from ruthless dictators bent on regional domination. Advances in communication facilitate the ability of these dictators to threaten countries near and far. Iraq comes to mind. The elimination of a large portion of Iraq's considerable arsenal is seen by many as promoting world peace, which is itself a collective good. Ironically, the Iraqi arsenal was acquired from some of the same nations that fought against Iraq during the Gulf War. Obviously, each of these nation's pursuit of arms trade profits and other nation-specific agendas created a collective action problem that required a collective response.

The expansion of the world's population has also made the world seem smaller and has increased the need for collective action. Food and fuel needs have led to wholesale destruction of tropical rain forests, a destruction that has caused widespread flooding in lowland areas (e.g., Bangladesh in the late 1980s and early 1990s) and added to the global warming problem. Since forests absorb carbon dioxide, their destruction augments the accumulation of carbon dioxide and, with it, global warming. Population expansion has created monumental garbage problems and caused resource pools to be used at alarming rates. Myriad forms of pollution, stemming from increased population needs and industrial demands, have threatened air quality as well as surface water and groundwater supplies. The depletion of the protective ozone layer has been due, in part, to the accumulation of chlorofluorocarbons in the upper atmosphere. This accumulation has arisen from increased population demands for refrigeration.

1.1 Basic Premise of Collective Action

Although *Logic* is rich in propositions, analysis, and applications, the book rests on a single basic premise: *individual rationality is not sufficient for collective rationality.* Individual rationality is operationally defined by the usual assumptions or axioms of consumer behavior[2] (see Alchian and Allen 1972, chap. 3, or Deaton and Muellbauer 1980). These consumer assumptions require individuals to maximize their satisfaction or utility subject to their income and market data in terms of prices. Commodities that augment satisfaction are desired. Moreover, consumer tastes must be consistent, to allow for predictability, and must also be "continuous" to permit all available market baskets to be comparable. Finally, a consumer's willingness to trade between commodities is dependent on the amount of each good already acquired. Ceteris paribus, a consumer is more generous when trading away some of a commodity in relatively great supply. In simple terms, rationality implies predictability, so that changes in constraints lead to foreseeable behavioral changes. Moreover, rationality implies that properly informed individuals do their best given their constraints; they do not choose feasible (affordable) market baskets that are inferior to other available baskets. Similarly, collective rationality implies both predictability and efficient outcomes. If a collective were to choose an outcome inferior to other available outcomes, then a collective failure or irrationality is evident.

An interesting and often-cited example of collective failure is the so-called Prisoner's Dilemma, in which two (or more) suspects are made to turn state's evidence by confessing to a crime that they may or may not have committed. The storyline of the Prisoner's Dilemma involves two individuals apprehended near the scene of an armed robbery. The district attorney has sufficient evidence to convict them of a lesser crime, say carrying a firearm, but cannot convict the suspects of the robbery unless at least one confesses. To elicit the confession, the district attorney separates the prisoners and promises each less than the maximum sentence for the robbery (but greater than the firearms charge) provided that both confess. If, however, only one confesses, then the confessor receives a light sentence (less than the firearms charge) and the nonconfessor gets the maximum penalty. When neither confesses, they both receive a moderate penalty for the firearms charge. Each of the prisoners is interrogated separately and is thus denied an opportunity to communicate with the other.

Suppose that the robbery charge carries a ten-year sentence and the firearms charge carries a two-year sentence. Suppose further that the district

---

2. Roughly speaking, these axioms require monotonicity, transitivity, continuity, and convexity of preference orderings. Monotonicity requires an individual to prefer a market basket that has more of at least one good and no less of any other good. Transitivity is a consistency requirement that indicates if bundle A is at least as good as bundle B, while bundle B is at least as good as bundle C, then bundle A must be at least as good as bundle C. Continuity implies that all bundles can be ranked by the ordering. Finally, convexity requires a person's willingness to trade one good for another to depend on his or her relative holdings of the goods: goods in relatively great supply have a lower substitution value.

attorney reduces the robbery sentence to seven years provided that both prisoners confess. When only one prisoner confesses, the confessor gets off with a one-year sentence. The options before each of the prisoners are: by confessing, he or she receives a seven-year sentence when his or her buddy also confesses and a one-year term when his or her buddy does not confess. On the other hand, by not confessing, the prisoner receives either a ten-year or two-year sentence depending on what his or her buddy does. Not knowing what his or her buddy will do, it is clear that the sentences or outcomes for either prisoner are such that each chooses to confess to the robbery. From each prisoner's isolated viewpoint, he or she is better off confessing regardless of the other prisoner's action; confessing is a *dominant* strategy because it gives a smaller sentence (higher payoff) for each choice or action of the other prisoner. Ironically, when both prisoners use their dominant strategy, each receives a sentence greater than had they both not confessed. Although the cooperative, no-confession solution could make them both better off, individual incentives motivate each prisoner to reach an inferior position. The Prisoner's Dilemma is discussed more fully in chapter 2 and is presented to illustrate that the pursuit of individual self-interest may imply an outcome for the collective that is inferior to other feasible outcomes.

Olson's *Logic* is most concerned with elucidating cases in which collective failure results when individuals pursue their self-interest. This collective failure stands in stark contrast to Adam Smith's invisible hand proposition, which indicates that an individual pursuit of self-interest in competitive, private good markets will further the collective interest. No contradiction is implied, because collective action problems arise in situations when goods are not private and/or markets are not competitive. Olson's *Logic* primarily concerns pure public goods, impure public goods, and externalities (uncompensated interdependencies).

Since these latter classes of goods are crucial for the understanding of collective action and may not be familiar to all readers, I define each at the outset. Two essential terms—nonexcludability and nonrivalry of benefits—must be defined first. Benefits of a good, available to all once the good is provided, are called *nonexcludable*. If the benefits of a good can be withheld costlessly by the owner or provider, then benefits are excludable. The food we eat and the clothing we wear are excludable, while the appearance of our house or garden is not excludable unless we want to build a very high fence. When, however, an exclusion cost is so prohibitive that exclusion is not practical, the good's benefits are nonexcludable and, hence, available to anyone who wants to take advantage of them. Pollution removal is a nonexcludable good, since once pollution is cleaned up, persons in the once-polluted area benefit regardless of whether they supported the cleanup or not. An individual cannot be kept from breathing the cleaner air. Other examples of nonexcludable goods include mine-sweeping operations, open access fisheries, fireworks displays, and nuclear deterrence. In the national defense case, all residents of a nation or of an alliance of nations are protected by a nuclear deterrent force, irrespective of whether they pay taxes or believe in defense. The threat to any would-be aggressor, embodied by the nuclear deterrent, is made on behalf of everyone. It is not possible to protect selectively some lives and property within a nation.

The second essential concept used to define goods is the nonrivalry of benefits. The benefits of a good are rival when the consumption of a unit of the good by a person uses up all of the available benefits. Food and fuel are perfectly rival. A good is *nonrival* or indivisible when a *unit* of the good can be consumed by one individual without detracting, in the slightest, from the consumption opportunities still available for others from that *same* unit. In the case of a nuclear deterrent force, additional people can migrate or be born into the country without diminishing the benefits derived from the deterrent by each individual. The weaponry's technological capabilities to put enemy targets at risk, not the number of lives protected, determine the ability of the weapons to forestall enemy aggression. Nonrivalry characterizes benefits derived from pollution-control devices, weather-monitoring stations, scientific discoveries, crisis-warning monitors, information-dissemination systems, and disease eradication. In the latter case, once a cure is found, the ability to apply the cure to one patient does not diminish the ability to apply the cure to others. Similarly, a scientific breakthrough can be used by one individual or nation without diluting the potential benefits available to other users.

A pure public good provides benefits that are nonexcludable *and* nonrival or indivisible between users. The removal of pollution is a pure public good, as are mine-sweeping operations along an international waterway (e.g., the Persian Gulf). A nuclear deterrent arsenal is also a pure public good.

In contrast to a pure public good, a private good possesses benefits that are fully excludable and rival between prospective users. Food, clothing, and paper are apt examples. Some goods may be nonrival but excludable, such as concerts, information, scientific discoveries, and weather forecasts; others may be nonexcludable but rival, such as oil pools beneath more than a single country or migratory resources (e.g., whales or salmon). For concerts, turnstiles and ticket takers can bar nonpayers, and, until the concert hall capacity is reached, additional people can listen to the same performance without necessarily detracting from the enjoyment of other concert goers. For the oil pool example, both nations can draw from the same resource reservoir owing to open access, but a barrel more of oil for one country is one less for the other country. Impure public goods possess benefits that are partially rival and/or partially excludable. If, therefore, a good does not display both excludability (nonexcludability) and rivalry (nonrivalry) in their pure forms, the good is called impurely public. Impure public goods include those whose benefits are excludable but partially nonrival; these goods are *club goods*. Examples include recreation facilities, national parks, and highways, since exclusion can be practiced and, although nonrival at low levels of usage, they are partially rival because crowding occurs when more intensively used.

An externality arises when the action of one agent influences the welfare, in terms of utility or profit, of another agent and no means of compensation exists. When the playing of loud music in one apartment disturbs the sleep of someone in another apartment, an externality is present. If production activities in one nation create pollution (e.g., acid rain) in another, downwind nation, a transfrontier externality results.

By focusing on collective failures stemming from the pursuit of individual well-being, *Logic* concerns market failures. Market failures arise, in part, from public goods and externalities, which, in turn, involve quantity-constrained behavior. For example, the public good provided by the rest of the community is not a choice variable to someone who is deciding his or her own public good provision level and, consequently, represents a quantity constraint additional to the standard resource or budget constraint (Cornes and Sandler 1986, chaps. 3, 5, 17). The presence of a quantity constraint can cause uncoordinated individual actions or decisions to reach suboptimal positions from which all individuals could have their well-being improved. If the participants can agree to coordinate their choices so that the consequences of each quantity choice (e.g., voluntary contributions to a public good) reflect the interests of the entire group, then collective action will, even in the presence of public goods and externalities, provide better outcomes from the standpoint of the collective. When choices are interdependent but individual decisions are made independently, a collective failure, as in the Prisoner's Dilemma, may arise.

1.2 The Purposes of the Book

This book has a number of purposes. First, it is intended to take stock of the state of knowledge regarding collective action. To accomplish this purpose, I distill three basic themes from *Logic* that identify important factors or influences related to the notion of collective failures. In particular, group size, group composition, and institutional design are related to the performance of the collective in optimizing their members' welfare. Second, each of the themes is developed and brought up to date. The validity of the collective action propositions, associated with *Logic*'s themes, is shown to depend on one or more of the following: (*a*) the form of the agent's utility function, (*b*) the *technology of public supply* (i.e., how individual contributions add to the total public supply achieved), (*c*) the strategic assumption (i.e., how agents expect others to react to their choices), and (*d*) the constraints of the problems. These ingredients are crucial in determining the underlying game structure, which describes how agents' choices are interrelated in terms of outcomes. Third, I indicate areas in the study of collective action that require further development. Fourth, an overview of relevant empirical methods and studies is given. As a scientific endeavor, the theory of collective action must be subject to testing, evaluation, and reformulation, and empirical results are pivotal to this ongoing process. Fifth, I present an evaluation of a host of applications that include the study of common property resources, military alliances, strategic trade policy, labor unions, foreign aid, public inputs, infrastructure, and others.

With the recent interest shown in strategic behavior and game theory, the field of collective action will surely grow in importance as new game-theoretic insights are uncovered. With the passing of twenty-five years since the publication of *Logic,* it is now a good time to assess what has been learned, how the associated theory has been applied, what has been gained from the empirical studies, and what the unanswered questions are. There is no attempt here to provide an exhaustive survey of the vast literature spawned by *Logic.*[3] Rather, I refer selectively to pivotal contributions or representative articles. In doing so, a large number of references are, nevertheless, given.

1.3 The Basic Themes: A Brief Overview

By way of introduction, the basic themes and their subcomponents are now sketched. A fuller analysis is provided in chapters 2 and 3. For a book of the scope and intellectual achievement of *Logic,* it is, indeed, a difficult task to condense the work's message to a few simple themes. Nevertheless, I have attempted to accomplish this reduction by identifying three simple, basic themes and subcomponents. A list of these themes is presented at the outset to provide a ready reference for the reader to turn back to when the need arises. Each of these themes are listed below, accompanied by relevant subcomponents.

1. Group size is, in part, a root cause of collective failures.
   a) Large groups may not provide themselves with a collective good;

---

3. The reader should consult Hardin 1982 for an earlier survey of collective action and a more exhaustive list of references. Even though Hardin provides many worthwhile insights (in particular, his analysis of contracting by convention), I view many problems (e.g., the relationship of collective action and the Prisoner's Dilemma) differently. The study of collective action has advanced greatly since 1982 due, in part, to the reemergence of game theory in economic thought.

The reader should also consult the excellent survey of public goods by Blümel, Pethig, and von dem Hagen 1986. This survey also contains a very useful list of references, as does Pethig 1985.

hence, no individual or coalition within the group may satisfy the sufficient condition of a *privileged group* (see definition below).

  b) The larger the group, ceteris paribus, the greater the departure of individual uncoordinated behavior (also known as independent adjustment)[4] from optimality; that is, the more suboptimal is the equilibrium.

  c) The larger the group, the smaller the collective provision level.

2. Group asymmetry, in terms of individuals' tastes and/or endowments, is related to collective failures.

  a) Larger members (those with the greater endowments) will bear a disproportionate burden of collective provision. "There is a systematic tendency for exploitation of the great by the small" (Olson 1965, 35).

  b) Asymmetric groups are more likely to be privileged.

3. Collective failures may be overcome through selective incentives (giving private benefit inducements) and institutional design.

Before remarking briefly on each of these themes, I present a few definitions. Olson (1965) uses collective action, in a general sense, to refer to any problem that provides benefits and/or costs for more than one individual, so that some coordination of efforts is required. Although *Logic*'s general propositions are valid for many collective action scenarios, they give researchers wide latitude to construct specific cases that might violate the propositions' implicit assumptions; for example, public goods characterized by negative income elasticities (Cornes and Sandler 1984a and 1986, chap. 5), public goods whose contributors use strategic assumptions at variance with those of Olson (Guttman 1987), or public goods with unique technologies of aggregation (Hirshleifer 1983, the weakest link case).

The first and second themes, in part, refer to a privileged group, a key determinant of collective action. A *privileged group* contains at least one individual or coalition whose benefits from collective action exceed the associated costs, even if these costs are solely borne by the individual or coalition. When this sufficiency condition for privileged groups is not met, but the group is sufficiently small that members are aware of those who assist collective action, the group is *intermediate* and may still form. If, however, the group is neither privileged nor intermediate, then it is *latent* and does not form. From a practical standpoint, there is no operational definition given for an intermediate group. By examining the net benefits for each potential participant (indi-

---

4. Another term for Nash behavior is independent adjustment, whereby each individual chooses his or her best response in relation to those of the other agents. Nash behavior is defined more fully later in the chapter. Optimality refers to Pareto optimality, in which no one's welfare can be improved without decreasing the welfare of at least one other individual.

vidual or coalition), one can determine whether the group is privileged or not, but the notion of intermediacy has never been given a clear-cut criterion for identification. If, say, a group of four is not privileged, it may still be intermediate and, thus, form. Intermediacy in these cases can only be determined by inspection to see whether the group provides itself with the collective good. Since I intend to analyze equilibria using explicit criteria, I must eschew the concept of intermediate group and distinguish solely between privileged and latent groups.

Theme 1, concerning the relationship of group size to collective provision and efficiency, has received much attention in both the theoretical and experimental literature.[5] For many cases, an increase in group size is associated with a deterioration in the performance of the collective in providing for the participants' welfare. In particular, an increase in group size is thought by Olson (1965) to limit individual contributions so that total provision levels actually decline as the group grows. With sufficiently large groups, *Logic* suggested that each person may view his or her share of the gain to be so small that *each* person refrains from contributing to the collective good and, in consequence, none of the collective good is provided (i.e., the group is latent). When an increase in group size curtails contributions, *and* when total benefits of collective action directly relate to group size, an increase in group size may cause a deterioration in optimality as hypothesized in *Logic*. In general, the theoretical literature has identified some bounds to the truth of the propositions that underlie theme 1. If, for example, a well-endowed individual gains great benefit from a collective action, he or she might provide the action so that the group is privileged, regardless of group size. For instance, an individual may derive sufficient benefits from the restoration of a monument in the town square, especially if it depicts an ancestor, that he or she will restore the statue at his or her own expense. The size of the town and, hence, the number of potential other contributors does not influence the contributor's decision. When, in other situations, the smallest contribution determines the overall level of the collective action experienced, an increase in group size may not be associated with smaller provision levels.

The composition of the group, in terms of the members' endowments (or wealth) and tastes, is behind theme 2 of *Logic*. Collectives may be homogeneous in that all members have identical tastes and income, or collectives may be heterogeneous in that members have either different tastes and/or different incomes. In the real world, both kinds of collectives exist. The members of prestigious neighborhoods or exclusive country clubs are often homogeneous, while the users of national parks are heterogeneous. Olson (1965)

---

5. For theoretical treatments, see, e.g., Chamberlin 1974; McGuire 1974; Andreoni 1988a. For experimental treatments, see, e.g., Isaac, Walker, and Thomas 1984; Kim and Walker 1984; Isaac and Walker 1988a.

argued that heterogeneous memberships would confront an exploitation problem, whereby the better-endowed members would carry the burdens of the less fortunate. On the positive side, Olson (1965) thought that heterogeneity might promote a group being privileged, since great disparity between potential contributors may ensure that at least one member (i.e., the wealthiest) might derive sufficient benefits to bear the entire burden of collective provision alone.

Theme 2 concerning asymmetry has generated an empirical literature following Olson and Zeckhauser's (1966) study of the NATO alliance. The manner in which membership asymmetry or heterogeneity is handled is crucial for the establishment of the associated propositions in subsequent contributions (e.g., Bergstrom, Blume, and Varian 1986). If all goods are normal with positive income elasticities so that purchases of all goods rise with income *and* if tastes are identical, then contributors can be rank ordered from highest to lowest based solely on income levels (Andreoni 1988a). In this case, theme 2 then holds as Olson hypothesized: wealthier persons contribute more than poorer persons. The wealthy (great) consequently carry the burden of collective provision for the poor (small). When, however, tastes differ between agents, matters become more complex. Theme 2 may no longer hold, because a relatively strong preference for the collective action may motivate even a poor individual to support the action on par or better with a wealthier person who is less inclined toward it. For the Israeli-U.S. military alliance, Israel (the poorer partner) allocates approximately 20–25 percent of its gross domestic product (GDP) to defense, while the United States allocates approximately 5–7 percent of GDP. Obviously, Israel places great value on its defense.

In terms of the policy-oriented theme 3, much work has been done in analyzing the influence of joint products, *in which the collective activity yields multiple outputs that vary in their degree of publicness.*[6] Some outputs may be private, while others may be purely or impurely public. Much less attention has been paid to the more important policy component of theme 3—that is, the design of institutional rules to provide the proper incentives to surmount collective action impediments. In *Logic,* Olson focused on the use of federated structures that fostered closer contact between participants and that reduced the size of subgroupings. Federal structures characterize labor unions and some charities (e.g., the United Fund). In recent years, investigators have examined the effects of institutional rules on the underlying game structure.[7] Theme 3 is also associated with the use of coercion to engineer group com-

---

6. See, e.g., Andreoni 1987, 1989, 1990; Cornes and Sandler 1981, 1984a, 1986; Murdoch and Sandler 1984; Sandler 1977; McGuire 1990; and Sandler and Murdoch 1990.

7. See Ostrom and Nitzan 1990; Cornes and Sandler 1984b; de Jasay 1989; Guttman 1987; Runge 1984; Lipnowski and Maital 1983; Sen 1967.

pliance. As Guttman (1978) has recognized, coercion must itself be financed, and this raises other issues concerning the manner in which resources are earmarked toward coercion.

1.4 On the Validity of Olsonian Propositions

Given the wide range of activities encompassed by collective action, it is nearly impossible to formulate simple propositions with general validity. Two or more collective action problems may require vastly different models and assumptions. The failure of Olson's propositions to have universal validity does not significantly detract from his great achievement in elucidating some of the principles of collective action. Since its publication, researchers have devised exceptions to each of the propositions. If *Logic* does not contain universally valid propositions, then why has it had such a significant effect? Why do people continue to read the book? The answers surely relate to the numerous specific cases in which the propositions are, indeed, valid. I would argue that it is these special cases that most clearly apply to real-world problems that arise daily. Had Olson qualified his propositions in such a manner as to yield airtight propositions, *Logic* would not, I am convinced, have generated the interest that it has. Olson's bold, sweeping, and provocative propositions enticed researchers to search further to draw better boundaries to the statements. Moreover, the uncomplicated and simple language and notions, embodied by the propositions, were accessible to a wide audience in related disciplines. If the relevant valid cases had been unimportant or irrelevant to political, economic, and sociological problems, the propositions would have been long forgotten. Instead, notions of free riding, unfair burden sharing, and the exploitation of the great by the small have begun to permeate our everyday language and thought.

By examining the validity of the propositions, one may be able to explain why, in some instances, collective action is forthcoming, while it is not in others. When faced with disasters (e.g., forest fires threatening multiple western states), collective action is often accomplished. Billions of dollars are raised each year by charities, even though philanthropic activities have pure public good aspects. Brutal dictators are overthrown, and revolutionaries liberate oppressed peoples. Yet in other cases, collective action does not materialize. For example, individuals do not conserve water or energy unless coerced to do so through prices or sanctions. Otherwise law-abiding citizens do not maintain pollution control devices on their automobiles and, in some cases, disconnect them to increase performance, even though automobile emissions destroy the environment for everyone. Commons (e.g., hunting grounds, fisheries, oil pools) are often depleted at inefficiently high rates. Military burdens are shared unequally among allies in times of peace, but burdens are shared on a more equal footing in times of war. Operation Desert Shield (Storm) may be an excellent example of this phenomenon. This book is meant to explain the forces behind these and other collective action successes and failures. An analysis of the basic themes holds the answers.

1.5 The Methodology of the Book

Since this book is intended to interest researchers and students drawn from economics, political science, sociology, and anthropology, the analysis is purposely kept uncomplicated. Much of the analysis relies on basic micro-economic principles that are taught at the intermediate level. In many places throughout the book, collective action problems are examined using elementary ideas drawn from the analysis of games. Simple tables, displaying the rewards or payoffs associated with various strategy combinations, are employed. Such tables are known as the normal-form or matrix representation of games; the simplicity of this representation should appeal to a wide audience. In other places, I utilize basic notions of optimization. The appendix at the book's end also reviews some of these notions; the interested reader should consult either Chiang (1984, chaps. 9, 11, 12, 21) or Dixit (1990) for further details. Sophisticated derivations are relegated to chapter appendixes.

1.6 Some Definitions and Basic Concepts

This section presents some key definitions and concepts that will be utilized from the outset of chapter 2. Readers familiar with Pareto optimality and Nash equilibrium are advised to skip directly to chapter 2.

1.6.1 Pareto Optimality

In studying collective action, a behavioral standard is needed to judge whether a group has managed to do well by its members. In economics that standard is *Pareto optimality.* An allocation or assignment of resources is Pareto optimal when it is not possible to improve the well-being of one individual without harming at least one other. When an alternative allocation exists so that it is possible to improve at least one person's well-being while harming no one else, the normative implication of the Pareto criterion is that the alternative allocation should be implemented. One state or allocation *Pareto dominates* (or is *Pareto superior* to) another if at least one individual has his or her welfare improved and no one has his or her welfare lowered. Similarly, allocation A is *Pareto dominated* by (or *Pareto inferior* to) allocation B, if, at allocation A, at least one person's welfare is smaller and no one's welfare is higher when compared to allocation B. Pareto-optimal allocations are said to be optimal, while Pareto-inferior or Pareto-dominated outcomes are called suboptimal.

Although Pareto optimality has much intuitive appeal as a normative standard, it is not without shortcomings. First, the Pareto criterion of preferring Pareto-optimal positions does not give a *complete ordering*, whereby all states or allocations can be compared. In particular, two Pareto-optimal positions cannot themselves be compared or ordered. Moreover, an inefficient position may be noncomparable to a Pareto-optimal position if the income distribution makes at least one person worse off in the Pareto-optimal position when compared to the inefficient allocation. Second, the Pareto optimality criterion is silent about whether an income distribution is better or worse. This latter judgment requires a *social welfare function* that relates individual utilities to societal well-being. Such a function aggregates the utility levels of individuals into a single index that reflects how well off society is supposed to be. Different allocations of resources can then be compared by the size of this index. Third, the Pareto-optimal criterion often favors the status quo. A stark example of this is an allocation whereby one person has everything and no one else has anything. If the fortunate person is not altruistic, then any redistribution away from the status quo that benefits others would fail the Pareto criterion, since the fortunate person becomes worse off. Even an outward shift of the entire production possibility frontier owing to, say, a technical improvement may lead to noncomparable positions if someone is made worse off.

Despite its shortcomings, Pareto optimality remains the normative standard in economics. This is probably due to a reciprocal relationship between a competitive market equilibrium with private goods and the criterion of Pareto optimality. This relationship is characterized as the first and second fundamental theorems of welfare economics. The first theorem states that every competitive equilibrium is Pareto optimal. As each firm maximizes profits subject to its technology, and as each consumer maximizes utility subject to tastes and the budget constraints, the resulting equilibrium satisfies all of the requirements of a Pareto optimum (Cornes and Sandler 1986, 14–17). In particular, exchange efficiency is achieved so that it is not possible to improve the well-being of one person without lowering the well-being of another through exchange. Moreover, production efficiency must be satisfied at a competitive equilibrium. Thus, resources are allocated between industries so that it is impossible to increase the output of one industry without decreasing the output of another. All points on a transformation or production possibility frontier satisfy production efficiency. Finally, a top-level Pareto condition is fulfilled at a competitive equilibrium. The top-level condition ties together the exchange and production sides so that it is impossible to improve someone's well-being without hurting someone else's through a production and exchange reallocation. The first theorem is often known as Adam Smith's invisible hand theorem. In the *absence* of externalities, public goods, wrongly shaped utility and production functions, and information failure, individuals' pursuit of their selfish interests leads to the well-being of the community. As such, no collective action problem arises.

The second fundamental theorem of welfare economics indicates that *any* Pareto optimum can be sustained by a perfectly competitive economy through a suitable lump-sum transfer of resources (i.e., a transfer that does not distort prices). Technical requirements, in terms of the convexity or shape of production and consumption sets, are more stringent under this second theorem.

To derive a Pareto-optimal position, one agent's utility function is maximized subject to the constancy of the utility levels of the other individuals and to the relevant resource constraints. Each of the three Pareto conditions can be related to an equality of marginal conditions. In the case of exchange efficiency, the marginal rate of substitution (MRS) between each pair of goods must be equated across all consumers of the goods. The MRS is the negative slope of an indifference curve and indicates how a person is willing to trade one good for another while maintaining a constant level of utility. Production efficiency is achieved when the marginal rate of technical substitution (MRTS) between each pair of inputs is equated across all industries using these inputs. The MRTS is the negative slope of a firm's isoquant and depicts how a firm can trade one input for another while maintaining constant output. The fulfillment of production efficiency means that each firm is operating on its marginal cost (MC) curve and that MC is equated across all firms or plants in the industry.[8] The Pareto top-level condition equates the common MRSs of the consumers to the marginal rate of transformation (MRT) of the economy for every pair of produced goods. The MRT is the negative of the slope of the transformation frontier. Points along the transformation function correspond in a one-to-one fashion to points along the contract curve of an Edgeworth-Bowley box in input space. As such, every point on the transformation frontier is production efficient and fulfills the MRTS equality.

1.6.2 Nash Equilibrium

An important solution concept for noncooperative games, in which individuals pursue their own best payoffs without coordinating with others, is the *Nash equilibrium*. A Nash equilibrium results when an agent chooses his or her best or optimizing choice for one (or more) variables, given that the other players have chosen their optimizing or best responses for this (or these) variables. In, say, a pure public good situation, a contributor decides his or

---

8. Marginal cost is the change in cost resulting from a unit change in output.

her contribution level when confronted with the optimizing contribution levels of everyone else. If, say, everyone else in aggregation would provide ten units of the public good, then an individual takes these ten units as given and decides whether to contribute additional units. At equilibrium, all optimizing choices are mutually consistent in the sense that no one would want to change his or her behavior alone.

In its standard form, a Nash equilibrium is without an explicit temporal structure; conceptually, all of the choices are made simultaneously. Of course, a temporal structure could be added that permits a sequence of moves between or among the agents. An explicit temporal structure often brings with it the notion of repeated games, whereby the actions and responses of the agents are examined over a number of periods.

Since actions are not coordinated in the usual Nash depiction, *independent adjustment* is said to characterize Nash behavior. In the standard, well-behaved, competitive market equilibrium, independent adjustment leads to Pareto optimality. In the pure public good model, Nash behavior leads to an equilibrium in which too little of the good is provided (see the proofs in chapter 2). The resulting suboptimality is with respect to a Pareto-optimal standard. An explicit welfare comparison between the Nash and Pareto optimum would require a knowledge of the distribution of income or utility. Typically, one settles for a qualitative statement that the public good is under-supplied in the Nash equilibrium.

When a public good is impure owing to excludability and/or jointly produced private benefits, Nash behavior need not imply suboptimality. Excludable public goods or club goods can be voluntarily provided by members to satisfy Pareto optimality. Clubs are a private alternative to government provision of public or collective goods. Examples include recreation facilities, movie theaters, military alliances, golf courses, parks, swimming pools, and health clinics.

Club goods are often partially rival in their benefits owing to congestion or crowding. Crowding simply means that one user's utilization of the club good decreases the benefits or the quality of service still available to the remaining users. As such, crowding depends on some measure of utilization, which could include the number of members, the number of visits, or the average utilization rate. Club crowding may assume various forms, including longer travel times on highways, longer waits for service, higher noise levels, more frequent breakdowns of equipment, greater bacteria levels in swimming pools, reduced views at movies, and increased safety risks on highways. Two types of clubs or groups can be distinguished, as in *Logic,* based on the notion of rivalry. If the club good is completely nonrival so that crowding costs are zero regardless of the number of users, then the club is *inclusive* and should involve everyone who wants to join. Since, in this case, an additional member can reduce everyone's cost payment through sharing (i.e., total costs are spread over a greater number of payers) without detracting from the club's benefits, all willing participants should be included. In other words, additional members augment the collective benefit through reduced cost shares without increasing collective costs; thus, collective group size should be unrestricted.

In contrast, an *exclusive club* limits membership size and imposes a membership size restriction. An exclusive club shares a partially rivalrous good, whose benefits decrease for the members as group size expands. Roughly speaking, membership is increased until the marginal benefits from cost spreading equal the marginal crowding costs that the entrant imposes on the club. The membership restriction equates benefits and costs at the margin that arise from increased membership.

1.6.3 Free-Riding Behavior

Each year, Public Broadcasting Stations in the United States run a fund-raising campaign to ask viewers to contribute to support programming. Although many pledges are forthcoming, a large proportion of the viewers never send in anything. Such individuals are free riders since they rely on the contributions of others to support programs that these free riders view but do not help finance. In a broad sense, a free rider is anyone who contributes less than his or her true marginal value derived from a nonexcludable public good. If everyone contributes his or her true willingness to pay (i.e., his or her MRS), there would be no free riders. When a good is nonexcludable, many people will fail to contribute, because they will get the good's benefits free once provided by others. In doing so, free riders save income that could be used to buy other excludable goods.

Although the term *free riding* is never used per se in *Logic,* free riding is associated with Olson's seminal book. The nearest Olson comes to using this terminology is in the following.

> Once a smaller member has the amount of the collective good he gets free from the largest member, he has more than he would have purchased for himself, and has no incentive to obtain any of the collective good at his own expense. (Olson 1965, 35)

The term *free riding* is used rather loosely in the literature and applies to distinct, but related, phenomena (see McMillan 1979a, 96–97). At times, free riding refers to the suboptimality that often characterizes the Nash or non-cooperative equilibrium associated with the provision of a public good. At other times, especially with respect to empirical studies, it relates to the inverse relationship between an agent's contribution and those of the other agents. Free riding also relates to the failure of individuals to reveal their true preferences for the public good through their contributions. Finally, it denotes the tendency for marginal and average contributions to decline with group size.

1.7 The Plan of the Book

The remainder of the book contains six chapters. In chapter 2, each of the basic themes are examined and developed in light of the advances made in the last twenty-five years. This chapter forms the theoretical underpinning for the book. Chapter 3 focuses on more recent developments concerning collective action. The chapter opens with a discussion of the neutrality theorem, which states that suboptimal Nash provision levels for some types of collective good cannot be corrected by standard income and tax policies unless the set of contributors is affected. Chapter 3 also investigates the importance of the technology of the public good, which transforms the amounts of individual contributions into an aggregate consumption amount for the collective good. The theory of clubs, dynamic considerations, uncertainty, and strategic behavior are also studied. Chapter 4 analyzes a host of applications that are topics of current professional interest in both political science and economics. Chapter 5 reviews empirical attempts to test propositions from *Logic* (this chapter assumes a knowledge of basic econometrics and should be skipped by the unprepared reader). Chapter 6 analyzes some current contingencies with the use of collective action theory. These include burden sharing among nations involved in Operation Desert Storm and three different global collective problems (i.e., ozone depletion, global warming, and acid rain). Chapter 7 provides directions for further research and concluding remarks.

CHAPTER 2

Basic Themes and the Theory of Collective Action

For a moment, imagine a world devoid of collective action. There would be no nations, no immigration restrictions, no armies, no parks, no public education, no emergency-warning systems, no governments, no lobbies, and no police. To protect property against theft or invasion, each person would have to devise his or her own defenses. If a road is needed, then a person would have to level and clear his or her own path. This would be a hostile environment. Much of each person's time would be spent in the unproductive activity of guarding possessions. Collective action would soon evolve from this natural state. If some individuals (i.e., the thugs) specialize in providing protection, and if this protection is offered for fewer resources than those required to provide one's own defenses, then defense would be collectivized. Individuals who specialize in providing defense would amass weapons and armies, and would become the government. Over time, the protectors would acquire other collective activities. Some collective action would evolve between small groups of individuals without the intervention of a government. If, for example, two people have reasons to interact often, they may both pitch in to build a path between them. Judging from history, I suspect that there would be a natural tendency toward some collective action.

The study of collective action examines the factors that motivate individuals to coordinate their activities to better their collective well-being. Why are some forms of collective action (e.g., the adherence to driving on the right-hand side of the road in North America) self-enforcing, while other forms (e.g., not confessing to a crime in a Prisoner's Dilemma situation) are not? What are the underlying parameters or considerations behind people's willingness to act so as to achieve a collective goal? In this chapter and the next, I identify some of the factors behind successful and unsuccessful collective action. In doing so, the theoretical development of collective action analysis is surveyed. This chapter focuses on the three themes of *Logic* that relate group size, group composition, and institutional design to the outcome of collective action. The analysis shows that important exceptions exist to these themes and their underlying propositions. For example, the extent of suboptimality may be independent of group size. Large, homogeneous groups may be privileged, and their provision levels may increase with group expansion.

The small need not exploit the large, and, in some scenarios, the large do the exploiting. Nash equilibria may, at times, be Pareto optimal. In many instances, the underlying game structure, as reflected by the pattern of payoffs associated with the various individual strategies, determines the outcome of collective action.

The remainder of the chapter is divided into six major sections. The first section presents a more detailed examination of the two-person Prisoner's Dilemma with the help of a matrix. In section 2.2, the requirement for being a privileged group is investigated, and the inherent suboptimality for Olson's generic collective action problem is established. Readers who wish to avoid the mathematical presentation should skip section 2.2.1. Section 2.3 concerns the first theme of *Logic*. This section also presents the technology of public (or collective) supply, a key factor behind all of the themes. Quite simply, the technology of public supply concerns how individual contributions to the collective action are aggregated to arrive at the amount of the collective good that is available to all to consume. Section 2.4 investigates group composition and collective action, while section 2.5 studies means for overcoming collective action failures. Concluding remarks are found in the last section.

2.1 The Prisoner's Dilemma Once Again

Let us return to the district attorney and the two forlorn prisoners, suspected of armed robbery. Unless the district attorney can convince one or both suspects to confess, there is not sufficient evidence to convict them on the robbery charge. The district attorney has, however, enough to convict them of a lesser firearms charge. The robbery charge carries a maximum penalty of ten years in jail, while the firearms charge carries a maximum penalty of two years. To elicit a confession, the district attorney promises the prisoners during separate interviews that if they confess and their companion does not, then the confessor receives a one-year sentence, while the nonconfessor gets the maximum ten-year sentence. If, however, both confess, they would each receive reduced sentences of seven years for the robbery. Only when a single prisoner confesses, does the confessor get off with a light sentence. Inasmuch as the district attorney cannot convict without the assistance of at least one suspect, one might think that neither will confess, but, in fact, both are likely to confess much to their collective dismay.

In figure 2.1a, the matrix indicates the jail sentences for the four possible scenarios: no confession (cell *a*), just prisoner 2 confesses (cell *b*), just prisoner 1 confesses (cell *c*), and both prisoners confess (cell *d*). The first payoff (or prison sentence) in each cell is that of prisoner 1, while the second is that of prisoner 2. In the matrix, the rows indicate the two strategies of prisoner 1, while the columns depict the two strategies of prisoner 2. When player 1's

2

Don't
Confess   Confess

Don't   *a*   *b*
Confess   2,2   10,1

1

           c   *d*
Confess   1,10   7,7

a. Cardinal Representation;
numbers refer to years in jail

2

Don't
Confess   Confess

Don't   *a*   *b*
Confess   3,3   1,4

1

           c   *d*
Confess   4,1   2,2

b. Ordinal Representation;
numbers refer to rankings
in prisoners' preferences

Fig. 2.1. Two-person Prisoner's Dilemma

payoffs in a row exceed *all* corresponding payoffs in the other row(s), player 1 is better off playing the row or strategy with these higher payoffs. When, analogously, player 2's payoffs in a column exceed all corresponding payoffs in the other column(s), player 2 is better off playing the column with these higher payoffs. In figure 2.1a, the "confess" row (column) has this property and is considered to be a *dominant strategy*. A dominant strategy gives a greater payoff regardless of the other player's actions. Prisoner 1 has a dominant strategy to confess, since no matter what prisoner 2 does, prisoner 1's payoffs for confessing (one year or seven years) are better than the corresponding payoffs for not confessing (two years and ten years). Because the game is symmetric, prisoner 2 views confessing as a dominant strategy—that is, best regardless of the other prisoner's action. By playing their dominant strategy, each prisoner confesses and ends up in cell *d* with seven years in jail. Ironically, the outcome in cell *d* is Pareto inferior to the no-confession case in which each serves two years. This follows because each prisoner receives seven years by confessing rather than two years by not confessing. Cell *d* is also a Nash equilibrium because, given the best response of the other player (i.e., to confess), the player's own best response is to confess. At cell *d*, neither prisoner would *unilaterally* want to change his or her strategic choice if given the chance. Such a change would yield a ten-year sentence as cells *b* and *c* indicate.

Obviously, there are many patterns of payoffs for even two-person games. Thus, we need a ready means for glancing at a matrix game and identifying a Prisoner's Dilemma. This is easily accomplished by ranking payoffs from best to worst and drawing up a new matrix with these ranks in the place of payoffs. This procedure yields the *ordinal form* for the matrix. The best payoff is assigned a 4, the next best a 3, and so on. Since longer prison terms are less desirable, the one-year sentence is the highest ranked alternative with a 4. The other entries in figure 2.1b are calculated similarly; hence, for example, the ten-year jail term is ranked lowest, with a 1. Any two-person payoff matrix that has the same ordinal payoffs as those shown in figure 2.1b is a prisoner's dilemma. Other ordinal payoff arrays imply a different game. For instance, changing the 1s to 2s and vice versa corresponds to the game of Chicken, which does not possess a dominant strategy.

2.2 On Suboptimality

Collective action fails when the pursuit of individual gains results in a suboptimal or inefficient outcome, based on the Pareto criterion. The Prisoner's Dilemma is an apt example. Each prisoner pursues his or her best individual strategy but ends up with an outcome in which *both* prisoners' payoffs (sentences) are smaller (greater) than those of some other strategy combination (cell *a*). If collective action results in a Pareto-inferior position, then a collective failure has occurred, since another strategy combination (i.e., the cooperative strategy of not confessing) could have made the participants better off by five fewer years of prison time. A collective action failure is especially troublesome when it corresponds to a stable equilibrium, from which attempts to alter the situation are met with a natural tendency to return to the original, suboptimal position. Consider the Prisoner's Dilemma and its stable (suboptimal) equilibrium. Suppose that the prisoners are released at the end of seven years. To celebrate, they take a vacation together and, as chance would have it, are near the scene of yet another armed robbery. As paroled felons, they are naturally suspected and arrested. Once again, they have a weapon, but the district attorney has insufficient evidence to convict them on the robbery charge. Suppose that the prisoners are again separated and given the same options as before. What is likely to happen? Given the same payoff matrix, each prisoner is apt to confess. Although the confession equilibrium is suboptimal, it is, nevertheless, stable and difficult to escape. Neither prisoner can trust the other to cooperate and not confess. As shown later, the suboptimality may worsen for an *n*-person Prisoner's Dilemma as *n* increases, because dissembling is a dominant strategy.

The Prisoner's Dilemma is important because it may yield a payoff structure identical to some important market failures, including pure public goods, the exploitation of common property resources, and externalities. In each of these cases, an individual's pursuit of his or her well-being results in a Pareto-inferior equilibrium, from which all participants could increase their well-being if better coordination of efforts were achieved. The Prisoner Dilemma also demonstrates that, in the case of a pure public good, none of the good might be provided. The pure public good case and its inherent suboptimality is illustrated in this chapter, while other relevant market failures are analyzed in other chapters.

*2.2.1 Olson's Formal Model

Much of Olson's (1965) treatment of collective action is presented without the explicit use of mathematics. In the early portion of *Logic*, Olson puts forth a formal model to support the rationale behind a number of his propositions. I utilize this model to depict Olson's notion of a privileged group and to investigate suboptimality with respect to collective action.

By presenting Olson's mathematical model, I hope that the reader gains an insight in terms of how many important details of modern-day analyses of collective action were not provided by Olson's formal model. For example, the utility function and the technology for aggregating collective benefits among participants were subsumed by Olson in a value function, which indicated the benefit that an individual derived from the collective good. Costs were treated as a simple, linear function of the level of collective provision. All collective-action problems were analyzed by a generic representation.

Olson's formal model (1965, 22–36) concerned a group sharing a public or collective good whose rivalry aspects were never made explicit. The provision level of the collective good is denoted by Q. Three different costs of collective provision are distinguished: (*a*) the total cost of collective provision, C; (*b*) the cost of collective provision for the ith individual, C_i; and (*c*) the cost of collective provision for a subset (Ω) of individuals, C_Ω. A subset of individuals is called a coalition and consists of members from the group or collective, G, who benefit from the collective good; hence $\Omega \subset G$.

The benefit or value that the ith individual derives from the collective good is denoted by V_i. For the coalition, this value is represented by V_Ω, and, for the group, it is indicated by V_g. The net gain that an individual derives from the collective good is A_i, which is the difference between the value of the benefit and its cost—that is, $A_i = V_i - C_i$. For a coalition, the net gain is denoted by A_Ω. Olson defines the "size" of the group, S_g, in terms of the gain per unit of provision, so that the value of the group (not accounting for cost) is

$$V_g = S_g Q \ . \tag{2.1}$$

Equation 2.1 relates collective provision to group gains, in which the derived benefit to the group is the product of its gain per unit of provision times the number of units provided. Olson's notion of group size, as the gain per unit of provision, is at odds with the standard notion of the number of individuals.[1]

Olson defines the ratio of individual gain to group gain as the *fraction* of group gain, F_i, of the ith individual:

$$F_i = V_i/V_g \ . \tag{2.2}$$

Similarly, F_Ω denotes the fraction of group gain, derived by coalition Ω, and is the ratio of V_Ω to V_g. Equation 2.2 relates to the distribution of collective benefits in which each individual receives a fraction of group benefits, so that $V_i = F_i V_g$. Since equation 2.2 embodies both the utility function and the manner in which individual contributions to collective provision are aggregated (i.e., the technology of public good), the exact nature of rivalry, if any, is not clear. This is clearly a drawback of the Olson model and explains why alternative models have been developed.

For convenience, table 2.1 lists the notation used to represent Olson's model. This table can be consulted in later chapters, when I refer to the Olson model.

A group is privileged if at least one subset of individuals can make a net gain in providing the collective action alone. The sufficient condition for a privileged group is met provided that

$$A_\Omega = V_\Omega - C_\Omega > 0 \tag{2.3}$$

for at least one subset or coalition drawn from the group ($\Omega \subset G$). Since equation 2.3 considers all subsets, it accounts for the case where a single individual meets the condition ($A_i = V_i - C_i > 0$).

---

1. This difference is also noted in Ostrom 1987, in which four distinct notions of group size are identified from *Logic*.

TABLE 2.1. Notation of the Olson Model

Variable	Definition
Q	Provision level of the collective good
q^i	Individual contribution to the collective good
$\bar{Q}$	Contribution of the rest of the group to the collective good
C	Cost of total collective provision
$C_i,\ C_\Omega$	Cost to the individual, cost to the coalition
S_g	"Size" of the group in terms of the gain per unit of provision
$V_i,\ V_\Omega,\ V_g$	Value to the individual, value to the coalition, and value to the group
$A_i,\ A_\Omega$	Net gain to the individual, net gain to the coalition
$F_i,\ F_\Omega$	Fraction of group gain to the individual, fraction of group gain to the coalition
G	The set of group members
Ω	Subset of the group members

The general suboptimality of the collective action problem posed by Olson is established by comparing the Nash equilibrium and the Pareto optimality condition. I first present the Nash equilibrium for collective provision. This equilibrium requires the representative individual to choose his or her contribution, q^i, to the collective good to maximize his or her net gain, A_i. By equations 2.1 and 2.2, the objective function for the Nash problem of the representative individual can be written as

$$\max_{q^i}[F_i S_g Q - C_i(q^i)] \ ,$$

where individual cost, C_i, is assumed to be an increasing linear function of provision. Furthermore, total provision for the group is the sum of individual i's provision, q^i, and the aggregate provision of the other individuals, $\bar{Q}$, so that $Q = q^i + \bar{Q}$. For independent adjustment or Nash behavior, each individual treats the optimizing provision level of the rest of the group as a parameter so that $\bar{Q}$ is held constant when maximizing. The cost function for the individual and that for the group are assumed identical with constant marginal cost, so that $dC/dQ = dC_i/dq^i = k$ for all Q and q^i, where k is a constant. The first-order condition[2] (FOC) for the Nash problem is

$$F_i dV_g/dQ - dC_i/dq^i = 0 \ , \tag{2.4}$$

---

2. Second-order conditions are satisfied since $C_i(q^i)$ is convex and V_g is strictly concave. Thus, the objective function is strictly concave.

in which the concave benefit function V_g has replaced S_gQ. The concavity of V_g merely indicates that the marginal benefit for the group declines as provision increases. Since S_g can itself depend on Q, V_g does not have to be linear in Q. Henceforth, I assume that V_g is a strictly concave function of Q. In equation 2.4, the individual's marginal benefit equals the marginal cost of provision. When equation 2.4 holds for *each i*, a Nash equilibrium is achieved. The *simultaneous* satisfaction of the system of FOCs in equation 2.4 determines an optimizing vector of q^i's. The sum of these optimizing q^i's is the Nash quantity, Q^N, that satisfies equation 2.4 for each *i*. This Q^N can be compared with the Pareto-optimizing quantity to establish suboptimal Nash provision.

A Pareto optimum corresponds to

$$\max_Q (V_g - C) \, ,$$

where collective provision is chosen to maximize the group's net benefits. The Pareto optimum must fulfill the following FOC.

$$dV_g/dQ - dC/dQ = 0 \, , \tag{2.5}$$

so that the group's marginal benefit from provision equals its marginal cost of provision. Denote Q^* as the argmax$(V_g - C)$, or the provision level that satisfies equation 2.5. If the Nash quantity, Q^N, that satisfies equation 2.4 is used to evaluate the left-hand side of equation 2.5, then we have

$$\frac{dV_g(Q^N)}{dQ} - \frac{dC(Q^N)}{dQ} > 0 \, , \tag{2.6}$$

since the marginal benefit evaluated at Q^N equals $F_i \cdot dV_g(Q^N)/dQ$ by equation 2.4,[3] where $0 < F_i < 1$. By equation 2.6 and the strict concavity of the objective function, we then have

$$Q^N < Q^* \, ,$$

so that the Nash quantity implies too little provision and, hence, suboptimality.[4] Group utility can be increased with provision at Q^* rather than Q^N, since marginal benefits are greater than marginal costs at Q^N by equation 2.6.

---

3. This assumes that $dC_i/dq^i = dC(Q^N)/dQ$, since marginal cost is assumed constant. With nonconstant marginal cost, the comparison of the Pareto and Nash conditions is less clear-cut and requires knowledge of the marginal cost functions. In *Logic*, Olson (1965, 24) did not distinguish between group and individual cost functions.

4. The more traditional approach for establishing suboptimal provision for a Nash equilibrium is to examine the maximization of utility subject to a resource constraint, in which

Although suboptimality follows immediately from Olson's model, the effect of group size (in terms of the number of people, n, in the collective) on the degree of suboptimality (i.e., the relationship between Q^N/Q^* as n changes) is not dealt with explicitly, because the relationship of cost and benefit to group size is not given. Without these relationships, an explicit theory of clubs cannot be established formally (see chap. 3). Olson's setup has insufficient details to distinguish between different cases of collective action. For example, an externality may be depicted in myriad forms depending upon the nature of the uncompensated interdependency. That is, an externality may be unidirectional if one individual's actions affect others, but the actions of others do not affect the externality generator. In contrast, externalities are reciprocal when all individuals are both recipient and generator of uncompensated interdependencies. The nature of the interdependency associated with a collective action problem is hidden in Olson's value function.

2.2.2 A Graphic Presentation

A graphic analysis of a collective action problem often proves burdensome because at least three dimensions are required. In the case of a pure public good (e.g., pollution removal or a fireworks display), axes must be assigned to each agent's provision of the public good and to the private (noncollective) activity. For two individuals, three axes are involved, since both a private and a collective good must be included to make the agent's budget allocation process nontrivial. Even a two-person externality requires three axes—one for the private nonexternality-generating activity, and one each for the externality-generating activity and the externality. To depict the problem in two dimensions, as I intend, a choice must be made in terms of which good to hold constant when displaying a *projection* of the requisite objective (e.g.,

$$U^i = U^i(y^i, Q)$$

is the ith individual's utility function and y^i is the ith person's consumption of a private good. For a linear resource constraint, the Pareto optimal FOC is

$$\sum_{i=1}^{n} \mathrm{MRS}^i_{Qy} - (p/p_y) = 0 \, ,$$

in which MRS^i_{Qy} denotes the ith individual's marginal rate of substitution between the public and private good, p is the per-unit price of the public good, and p_y is the per-unit price of the private good. The FOCs of the Nash equilibrium satisfy

$$\mathrm{MRS}^i_{Qy} - (p/p_y) = 0, \qquad i = 1, \ldots, n \, .$$

When the Q^N that solves the Nash equilibrium is used to evaluate the Pareto-optimal FOCs, the resulting positive inequality implies that $Q^* > Q^N$.

utility or profit) surface onto two dimensions. In the case of the pure public good, the private good and *one* of the two public good contribution axes have historically been used (see, e.g., Samuelson 1955; Pauly 1970). Changes in the public good contribution of the other agent(s) then shift the curves in the two-dimensional diagram. Because the allocation decision of interest is the agents' provision or contribution to the public good, additional insights can be gained if the private good level is held constant and the axes are assigned to the agents' contributions to the public good (Cornes and Sandler 1984b and 1985), as I do below.

The diagram to be presented can be used in a large number of collective action scenarios, including pure public goods, common property resources, impure public goods, and externalities. For purposes of illustration, I focus my presentation on the pure public good case; small modifications would be required to treat the other cases (see, e.g., Cornes and Sandler 1986). The analysis could relate to the removal of a pest (e.g., mosquitoes) along a lake shared by two individuals. Mosquito removal is nonrival, since one less insect provides a benefit to each individual that is independent of the number of people enjoying its absence. Moreover, once the mosquito is eliminated, no one in the vicinity of the lake can be excluded from the benefit that results. Only two individuals are assumed to "subscribe" or contribute to the private provision of the public good, Q. The diagrammatic analysis can be extended to accommodate more individuals in two ways: (1) by assuming that $n - 1$ individuals can be treated as a single entity, or (2) by assuming that all individuals are identical.

Each of the two agents derives satisfaction from a private good and a public good, Q. The ith agent's utility function is

$$U^i = U^i(y^i, Q) , \tag{2.7}$$

where the total amount of the pure public good is the simple sum of the individuals' contributions ($Q = q^1 + q^2$) owing to nonexcludability and nonrivalry. The summation "technology" implies that the public good is completely substitutable between providers. This might be an appropriate assumption, for instance, with respect to mine sweeping or pollution removal in a shared waterway, since it does not matter who removes the mines or pollution. For other public goods, the identity or location of the provider (e.g., conventional forces along a shared perimeter) may make a difference. Other technologies of public supply could be incorporated into the graphic analysis to account for these cases. For example, weights, w^i, could be applied so that total provision is a weighted sum of the individuals' contributions (see section 2.3). To facilitate exposition, the graphic analysis focuses on the summation technology where each individual is constrained by a simple linear budget constraint,

$$I^i = y^i + pq^i ,$$ (2.8)

in which the private good's price is set equal to 1 to simplify the presentation and the public good's price is p.

From the viewpoint of either individual, the basic subscription problem involves two constraints: the budget constraint and the level of contributions of the other subscriber. For individual 1, this problem is as follows:

maximize $U^1(y^1, q^1 + q^2)$

subject to

$$I^1 = y^1 + pq^1 ,$$

with q^2 fixed. The fixity of q^2 is the quantity constraint alluded to in chapter 1 and is identified with the Nash "conjecture" that each agent picks an optimizing level of contributions based on the choice of others. The FOC necessary for an optimum requires the contributor to satisfy

$$MRS^i_{Qy} = p ,$$ (2.9)

in which MRS^i_{Qy} is the ith individual's marginal rate of substitution between the public good and the private good and, as such, denotes the marginal benefit derived from the public good. The MRS involves a ratio of marginal utilities, in which each is evaluated at the optimizing (fixed) level of q^2. The condition in equation 2.9 is analogous to the consumer's optimizing choice between two private goods (see the appendix at the end of the book), where the MRS is equated to the price ratio. Unlike the private goods case, the condition in equation 2.9 does not necessarily imply a Pareto-optimal outcome, since benefits conferred on others by an agent's action are not taken into account, as shown below.

Using a standard consumer indifference diagram, I illustrate equation 2.9 for agent 1 in figure 2.2. The private good consumption of individual 1 is measured on the vertical axis of figure 2.2, while public good contribution (q^1) and consumption (Q) of individual 1 are on the horizontal axis. The budget line of agent 1 when $q^2 = 0$ is AC with a slope equal to $-p$. Only individual 1 contributes to the public good when AC applies. Curves I^1I^1, I^2I^2, and I^3I^3 represent three from a family of indifference curves for agent 1. An indifference curve denotes all combinations of private and public good consumption bundles whereby the agent's satisfaction or utility is unchanged. An indifference curve that is to the right and above another (such as I^2I^2 in relationship to I^1I^1) depicts a greater level of satisfaction. The negative of the slope of the indifference curve is the MRS, which indicates the ratio at which

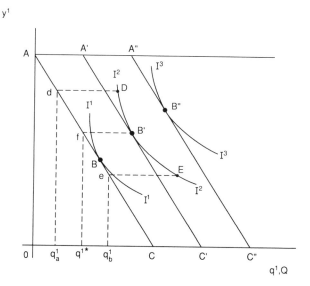

Fig. 2.2.   Effects of spillovers on provision decisions

the consumer can trade the two goods and still maintain a fixed utility. If, say, the marginal utility of the public good is high relative to the private good, then the individual is willing to trade a relatively large quantity of the private good for an additional unit of the public good—that is, I^1I^1 is relatively steep. A convex-to-the-origin indifference curve implies that the MRS decreases as Q is acquired.

In the absence of any q^2, condition 2.9 is satisfied at the tangency between AC and I^1I^1 at point B in figure 2.2. If, however, q^2 equals AA', then the relevant budget line incorporating this nonzero q^2 contribution is $A'C'$ with slope $-p$. Condition 2.9 is now satisfied at the tangency between I^2I^2 and $A'C'$ at B'. If q^2 equals AA'', then condition 2.9 corresponds to the tangency between I^3I^3 and $A''C''$ at B''. At, say, point B', agent 1 contributes q^{1*} to the public good, since AA' $(=fB')$ is derived from agent 2's contribution.

To display figure 2.2 in public good space, we first substitute the budget constraint into the utility function so that the subscription problem confronting individual 1 becomes:

$$\text{maximize } U^1(I^1 - pq^1, q^1 + q^2)$$
$$q^1$$

for fixed q^2. This problem permits us to express *budget-constrained* utility as

$$U^1 = U^1(I^1 - pq^1, q^1 + q^2) \tag{2.10}$$

$$= U^1(q^1, q^2; I^1, p) \ .$$

According to equation 2.10, utility can be displayed in (q^1, q^2) space for a given income level and public good price. Since q^2 adds to individuals 1's satisfaction, an increase in q^2 for a constant level of q^1 corresponds to a higher utility level. In figure 2.3, v^1v^1, v^2v^2, and v^3v^3 depict three isoutility curves for constant income and prices, where q^2 is measured on the vertical axis and q^1 on the horizontal axis. The slope of each isoutility curve can be shown to equal[5]

$$\frac{dq^2}{dq^1} \bigg|_{U^1 = \bar{U}^1} = (-1) + (p/\mathrm{MRS}_{Qy}^1) \ . \tag{2.11}$$

In figure 2.3, curve v^2v^2 depicts a higher level of utility than v^1v^1 since, for a given q^1 level, the amount of agent 2's contributions to the public good is larger. Higher isoutility curves denote greater utility levels; hence, the cross-hatched regions above each isoutility curve are preferred points to those on the curve. For a given level of public good subscription by agent 2, say level $\hat{q}^2$, condition 2.9 is obtained when v^1v^1 has a zero slope, since MRS_{Qy}^1 then equals p by equation 2.11. The zero-sloped points on the isoutility curves satisfy the Nash FOCs for various q^2 levels. Connecting these zero-sloped points yields a Nash reaction path for individual 1, showing his or her best response to various subscription levels of his counterpart. Vertical line I^1/p bounds individual 1's maximum contribution to the public good and corresponds to the case where the entire income is devoted to the public good.

The U-shape of the isoutility curves can be justified by consulting related points in figure 2.2. For example, B' in figure 2.2 corresponds to point F in figure 2.3 if $\hat{q}^2 = AA'$. If, in figure 2.2, the agent is constrained to utility I^2I^2 and alters his or her contribution away from ideal level q^{1*} associated with point B', then the individual must be compensated with more q^2 as shown at point D or E on I^2I^2. At D, the agent contributes $q_a^1 < q^{1*}$, while at E, he or she contributes $q_b^1 > q^{1*}$. Thus, in figure 2.2, lower (higher) q^1 contributions must be matched with higher q^2 levels if utility is to be maintained. In consequence, the isoutility curves are U-shaped in figure 2.3.

---

5. Differentiating the top expression of eq. 2.10 for a constant utility level gives

$$-pU_y^1 dq^1 + U_Q^1 dq^1 + U_Q^1 dq^2 = 0 \ ,$$

where $U_y^1 = \partial U^1/\partial y^1$ and $U_Q^1 = \partial U^1/\partial Q$. Equation 2.11 follows immediately from this expression since $\mathrm{MRS}_{Qy}^1 = U_Q^1/U_y^1$.

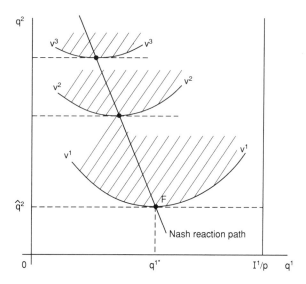

Fig. 2.3.   Isoutility curves and Nash reaction curves

The Nash equilibrium for the two-agent model is depicted in figure 2.4, where two of agent 2's isoutility curves, ii and i^1i^1, are displayed along with agent 1's isoutility curves II and I^1I^1. Agent 2's isoutility curves are U-shaped with respect to the q^2 axis and has a slope equal to the reciprocal of $(-1 + p/\text{MRS}^2_{Qy})$, since agent 2's curves are translated through 90 degrees: N^1N^1 is the Nash reaction path for individual 1, while N^2N^2 is the corresponding path for individual 2. At the intersection of the two reaction paths (i.e., point E), both agents' Nash condition (eq. 2.9) are mutually satisfied; hence, neither has a motivation to alter his or her contribution and an equilibrium is obtained. At this equilibrium, agent 1's isoutility curve has a zero slope and agent 2's isoutility curve has an infinite slope. Point E is Pareto inferior to points in the cross-hatched region in figure 2.4, which denotes points where both agents' utility levels are higher than at E. Thus, suboptimality of a Nash equilibrium for the provision of a pure public good is established graphically. The dotted curve in figure 2.4 depicts the Pareto-optimal subscription points where $\Sigma\text{MRS}^i_{Qy} = p$ and corresponds to the tangencies between the agents' isoutility curves.[6] At the Pareto-optimal subscription level, the sum of the marginal benefits to the entire group is equated to the public good's price or marginal cost. This sum of marginal benefits is merely the sum of MRSs between the public good and the private good. At a Nash equilibrium, subop-

---

6. Since the slopes are equal, we have $-1 + (p/\text{MRS}^1_{Qy}) = [-1 + (p/\text{MRS}^2_{Qy})]^{-1}$. Clearing fractions and simplifying give $\Sigma\text{MRS}^i_{Qy} = p$.

q^2

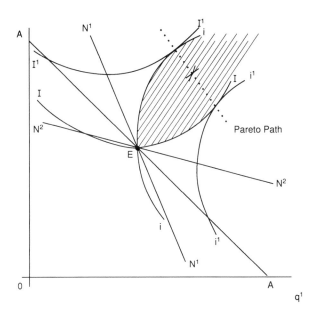

Fig. 2.4. Pareto and Nash paths for two agents

timality results since an individual equates his or her marginal benefit to marginal cost and ignores the marginal benefit that his or her contribution confers to others. In other words, individual i does not account for MRS^j_{Qy} when deciding contributions.

To show the total amount of the public good associated with the Nash equilibrium at E, we draw line AA with a slope of -1 through point E, so that this line makes a 45-degree angle with the two axes at their intercepts. Distance $0A$ along either axis then measures the total contribution to the public good, since the sum of the coordinates along a line with slope -1 is constant. The intercepts of such negatively sloped 45-degree lines through points on the dotted Pareto path are greater than those of line AA, thereby confirming the underprovision hypothesis. Clearly, Olson's underprovision hypothesis holds in well-behaved pure public good situations. But since collective action involves scenarios other than *pure* public goods, other cases and technologies of public supply must be examined, as done throughout this chapter and the next, to determine whether underprovision is a general proposition.

The diagrammatic apparatus can be modified to examine n-person symmetric equilibria, where all agents have identical tastes and endowments (see

34   Collective Action

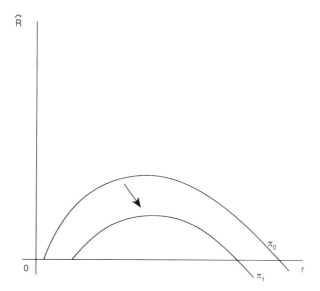

Fig. 2.5. Isoprofit contours for the commons

Cornes and Sandler 1986, 82–84) and make identical contributions at the equilibrium. If the contributions of all agents but one are summed

$$\left(\tilde{Q} = \sum_{j \neq i} q^j \right)$$

and placed on the vertical axis, then an n-person case can be displayed in terms of a representative individual's isoutility diagram analogous to figure 2.3.

Some collective action problems, such as the tragedy of the commons (Hardin 1968) where unrestricted or open access to a resource can lead to overutilization, require an alteration in the shape of the curves. For the commons, isoprofit curves would appear as hills rather than U-shaped contours. If the total exploitation of others, $\tilde{R}$, is placed on the vertical axis and the representative individual's exploitation effort, r, on the horizontal axis, as in figure 2.5, then movements in the direction of the arrow would lead to higher profit levels, in which the combined efforts of others is smaller for each r level (Cornes and Sandler 1983). The shape of these isoprofit curves are the mirror image of isoutility curves, since an increase in the variable on the vertical axis decreases the agent's objective in terms of profits. An analysis of public inputs (e.g., bridges, drainage systems, highways) that benefit two or more firms simultaneously could be displayed with diagrams analogous to figures 2.3 and

2.4. Technologies of public supply other than summation would affect the slope of the isoutility and isoprofit curves since the MRS expression of equation 2.11 would have to be weighted or transformed in some fashion.

In figure 2.4, the graphic analysis depicts an interior solution in which each individual contributes to the public good in equilibrium. Many Nash equilibria may be corner solutions in the sense that no one contributes or, in the case of two individuals, only one person contributes. This point has been emphasized by Jack and Olson (1991) in a paper that presents a different graphic device. With the Cornes-Sandler diagram, a corner solution would occur when one agent's Nash reaction path, say agent 1's, is everywhere to the right of agent 2's reaction path. In this case, the Nash equilibrium is at the horizontal intercept of agent 1's reaction path, so that agent 1 contributes and agent 2 does not. Moreover, agent 1's contributions are suboptimal, because he or she does not account for the benefits derived by agent 2.

2.3 Theme 1: The Influence of Group Size

2.3.1 Group Size and Being Privileged

Whether any of the collective good is provided or not depends on the notion of privilege. A group is privileged when at least one individual derives sufficient net benefits from the collective action to go it alone. If some individual or coalition views a collective action as providing positive *net* benefits, even though no one else contributes, then the group is privileged. The U.S. provision of a nuclear deterrent in NATO is an example. In theme 1, Olson (1965, 33–34, 48) argued that larger groups are less likely, ceteris paribus, to be privileged than smaller groups, since an individual's (coalition's) share of the group benefit from collective action declines with group size. If this share, denoted by F_Ω, decreases with group size and if, moreover, the group's benefits and costs are independent of group size, then Olson's relationship would hold (see eq. 2.3). This follows because the individual's (coalition's) benefit declines with group size but costs remain unchanged. If, however, an individual's (or a coalition's) cost also decreases with overall group size, then the fall in an individual's (or a coalition's) fraction of the group gain may be offset by the decline in cost, thereby ensuring that the group remains privileged. Institutional rules may play a role here. If, say, provision costs are shared among group members regardless of the contributor, then individual cost would indeed fall with membership size. In consequence, the requirements of being privileged may not depend on group size. The method of cost allocation as well as technological considerations play a role here.

The conditions for a privileged group may also hinge on the technology of publicness and its relationship to the underlying game structure or payoff matrix.[7] The technology of publicness refers to the manner in which individuals' provision or subscription levels are aggregated to yield a group provision or consumption level. Since the possible technologies are endless, we must focus on a few noteworthy cases. The most common technology is that of summation.

$$Q = \sum_{i=1}^{n} q^i , \qquad (2.12)$$

where q^i is the collective good's provision level of individual i, and n is group size in the more traditional sense of the number of individuals in the collective. Summation implies perfect substitutability between the q^i's. The elimination of pollution from a shared ecosystem abides by equation 2.12 as may nuclear deterrence derived from a strategic arsenal. When, however, the location or the identity of the provider influences the resulting level of the public good received by the group, simple summation is no longer an appropriate representation. For cases in which substitutability is less than perfect, individualized weights may have to be applied to the q^i's or else a different functional relationship may be needed. In the case of two individuals, total provision may have the following form.

$$Q = w^1 q^1 + w^2 q^2 , \qquad (2.13)$$

in which $0 \leq w^i \leq 1$ for $i = 1, 2$.

An important technology is that of the weakest link, in which

$$Q = \min(q^1, \ldots, q^n) , \qquad (2.14)$$

so that the smallest provision level of the group determines the collective provision (Hirshleifer 1983; Harrison and Hirshleifer 1989). The weakest link may apply to the scenario where a military alliance fortifies a perimeter against a common threat. If security depends on keeping the enemy from breaking through, then the poorest fortification along the front determines the level of collective security. Prophylactic actions to forestall the advance of a disease, a plague, or pest may also abide by the weakest-link technology. Hirshleifer (1983) gave the apt example of dike building. Beautification programs for neighborhoods or cities may also correspond to the weakest link, since the least-attractive yard or house may become the standard for assessing

---

7. See Runge 1984; Cornes and Sandler 1986, chap. 7; Ostrom and Nitzan 1990.

the entire neighborhood. Collective competitions (e.g., relay races, army inspections) may be heavily dependent on the weakest member's performance. The imposition of quality standards to integrated networks abide by the weakest link, since a crucially placed part or person (e.g., a bolt on a helicopter blade or a message relayer in a communications network) can solely determine the performance of the whole. In contrast, a best-shot technology,

$$Q = \max(q^1, \ldots, q^n) , \tag{2.15}$$

equates provision to the largest individualized effort. The discovery of a cure for a disease is an example of the best shot, as is the more fanciful example of dragon slaying. Other examples include the achievement of a research breakthrough or the intelligence acquired in espionage operations, in which the information sought is not cumulative. The best shot may also apply to an *offensive* alliance that initiates an attack, since the ally inflicting the heaviest damage may well determine the outcome of the war.

For the case of two agents, the technology in equation 2.13 corresponds to the weakest link when $w^1 = 1$, $w^2 = 0$, and $q^1 < q^2$; to the best shot when $w^1 = 0$, $w^2 = 1$, and $q^1 < q^2$; and to summation when $w^1 = w^2 = 1$. The weighting scheme in equation 2.13 could, of course, be generalized to n individuals by rank ordering the q^i's from lowest to highest. Whenever the weights are between zero and one, none of the three special technologies applies.

The technology of publicness is also behind the notion of selective incentives and joint products (as shown subsequently in section 3.6). It also plays a pivotal role in determining crowding in the modern treatment of clubs (see, e.g., Sandler and Tschirhart 1980). This follows because the crowding function indicates how the utilization of the public good and the quantity supplied influence the amount of the good that each individual gets to consume. As such, the crowding function is a technology of public supply (see section 3.1 for further details).

Once the technology of publicness is specified, it is substituted into the individual's utility function.

$$U^i = U^i[\min(q^1, \ldots, q^n), y^i] . \tag{2.16}$$

When equation 2.16 is optimized subject to the relevant constraints, the various equilibria (Nash or Pareto) can be found.

In the case of joint products, a collective action gives rise to multiple outputs. Suppose that each unit of q^i yields γ units of a private output, x, and δ units of a pure public benefit, z. For individual i, the technology implies

$$x^i = \gamma q^i ,$$ (2.17)

and

$$z^i = \delta q^i .$$ (2.18)

If the technical parameters do not differ between agents and if, moreover, total public output, Z, abides by summation, then the ith agent's utility function can be written as

$$U^i = U^i(y^i, x^i, Z) = U^i \left(y^i, \gamma q^i, \sum_{i=1}^{n} \delta q^i \right) .$$ (2.19)

The joint product model is sufficiently flexible to apply to many situations, including charity, foreign aid, police protection, education, or defense. Relevant situations involve those in which contributions to the collective action are motivated by private and public benefits.

2.3.1.1 Two-Person Games and Being Privileged
To illustrate how the technology of public supply, the institutional rules, and/or the configuration of costs and benefits affect whether the good is provided, I present a few noteworthy two-person, normal-form games that may arise from slight variations in a basic scenario. These simple examples demonstrate that a host of different collective action scenarios may ensue from a slight alteration in the configuration of costs and benefits. Some configurations imply that collective action will succeed automatically, while others indicate that collective action will yield a Pareto-inferior result unless intervention occurs. I am particularly interested in whether the group is privileged. In figure 2.6, six game forms are displayed. In each of the six matrices, player 1's strategies correspond to the row, while player 2's strategies correspond to the columns. As in figure 2.1, the first payoff in any box is that of player 1, while the second is that of player 2. Each player has two strategies: cooperate by contributing to the collective good or defect by not contributing.

If benefits abide by summation, and if, moreover, the individual cost of provision exceeds the individual benefit, then a Prisoner's Dilemma may apply. To see this, assume that each individual must decide whether to contribute a unit of the collective good. Further assume that each unit contributed gives a benefit of 5 to each and every individual, contributor and noncontributor alike, at a cost of 6 to just the provider. If both agents contribute, then each receives a net benefit of 4 (cell *a*), which corresponds to five times the number of contributors (i.e., two) minus the individual cost of 6. If, however, only

a. Prisoner's Dilemma

	2 Cooperate	2 Defect
1 Cooperate	a 4,4	b -1,5
1 Defect	c 5,-1	d 0,0

a. Prisoner's Dilemma

b. Fully privileged

	2 Cooperate	2 Defect
1 Cooperate	a 6,6	b 1,5
1 Defect	c 5,1	d 0,0

b. Fully privileged

c. Chicken

	2 Cooperate	2 Defect
1 Cooperate	a 4,4	b -1,5
1 Defect	c 5,-1	d -x,-x

c. Chicken; -x < -1

d. Coordination; Battle of the Sexes

	2 Cooperate	2 Defect
1 Cooperate	a 1,1	b 1,5
1 Defect	c 5,1	d 0,0

d. Coordination; Battle of the Sexes

e. Assurance 1

	2 Cooperate	2 Defect
1 Cooperate	a 4,4	b -3,-3
1 Defect	c -3,-3	d 0,0

e. Assurance 1

f. Assurance 2; No Refund game

	2 Cooperate	2 Defect
1 Cooperate	a 4,4	b -6,0
1 Defect	c 0,-6	d 0,0

f. Assurance 2; No Refund game

Fig. 2.6. Examples of 2 × 2 games

one person contributes, then the noncontributor receives the benefit of 5 without any cost, while the contributor receives -1 after the cost is deducted (cells b and c). When neither contributes, the payoffs are zero (cell d). The resulting array of payoffs in figure 2.6a is the Prisoner's Dilemma, as previously displayed in figure 2.1. The dominant strategy, which is the best individual response regardless of the other player's strategy, is to defect and not contribute; hence, the group remains latent unless other considerations (e.g., intertemporal or enforcement) are included. In the Prisoner's Dilemma, individual rationality leads to collective failure, since the Nash equilibrium in cell d is a Pareto-inferior outcome to the mutually cooperative situation in cell a. Even if the two players communicate and agree to cooperate, the agreement is not self-enforcing because each has the incentive to defect once the other player cooperates. This is easily seen in figure 2.6a. Once player 1 contributes, player 2 is better off not contributing, since 5 is a greater payoff than 4. Unless intertemporal considerations, which involve the number of times that the players are asked to contribute, are included (see chap. 3), the prognosis is bleak even with just two players.

When, however, individual benefits exceeds individual costs and summation applies, the group is fully privileged. For instance, suppose that each unit of the collective good yields a benefit of 5 to each and every individual at a cost of 4 to the provider. Once again, benefits are summed over the units provided. In figure 2.6b, full cooperation gives each player a net gain of 6 ($=$ $[5 \times 2] - 4$). If one person defects, then the contributor gains 1, while the defector gains 5. The dominant strategy is to cooperate; hence, there is no collective failure or irrationality and the group is fully privileged. With this payoff scheme, the number of players would have *no* effect whatsoever on whether the good is provided—group size is irrelevant. The irrelevancy of group size is driven, in part, by the linearity in benefits and costs.

A second important game form is the game of Chicken. This game derives its name from the following storyline. Two cars traveling in opposite directions are speeding down the middle of the road. Neither driver wants to be the first to swerve out of the way of the oncoming car. If no one swerves (cooperates), then the outcome is disastrous so that the mutual defect (noncooperative) payoffs are the lowest. The best payoff results for the driver who manages to hold his or her ground, while forcing the other driver to swerve. If both swerve (cooperate), then the payoff is below the best but above that associated with swerving first (i.e., being the chicken). The averting of national disasters and the provision of needed infrastructure may correspond to the game of Chicken, since the status quo of no action has significant penalties (see, e.g., Lipnowski and Maital 1983). The confrontation of superpowers in a crisis (i.e., brinksmanship) may also correspond to the game of Chicken

(Schelling 1960). Curbing the spread of a disease or limiting the progress of a forest fire are other instances where doing nothing leads to disastrous payoffs.

The game of Chicken can be generated by a slight alteration to the payoff arrangement in the Prisoner's Dilemma if a penalty $(-x)$ *greater than* the payoff of -1 (associated with cooperating when the other player defects) is imposed on both players for mutual defection. The 2×2 Chicken game has no dominant strategy, but it has two pure-strategy Nash equilibria in cells *b* and *c*.[8] At cell b, neither person would unilaterally change his or her strategy. By changing strategy, player 1's payoff would drop from -1 to $-x$, while player 2's payoff would drop from 5 to 4. A Nash equilibrium is, consequently, reached for cell *b*. The same holds for cell *c* with players' payoffs reversed. A sufficiently large penalty eliminates the latent group outcome as an equilibrium and, thus, ensures that some of the collective good is provided. Thus, game structures very similar to the Prisoner's Dilemma need not imply the absence of collective provision.

Next consider a Coordination game based on the best-shot technology. Suppose that the first unit of the collective good provided gives a benefit of 5 to each and every member, but that additional units add no benefit. Since each agent can provide only a single unit by assumption, the first unit provided denotes the best shot. Further suppose that each unit costs 4. In figure 2.6d, the associated Coordination game has no dominant strategy, but it does have two pure-strategy Nash equilibria in cells *b* and *c*. Mutual cooperation yields 1 to each person, as costs of 4 are subtracted from benefits of 5. If only one individual contributes, then the contributor receives a net gain of 1 ($= 5 - 4$) and the noncontributor gets the full benefits of 5 at no cost. If neither contributes, then each receives nothing. The Coordination game has a payoff structure reminiscent of the Battle of the Sexes game (Luce and Raiffa 1957, 90).[9] For the Coordination game, the players must decide how to *alternate* efforts because no provision as well as mutual provision are Pareto inferior to cells *b* and *c*. A Coordination game may result when a standard technology is being considered for a new consumer product (e.g., video recorders). In figure 2.6d, cooperation would then correspond to embracing 1's standard, while defection would correspond to embracing 2's standard. The adoption of a single standard is (weakly) preferred from both players' viewpoints. Although each player wants his or her standard adopted, each prefers some

---

8. There is also a mixed-strategy equilibrium in which each player randomizes his or her strategy. A mixed-strategy equilibrium is found by allowing each player to choose his or her probability based on the best probability choice of the other player. I do not analyze these mixed strategies here.

9. If the payoffs in cell a were 0,0, then the game would correspond precisely to the Battle of the Sexes.

standard to none (Farrell 1987).[10] Other examples of Coordination games concern adopting a new military technology or strategic doctrine (e.g., flexible response, mutual assured destruction) in a military alliance. A single doctrine is preferred by allies over pursuing multiple independent doctrines, even if an ally's own-favored doctrine is not the one adopted. Coordination games result in a privileged group for collective provision.

In figure 2.6e and 2.6f, two different Assurance games are displayed. In figure 2.6e, *two units* of the collective good gives benefits of 10 (5 per unit) to each and every player at a total group cost of 12 (6 per unit), which is *equally shared* with each person paying 6 for benefits of 10. Thus, mutual cooperation yields net benefits of 4 for each contributor. If, however, only a single unit is provided, then no benefits are received and each player must split the cost of 6, thus receiving -3 apiece. The Assurance game may relate to the scenario in which a minimal effort (here two units) must occur to receive any benefits.[11] In this example, both players must contribute if either is to receive benefits from their own actions. The fighting of a fire (forestalling a disaster) that neither player can put out (achieve) alone is an example. The Assurance game has no dominant strategy, but does possess two pure-strategy Nash equilibria in cells *a* and *d*. Cell *a* Pareto dominates cell *d,* but may not be the outcome unless the players can rely on one another.[12] When one player fulfills a pledge to cooperate, the contract is, unlike the Prisoner's Dilemma, self-enforcing, since the other player has strong incentives to carry out his or her own pledge. To do otherwise would result in a loss of 3 rather than a gain of 4. Even without an enforcement mechanism, contracting can overcome collective failure in assurance situations.

The second variation of the Assurance game differs in terms of an institutional rule—that is, costs are not shared but are solely assigned to the provider. Although the equilibria in pure-strategy space is unaffected as compared with Assurance 1, there are subtle changes that become more apparent when generalized to *n* persons. In Assurance 2, mutual defection is more likely, especially in mixed-strategy space, where probabilities are applied to the strategies. This Assurance game corresponds to the provision of a discrete public good without refund (Palfrey and Rosenthal 1984). That is, the good is only provided when both individuals contribute, and a single contributor does not get his or her money back even though no collective good materializes.

Figure 2.7 illustrates three 2 × 2 games when the weakest link applies and each agent can contribute up to one unit of the public good. In figure 2.7a,

10. Farrell (1987) demonstrated that, with mixed strategies and preplay communication (i.e., cheap talk), repeated plays decrease inefficiency but do not eliminate it.

11. See Palfrey and Rosenthal's (1984) analysis of discrete public goods, in which the good is either provided or not, and Schelling's (1973) study of minimal contribution sets.

12. See de Jasay 1989; Gardner, Ostrom, and Walker 1990; Runge 1984; Sen 1967.

	2	
	Cooperate	Defect
	a	*b*
Cooperate	1,1	-4,0
1	*c*	*d*
Defect	0,-4	0,0

a. Similar to Assurance 2;
No Refund game

	2	
	Cooperate	Defect
	a	*b*
Cooperate	1,1	-4,0
1	*c*	*d*
Defect	0,-4	-1,-1

b. Not fully privileged; small
penalties for status quo

	2	
	Cooperate	Defect
	a	*b*
Cooperate	1,1	-4,0
1	*c*	*d*
Defect	0,-4	-5,-5

c. Fully privileged; large
penalties for status quo

Fig. 2.7. Further examples of 2 × 2 games; weakest link

each player receives benefits of 5 provided that *both* contribute a unit or match one another's provision. When both contribute, each receives net benefits of 1 since each agent must deduct a cost of 4. If only one contributes, as in cells *b* and *c*, then the contributor loses his or her cost of 4 and the noncontributor gains nothing. Payoffs are zero when no one contributes. The ordinal structure of this game is identical to Assurance 2. The two pure-strategy Nash equilibria correspond to cells *a* and *d*, and involve matching behavior among agents. For identical individuals, the Nash equilibrium–matching outcome is Pareto optimal (Hirshleifer 1983; Harrison and Hirshleifer 1989; Mueller 1989, 21–25). Since units provided beyond the lowest individual provision amount add to cost with no resulting benefit, there is no incentive in the weakest link to outdo the smallest spender. Figures 2.7b and 2.7c are based on the same scenario except for penalties being incurred for mutual defection. In figure

2.7b, a small penalty (less than the unit cost) is imposed on the two players, while in figure 2.7c, a large penalty (greater than the unit cost) is imposed on the two players. With large penalties, cooperation is dominant and the group is fully privileged; with small penalties, mutual defection remains a pure-strategy, Nash equilibrium for the weakest link. Nature-imposed sanctions attached to the status quo can assist groups to a Pareto-optimal outcome.

Before generalizing these games to their n-person counterparts, a number of conclusions can be drawn. First, these examples indicate that collective action problems need not imply a Prisoner's Dilemma. I, thus, take issue with Hardin's (1982, 25) statement: "Indeed, the problem of collective action and the prisoner's dilemma are essentially the same." The two are not the same. Second, for small collectives, the existence of a privileged group may depend on the technology of public supply, the payoff structure, or the institutional rules. The form of the utility function, which translates units of the collective good into a utility index or payoff, may also play a role in determining whether a group is privileged. Third, since there are so many different combinations for joining cost structures, the technology of public supply, and tastes, it is not really possible to state *general* propositions concerning the feasibility for collective action, even in the case of only two people, unless constraints limit these combinations. Propositions concerning the best-shot technology may consequently be inappropriate for perfectly substitutable (summation), collective action scenarios. Fourth, each basic game structure may apply to more than one configuration of costs, technology, and tastes. Thus, the appearance of a game structure such as the Battle of the Sexes does not uniquely identify a collective action scenario. When experiments are used to confirm propositions drawn from collective action, the nature of the experimental setup determines such things as the technology of public supply. The conflicting results in the experimental literature are due, in part, to differences in the configuration of costs and/or technology of supply induced by the experimental design (see, e.g., Isaac, Walker, and Thomas 1984; Isaac and Walker 1988a and 1988b). For example, experiments involving minimal sets of contributors give game structures similar to assurance and, hence, often result in groups being privileged (van de Kragt, Orbell, and Dawes 1983).

2.3.1.2 N-Person Games and Being Privileged

Five of the six two-person games shown in figure 2.6 are generalized to n persons in figure 2.8. The first two rows of figure 2.8a correspond to the Prisoner's Dilemma where j denotes the number of contributors besides individual i. The columns refer to the actions of the other contributors, while the rows indicate the strategy of the ith player. The payoffs listed are those of individual i. In figure 2.8a, every unit of the collective good provided yields 5 in benefits to each and every individual at a cost of 6 to the contributor. Each

Number of cooperators in group besides i

	0	...	$j-1$	j	$j+1$	...	$n-1$
cooperates	-1		$5j-6$	$5(j+1)-6$	$5(j+2)-6$		$5n-6$
defects (Prisoners' Dilemma)	0		$5(j-1)$	$5j$	$5(j+1)$		$5(n-1)$
defects (Chicken)	$-x$		$5(j-1)$	$5j$	$5(j+1)$		$5(n-1)$

a. Prisoner's Dilemma and Chicken

	0	...	$j-1$	j	$j+1$	...	$n-1$
cooperates	1	...	1	1	1	...	1
defects	0		5	5	5	...	5

b. Coordination; Battle of the Sexes

	0	...	$j-1$	j	$j+1$	...	$n-1$
i cooperates	$-6/n$		$\dfrac{-6j}{n}$	$(5-\dfrac{6}{n})(j+1)$	$(5-\dfrac{6}{n})(j+2)$		$5n-6$
i defects	0		$\dfrac{-6(j-1)}{n}$	$\dfrac{-6j}{n}$	$(5-\dfrac{6}{n})(j+1)$		$(5-\dfrac{6}{n})(n-1)$

c. Assurance 1

	0	...	$j-1$	j	$j+1$	...	$n-1$
i cooperates	-6	...	-6	$5(j+1)-6$	$5(j+2)-6$		$5n-6$
i defects	0	...	0	0	$5(j+1)$		$5(n-1)$

d. Assurance 2

Fig. 2.8. **Examples of *n*-person games**

individual may contribute up to one unit of the collective good. A summation technology applies. If, in the top row of figure 2.8a, i contributes and no one else does, then i receives a net benefit of -1, the difference between a cost of 6 and a benefit of 5. When, however, i as well as $j - 1$ others contribute, i gets $5j$ in benefits at a cost of 6 for a net gain of $5j - 6$. The other entries in the top row are computed in a similar fashion. In the second row of figure 2.8a, i receives nothing when neither i nor anyone else contributes. A noncontributor gets $5(j - 1)$ when $j - 1$ people other than him or herself contribute to the collective action. Other entries in the second row are computed similarly. A comparison of corresponding entries in the first two rows indicates that the (noncontributing) *defect* strategy dominates, regardless of the number of contributors; hence, the Nash equilibrium implies a latent group in which no one contributes. Defect (do not contribute) dominates because its payoffs are greater by 1 than the corresponding cooperative payoffs. Everyone receives 0 in the Nash equilibrium, which is Pareto inferior to the full-cooperation strategy with payoffs of $5n - 6$ for each player when all contribute.

If, for the Prisoner's Dilemma, a penalty could be imposed on a defector, cooperation could be transformed into the dominant strategy. Any penalty larger than the *net gains* from defecting would work. These net gains are 1.0 in figure 2.8a. If, say, a penalty of 1.2 were imposed, then the cooperative strategy would dominate in figure 2.8a. The greater the net gain from defecting, the larger the required penalty for defecting. The institution of the enforcement mechanism raises collective action problems of its own. Although it is in each participant's self-interest to have an enforcement mechanism to operate on everyone else, each would prefer that the mechanism did not apply to him or her. One collective action problem has merely replaced another. The financing of the enforcement mechanism is also a concern, since resources must be diverted from cooperative gains (if any) to underwrite the mechanism. Schemes that spread the enforcement costs over the entire group might have the best chance for institution, since individual net gains are more apt to be maintained rather than if only the subset of cooperating agents is made to support enforcement.

In a recent experimental paper, Ostrom, Walker, and Gardner (1991) analyzed whether small groups could enforce commitments to cooperative strategies without an external authority. These experiments attempted to analyze the isolated influence of communication and sanctions as well as their combined influence. Experimental results showed that either communication or sanctioning or both improved collective action beyond outcomes predicted by noncooperative game theory.[13]

The Chicken game (the first and third rows of fig. 2.8a) differs from the

---

13. Also see Isaac and Walker 1988a.

Prisoner's Dilemma only in terms of the penalty when everyone defects. There are now a plethora of Nash equilibria—each with a single contributor; hence, the group should be privileged regardless of the size.

Figure 2.8b generalizes the previous Coordination game to n persons. Each individual can provide, at most, one unit of the collective good and, moreover, *only* the first unit provides a benefit of 5 to each person. Each unit now costs 4. If i contributes to the collective good, then i receives a net benefit of 1, since he or she must cover the cost of 4. Net benefits to i are 1 regardless of the number of other contributors, as only the first unit has any benefits to convey. If, however, i does not contribute, then he or she receives 5, provided that at least one person contributes. In figure 2.8b, the pure-strategy Nash equilibria for the Coordination game consist of the strategy combinations in which a single individual contributes and all others free ride. The group is again privileged even though n may be a large number.

The two Assurance games in figures 2.8c and 2.8d require at least $j + 1$ individuals to contribute before a benefit of $5(j + 1)$ is gained by all n players. Each contributor beyond $j + 1$ adds another 5 in benefits to each and every player at a provision cost of 6. Hence, a summation technology applies *once* the threshold of $j + 1$ contributors is reached. In Assurance 1, cost is equally shared; in Assurance 2, only the provider pays. Each person pays $6/n$ times the number of units provided in Assurance 1. Assurance 1 displays a greater extent of cooperation than Assurance 2. For Assurance 1, the cooperative strategy actually dominates defection if $n > 6/5$ *and* at least j players besides i cooperate. There are two pure-strategy Nash equilibria for Assurance 1: no one contributes or everyone contributes. The latter Pareto dominates the former. As n becomes infinite, the cooperate strategy weakly dominates defection, because the penalty for cooperating, when less than j others cooperate, approaches zero as cost is equally divided. An increase in n augments the likelihood that the group is privileged. This is especially true if mixed strategies are allowed. A glance at figure 2.8d indicates that n has no such effect in Assurance 2. For the latter game, the cooperative strategy yields a higher payoff only when the ith player is pivotal—that is, exactly j players besides i contribute. In consequence, the Nash equilibria in Assurance 2 correspond to the scenarios in which either no one contributes or precisely $J + 1$ persons contribute. There are $\binom{n}{j+1}$ Nash equilibria for Assurance 2 where the collective good is realized. Although the number of Nash equilibria is larger for Assurance 2 than for Assurance 1, the number of contributors is smaller. If simple alterations of institutional rules can reduce the gains from defection, as in Assurance 1, then cooperation is fostered. Institutional design can promote the proper incentives, thereby tipping the scales in favor of cooperation. For instance, preference-revelation mechanisms work on the principle of designing institutions so that cooperation (e.g., telling the truth) becomes a dominant strategy (Clarke 1971 and 1972; Groves 1973). This is accomplished by engineering sidepayments so that each individual faces the collective or social consequences of his or her failure to internalize (account for) the effect that his or her action confers on others. A properly designed incentive scheme simulates the collective choice payoff function. These preference-revelation mechanisms place each individual in pivotal roles that are analogous to the Assurance game structure.

Since collective action problems embrace a wide range of scenarios with various technologies of public supply, costs, and resulting payoff configurations, there is no *simple* relationship between being privileged and group size. For the special, but surely important case, in which per-unit provision costs exceed per-unit benefits from an agent's viewpoint, a Prisoner's Dilemma game applies and group latency is, indeed, a problem no matter how many people are involved. If group size is to be related to latency in the Olsonian tradition, nonlinearities are needed for the cost and benefit relationships so that net gain varies in a nonlinear fashion with group size. When arguing that large groups are likely to be latent, Olson (1965, 46–52) also indicated that transaction or organizational costs are directly related to group size. Transaction costs are associated with a mode or means of allocation (e.g., a market or a club). As such, they include the cost of organizing groups as well as the cost of communicating between or among members. Information and enforcement costs are part of transaction costs. As group size increases, the transaction costs associated with the initial formation of the collective rise and impede formation. To date, there has been almost no attempt to integrate transaction costs and their relationship to group size into the analysis.[14] Such an integration may well support Olson's hypothesis that group size inhibits formation. By introducing transaction costs, researchers could investigate why many collective action groups (e.g., the United Nations or NATO) often provide multiple collective goods. Economies of scope, which are cost savings that arise when activities have a common cost, may be behind this fact. Since, for example, an emergency communication network can be used by the police, fire, and ambulance services, the cost of such a network is common to these collective activities. In consequence, economies of scope are present. Once established, the bureaucratic structure of the United Nations can be used for collective activities other than promoting world peace. The common cost of the bureaucracy gives rise to economies of scope. Chapter 4 presents a more in-depth analysis of these economies of scope.

We have also seen that, when the underlying game structure is Chicken or Coordination, the likelihood of being privileged is independent of group size for the examples given. The requirement of being privileged is more

---

14. A notable exception is Cauley, Sandler, and Cornes 1986.

dependent on the underlying game structure, which, in turn, depends on tastes, costs, and the technology of publicness rather than the number of players involved. If institutional arrangements can give the "right" game structure, as might be the case in Assurance 1, then the group may be privileged even when membership is large.

*2.3.2 Group Size and Provision Levels

Up until now, the collective action decision has been treated as a discrete variable; either the person contributed or did not. The choice of a level of contribution was not permitted. In the case of defense expenditures, each nation of an alliance chooses the size of its defense expenditure. Many collective actions allow the determination of actual contributions once a participant decides to contribute. We now turn to this decision.

The discrete games presented previously do not aid in discovering the relationship between group size and provision level. Appropriate models must permit contributors to choose an optimizing provision level; hence, collective provision must be treated as a continuous variable. For such models, the total provision of a collective good need not *fall* with an increase in group size. When the collective good and the private good are normal (i.e., both increase with income), Chamberlin (1974, 712) and McGuire (1974, 112) proved that total provision increases in a symmetric equilibrium,[15] even though each individual's contribution falls with n. Thus, the increased provision of the entrant more than offsets the aggregate decrease in the collective provision of the existing membership. In the symmetric equilibrium case,[16] average contributions decline, while total contributions increase. This latter result is *opposite* to that conjectured by Olson and derives from income effects generated from the spillover of collective benefits from other participants.

The Chamberlin-McGuire result is established by aggregating individual reaction or expenditure functions over the group membership to derive an expression for total contributions. Reaction paths, illustrated in figures 2.3 and 2.4, correspond to an individual's optimal subscription for different levels of subscriptions by all others. The latter quantity is often called a *spillover* or *spillin*, and is equal to the summation term in equation 2.20 (below). Following McGuire (1974, 112–13), we assume that everyone is identical in endowments and tastes. Furthermore, the private and public good are assumed normal with positive income elasticities. Finally, linear reaction or expenditure functions,

---

15. In a symmetric equilibrium, identical players contribute the same amount. Players are identical when their tastes and endowments are the same.

16. The technology of public supply is summation. Different results are likely with other technologies.

$$q^i = K - \gamma_i \sum_{j \neq i}^{n} q^j , \quad i = 1, \ldots, n , \tag{2.20}$$

are invoked for each individual. In equation 2.20, K is the isolated purchase of the collective good and $1 - \gamma_i$ is the agent's marginal propensity to spend income on the collective good.[17] Since a symmetric equilibrium is assumed, the subscript on γ and superscript on q can be dropped, thereby allowing equation 2.20 to be rewritten as

$$q = K/[1 + \gamma(n - 1)] , \tag{2.21}$$

since $q^i = q^j$ for all i and j. When equation 2.21 is summed over all agents, an expression for the Nash equilibrium level of Q results.[18]

$$Q = nK/[1 + \gamma(n - 1)] . \tag{2.22}$$

Differentiating equation 2.22 with respect to n gives

$$dQ/dn = K(1 - \gamma)/[1 + \gamma(n - 1)]^2 > 0 . \tag{2.23}$$

Hence, total Nash provision rises, rather than falls, with an increase in group size when public good purchases increase with income. As n goes to infinity, total contributions in equation 2.22 approach K/γ by L'Hospital rule (McGuire 1974, 112)—a finite total provision is reached in the limit. This result is easily generalized to nonlinear reaction paths, provided that all goods respond positively to an increase in income.

In a recent contribution, Andreoni (1988a) has generalized the result of McGuire-Chamberlin to a case where individuals have identical tastes but differ in their income endowments according to a continuous probability

---

17. For a Cobb-Douglas utility function, $U = y^\alpha Q^\beta$, where y is the private good, and α and β lie in the open unit interval, the expenditure function is linear and equal to

$$q^i = -[\alpha/(\alpha + \beta)] \sum_{j \neq i} q^j + [\beta/(\alpha + \beta)](y/p) .$$

The reaction path is found by maximizing utility subject to the resource constraint and the quantity-constrained level of spillins $\left(\sum_{j \neq i} q^j \right)$. Solving the associated FOCs for q^i in terms of the exogenous variables yields the reaction path.

18. McGuire (1974) was very close to discovering the neutrality theorem, discussed in chap. 3. If, in eq. 2.22, K had been written in terms of income, then the *redistribution of income* among an unchanged set of contributors would immediately imply $dQ = 0$ and neutrality.

density function. The collective good is continuous and normal, and a summation technology characterizes public supply. Andreoni (1988a, 59–62) showed that the proportion of the population contributing to a pure public good declines monotonically with n and converges in the limit $(n \to \infty)$ to zero (also see Sugden 1982). The richest individuals are the contributors. Although average giving falls to zero, total contributions approach a finite limit as group size increases to infinity.

For a stylized model where utility functions are placed along a continuum or scale based on a *single* arbitrary taste parameter, Andreoni (1988a, 66) generalized the theorem to the case of heterogeneous tastes. Andreoni also proved that, as group size goes to infinity, a single (identical) class of contributors will characterize the equilibrium. Clearly, the convergence of the population's fraction of contributors to zero as group size increases is in the spirit of *Logic*'s first theme. The relationship between group size and provision levels is still an area for fertile research. Until now, the relationship has been examined solely for the summation technology; other technologies of collective supply are apt to have dramatically different results—some in line with Olson's hypothesized negative relationship and others not. For instance, with a best-shot (weakest-link) technology, the addition of more poorly (richly) endowed individuals, while increasing group size, would have *no* effect on provision when tastes are identical and positively related to income. Group size may, in some instances, be unrelated to provision for these technologies. Behavioral assumptions other than Nash need to be examined when relating group size to provision.[19] In addition, more work needs to be done for heterogeneous agents, because such models are highly stylized at this time. Heterogeneous group models are especially relevant for theme 2, to which we turn in section 2.4.

Since so many aspects of the collective action problem can influence the relationship between group size and provision, it is not surprising that the experimental literature has found mixed results. Marwell and Ames (1981) found little relationship between group size and provision, while Kim and Walker (1984) found strong evidence of a negative relationship, as hypothesized in *Logic*. In order to study this relationship, the researcher must be explicit about the underlying utility function, the technology of public supply, the membership composition, the strategic assumption (i.e., Nash-Cournot or otherwise), and the budget constraint. Even some of the best treatments have eliminated important interactions by assuming a separable utility function, thereby removing the all-important income effect that arises from spillins.[20] Because of experimental cost considerations, researchers are yet to tackle

---

19. See Sandler and Posnett 1991; Dasgupta and Itaya 1991.
20. See, for example, Isaac, Walker, and Thomas 1983; Isaac and Walker 1988a.

very large (unsimulated) groups in an experimental environment. Most experiments deal with just two alternative group sizes, rather than a continuum. There is no difficulty in controlling the endowments and constraints of the subjects, but there is difficulty in controlling the distribution of tastes of heterogeneous subjects.

*2.3.3 Group Size and Suboptimality

The issue most often associated with theme 1 of *Logic* concerns whether an increase in group size leads to a decrease in efficiency. To address this question, the equilibrium associated with independent-adjustment behavior must be compared with some standard of efficiency as group size increases. Nash behavior is typically used as the measure of independent adjustment, while Pareto optimality is the measure of efficiency.

Given the wide array of models encompassed by collective action, the inverse relationship between group size and efficiency cannot be established in any general sense. Nevertheless, some important cases have been shown to abide by Olson's hypothesis. Mueller (1989, 18–21) considered a model in which the technology of public supply is summation and all individuals are identical. When each individual's tastes are represented by a Cobb-Douglas utility function,

$$U = y^{\alpha}Q^{\beta}, \quad 0 < \alpha < 1, 0 < \beta < 1, \tag{2.24}$$

(where α and β are constant exponents and superscripts denoting individuals are suppressed), the ratio of the Nash equilibrium provision, Q^N, to the Pareto-optimum provision quantity, Q^*, equals[21]

$$Q^N/Q^* = (\alpha + \beta)/(\alpha n + \beta). \tag{2.25}$$

If n equals 1, then the two equilibria coincide; if, however, n increases, then the departure of the Nash equilibrium from efficiency increases. This specific example is consistent with Olson's hypothesized deteriorating efficiency with larger groups.

In the case of an open-access, common property resource (e.g., fishing grounds), Cornes and Sandler (1983, 788) showed that the symmetric Nash equilibrium increasingly departs from Pareto optimality as the number of exploiters increases (see chap. 4 for further details). Once again, a summation

---

21. In Mueller 1989 (21), this ratio is depicted as $(\alpha + n\beta)/(\alpha n^2 + n\beta)$ owing to an algebraic error when finding the Pareto-optimal provision amount. In a letter to the author, Mueller indicated his awareness of this error and also indicated the correct answer.

technology characterizes the interdependency, and all exploiters are assumed identical. Markets are assumed to be perfectly competitive, and a well-behaved, neoclassical production function is invoked.

Cornes and Sandler (1986, 83–84) also established the inverse relationship between group size and efficiency for a quasi-linear utility function,

$$U = y + f(Q) , \tag{2.26}$$

in which increments in income are entirely spent on the private good, so that the income elasticity of the public good is zero. In equation 2.26, the aggregate supply of the public good is the sum of the individual provision amounts. Increases in group size were shown to increase Q^*, while leaving Q^N unchanged.

The inverse relationship between group size and efficiency is also dependent on the technology of supply. By utilizing the Cobb-Douglas utility function in equation 2.24, Mueller derived the following expression for the ratio of equilibria.

$$Q^N/Q^* = (\alpha + \beta)/[\alpha(1 + w) + \beta] , \tag{2.27}$$

where $0 \leq w \leq 1$, and w denotes a parameter of public supply technology. In the Mueller example, the public good technology is

$$Q = q^1 + wq^2 , \tag{2.28}$$

which is a special case of equation 2.13 with $w^1 = 1$, and $w^2 = w$. Mueller's result in equation 2.27 depends on q^1 being less than or equal to q^2 and on individuals being identical in tastes and endowments. The Nash equilibrium corresponds to matching behavior $(q^1 = q^2)$; each individual effectively faces the social-optimizing problem. If $w = 0$, then the weakest link applies to the problem, so that equation 2.27 implies that the Nash equilibrium is efficient.[22] In fact, Mueller (1989, 25) was able to generalize equation 2.27 to the case of n individuals: when $w^i = 0$ for all but the smallest contributor, the ratio, Q^N/Q^*, is still one. If, however, the w^i's are greater than zero but less than one ($w^i = 1$ for all i implies summation), then an increase in group size would imply a decline in efficiency. The experimental literature confirmed nearly optimal results for the weakest-link case.[23]

The inverse relationship between group size and efficiency is also depen-

---

22. The weakest-link case is similar in its normative aspects to the perfect-complements, joint-product case (Cornes and Sandler 1986, 81).

23. Harrison and Hirshleifer 1989; van de Kragt, Orbell, and Dawes 1983.

dent on the notion of the independent adjustment that is employed. Guttman (1978 and 1987) specified a model that departed from an one-shot Nash equilibrium. He specifically formulated a two-stage game: in the first stage, the participants choose a flat contribution to the collective good; in the second, the participants choose matching rates based on the spillover of flat contributions from the first stage. A Nash equilibrium for the two-stage procedure is found by first solving for the matching rates and then solving for the flat contributions.[24] Guttman (1978) proved that a Pareto optimum could be achieved if all players are identical and a separable utility function represents tastes. Thus, in the absence of income effects, Q^N/Q^* equals 1 regardless of group size. A similar single-stage result was established for Kantian behavior by Sandler and Posnett (1991). With Kantian behavior, each agent acts as he or she would want others to act. A nonzero conjecture applies.

If the standard Nash equilibrium forms the basis of independent adjustment and, moreover, the technology of public supply corresponds to summation, then Olson's inverse relationship holds for some noteworthy symmetric equilibria. In some instances, bothersome income effects must be sanitized to derive Olson's inverse relationship.

In comparing Nash and Pareto equilibria, the ratio Q^N/Q^* or some variant (see the index of easy riding in Cornes and Sandler 1984a, 588) is employed. In consequence, the comparison is made in quantity space rather than utility space. In the latter, the ratio U^N/U^* from a social aggregation viewpoint must be measured. Since utility may be nonlinearly related to quantity, the comparison of Q^N/Q^*, while helpful in a qualitative sense, is not the true measure of inefficiency in terms of lost utility.

2.4 Theme 2: Group Composition and Group Asymmetry

The second basic theme concerns disproportionate burden sharing within small groups where "there is accordingly a surprising tendency for the 'exploitation' of the great by the small" (Olson, 1965, 35). Although theme 2 has greater general validity than theme 1, theme 2 is not universally true. In *Logic*, Olson (1965, 35) reasoned that if the largest member of a group satisfies his or her collective good demand, then smaller members are likely to have their own demands satisfied free without the need to contribute. This is the nearest that Olson comes to using the now-popular term of *free riding*. Clearly, Olson has a specific class of collective goods in mind—nonexcludable, pure public goods. The disproportionate burden sharing was developed further in Olson and

---

24. This equilibrium is a "perfect equilibrium" since each subgame is a Nash equilibrium. Perfect equilibria and subgames are discussed in chap. 3.

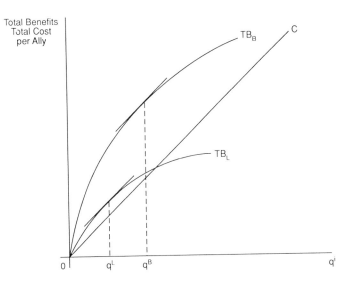

Fig. 2.9. Exploitation of the large by the small

Zeckhauser's (1966) seminal article on burden sharing in a military alliance. They used total benefit curves for two allies of disparate size to establish the exploitation of the large by the small. Although the diagrammatic exercise is correct, it depends on the implicit assumption of zero income effects.

The Olson and Zeckhauser study involved the sharing of deterrence by an alliance. Deterrence, as provided by a nuclear arsenal, is nonrival between allies because, once deployed, the associated retaliatory threat is independent of the number of allies. Moreover, tightly clustered allies cannot be excluded owing to nuclear fallout and misses in the event of an enemy attack—collateral damage to the providing allies brings a retaliatory response.

The Olson-Zeckhauser (1966) diagrammatic analysis is repeated in figure 2.9, where total benefits (costs) for each ally are measured on the vertical axis and each ally's provision of defense on the horizontal axis. In figure 2.9, TB_B denotes the benefits to the big ally, TB_L the benefits to the little ally, and C the cost of defense provision. Each ally determines a Nash-optimizing provision level by equating its marginal benefit (i.e., the slope of TB) and marginal cost (i.e., the slope of C). This procedure identifies the provision level associated with an ally's largest net benefits. Thus, the big ally wants to provide q^B, and the small ally wants to contribute q^L. Once the big ally provides q^B, there is no reason for the little ally to contribute anything, because its ideal demand for q^L is fulfilled through spillins—a free ride results. The large is consequently exploited by the small. With the diagrammatic procedure of figure 2.4, the reaction path of the big ally would lie everywhere beyond that of the small ally, giving the same free-rider outcome of figure 2.9. The Olson-Zeckhauser (1966) demonstration rests on many strict assumptions, including identical linear costs, zero income effects, summation technologies, Nash behavior, and marginal benefits being positively related to the participant's size. If, in terms of the technology of publicness, summation or perfect substitutability is lost, q^B may have little impact on the provision choices of the small ally. The weakest link, which leads to matching behavior, may eliminate exploitation entirely.

The concept of size is not unambiguous in Olson and Zeckhauser 1966; some have interpreted size to depend on resources or gross domestic product, while others have equated size to population.[25] In the absence of income effects, Dudley and Montmarquette (1981) have shown that, if spending on the collective good is proportional to population, the relative slopes of the players' reaction curves determine whether the large is exploited by the small. If the small player's reaction curve is sufficiently inelastic or unresponsive with respect to spillins (income), then the small player might provide more than the large player. Others have demonstrated that, if the small player's preferences for the public good are sufficiently strong, the natural tendency for disproportionate burden sharing need not apply. Supply considerations can also have an effect. When, for example, the small player (nation) has a supply-side comparative advantage over the large player in producing the collective good, then the exploitation hypothesis may also fail (Olson and Zeckhauser 1967; McGuire 1990).

Much of the empirical literature on disproportionate burden sharing has followed Olson and Zeckhauser 1966 and 1967 by examining NATO and other alliances.[26] This literature is reviewed more completely in chapters 4 and 5; a few of its important points are highlighted here. For the most part, the NATO allies have behaved according to the exploitation hypothesis, since the larger allies (the United States, the United Kingdom, France, and West Germany), in terms of gross domestic product (GDP), spent a greater proportion of their GDP on defense. The extent of disproportionate burden sharing, however, weakened after the adoption of a flexible response strategy, which placed greater importance on conventional arsenals. The latter produces more impure public and private (country-specific) outputs than the deterrence derived from nuclear weapons. Since the defense activity gives rise to multiple

---

25. The former includes Sandler and Forbes 1980; the latter includes Dudley and Montmarquette 1981.

26. The alliance literature is quite extensive and has shown significant growth in recent years. Contributions include Boyer 1990; McGuire 1982 and 1990; McGuire and Groth 1985; Gonzales and Mehay 1990; Murdoch and Sandler 1982 and 1984; Olson and Zeckhauser 1966, 1967; Palmer 1990; Sandler 1977; Sandler and Forbes 1980; Sandler and Murdoch 1990. See chaps. 4 and 5 for further details.

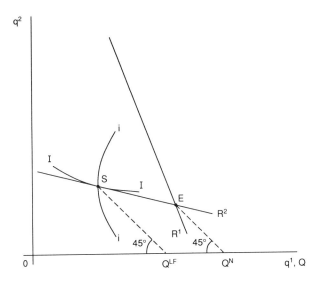

Fig. 2.10. Leader-follower behavior

outputs that vary in their degree of publicness, joint products are relevant.
Sandler and Murdoch (1990) have established that the presence of joint products, especially excludable ones, could work at odds to the exploitation hypothesis as burden sharing keys in on excludable, country-specific benefits.

Changes in the strategic assumption of Nash-Cournot can also work
against the exploitation hypothesis. In particular, Bruce (1990, 189) has
proven that leader-follower behavior could lead to an exploitation of the small
when the large country assumes the leadership role. With leader-follower
behavior, the follower takes the leader's collective provision level as given
and optimizes with respect to it, as in Nash behavior. The leader knows that
the follower will act according to his or her Nash reaction path and, hence,
will lead with a provision level that puts him or her in the best position
regarding the follower's reaction path. As compared with a Nash equilibrium,
a leader-follower equilibrium implies an increased (decreased) level of provision by the follower (leader), but a reduced aggregate level of provision
(Bruce 1990, 185–86). If the follower is the smaller agent, then his or her
increased share under leader-follower behavior can reverse the direction of
exploitation.

Leader-follower behavior and its implications are illustrated in figure
2.10 using the Cornes-Sandler graphic apparatus, in which the larger player is
agent 1. At the Nash equilibrium (point *E*), agent 1's reaction path, R^1,
intersects agent 2's reaction path, R^2, in such a way that agent 1 contributes
relatively more to the collective good. Total provision is Q^N at the Nash

equilibrium. For leader-follower behavior, the leader (agent 1) takes the follower's Nash reaction path as his or her constraint and optimizes with respect to this path. An optimum for the leader is obtained when his or her isoutility function II is tangent to the follower's reaction path at point S in figure 2.10. At S, the smaller agent now contributes relatively more and total provision declines to Q^{LF}. The standard exploitation hypothesis need not hold for big leaders and small followers. Total provision declines relative to the Nash equilibrium provided that all goods are normal and reaction paths are negatively sloped.

The most elegant proof of the Olson exploitation hypothesis for a summation technology and Nash behavior is found in Andreoni 1988a and Bergstrom, Blume, and Varian 1986. The former showed that, if all goods are normal and income is distributed continuously, the contributors will include only the richest individuals. Moreover, as group size increases without bound, the class of contributors will converge to a single type—the wealthiest. The richest individuals are, therefore, exploited by all others. Bergstrom, Blume, and Varian (1986, theorem 5, 38) demonstrated that, ceteris paribus, equalizing redistributions of endowments among a group of contributors would never increase total voluntary contributions for a given set of contributors. These Nash-Cournot results depend upon all goods being normal and represent strong (indirect) support for Olson's conjecture that asymmetric groups have a greater likelihood of being privileged, since the richest individual demand for the collective good will increase with his or her income level and disparity. As seen in section 2.3, the underlying game structure also has a role to play in whether asymmetry fosters groups being privileged.

2.5 Theme 3: Means for Overcoming Collective Action Problems

Logic (1965, chap. 6) suggested two means for overcoming collective irrationality: selective incentives and the design of institutional structures.

2.5.1 Selective Incentives

By selective incentives, Olson had in mind the tying of private benefits or inducements to the provision of the collective good. Such private benefits would motivate any member (of any size) to contribute, inasmuch as the private benefits can only be obtained by assisting provision. Although collective benefits are nonexcludable, the private benefits are excludable. The selective-incentive hypothesis spawned a large literature that equated selective incentives with a collective activity that provides joint products, some of which are agent specific.[27] Although there is yet to be a general proof that the presence of joint products reduces suboptimality, there is much evidence that joint products can increase total provision (Sandler 1977; Andreoni 1990) and make provision burdens coincide to a greater extent with benefits received (Sandler and Forbes 1980; Sandler and Murdoch 1990). A mere increase in the Nash provision level cannot, by itself, be equated with reduced suboptimality, since the relative position of *both* the Nash and the Pareto-optimal equilibria must be ascertained and compared for selective incentive cases.

In recent years, researchers have begun to appreciate the flexibility and realism of the joint-product model. There are, at least, five bases for favoring a joint-product model over the single-product alternative. First, the joint-product model is a generalization of both the pure public good and the private good model and, as such, is capable of displaying a wider range of results. If a joint-product model is used, empirical tests are now available to distinguish the appropriate model (see chap. 5 for details): pure or joint product.[28] Second, the joint-product model fosters realism, since most collective action situations yield private benefits (e.g., the control of domestic terrorism for allies or tax deductions for contributors to a charity). In the case of charities, private benefits have been examined empirically by Posnett and Sandler (1989). Third, if the joint products are complementary,[29] then private outputs have a privatizing effect, not unlike the establishment of property rights. This privatizing influence reduces the motives to free ride. If, moreover, the joint products are perfect complements so that they are consumed in a fixed ratio, then the Nash equilibrium may be Pareto optimal. Fourth, the game structure that underlies some joint-product scenarios may eliminate defection as a dominant strategy, thereby fostering the group's privileged status. If, say, the joint products are complementary, then failure to contribute might imply that the free ride associated with defecting could yield a smaller payoff than contributing, since the complementary private good is not then available. Its absence would lower the gain, if any, from free riding. The matrix payoff for two persons could then correspond to the fully privileged group shown in figure 2.6b, where cooperation is the dominant strategy. Substitute joint products could imply the payoff structure of Chicken or the Battle of the Sexes. Fifth,

---

27. See, e.g., Andreoni 1987, 1988a, 1989, 1990; Cornes and Sandler 1981, 1984a, 1986; McGuire 1990; Mishan 1969; Mohring and Boyd 1971; Murdoch and Sandler 1984; Posnett and Sandler 1986 and 1988; Sandler 1977; Sandler and Murdoch 1990; Sandler and Posnett 1991; Steinberg 1987.

28. See Sandler and Murdoch 1990; Khanna, Huffman, and Sandler 1990.

29. Goods are complementary when they enhance one another's services. Such goods are best consumed together. Examples include guns and bullets, and compact discs and compact disc players.

the joint-product model need not abide by the neutrality theorem,[30] which limits the effectiveness of redistribution and tax policies.

The neutrality theorem indicates that any redistribution of income among an unchanged set of private contributors of a pure public good will not affect the Nash equilibrium provision level for the group.[31] Two alternative proofs for the neutrality theorem are given in the appendix to chapter 3. When the neutrality theorem applies, suboptimal provision levels, associated with a Nash equilibrium, cannot be augmented by redistributing income from the low to the high spenders unless the set of contributors changes. Under the assumptions of the theorem, policy-engineered asymmetry will not have a desired effect, because income gainers would increase contributions commensurate to the decreases of the income losers. The neutrality theorem is considered further in chapter 3, where extensions to the collective action theory are presented.

Some researchers have expressed doubts concerning the tying of private benefits to collective outputs as a mean of motivating successful collective action.[32] In particular, these authors question whether the collective or public sector can compete against private sector firms that can provide the private benefits "separately." These critics recognize that if the collective has a monopoly over the private good provided, then their criticism does not hold. In fact, many private goods that are tied to collective provision problems (e.g., a journal given to members of a learned society or concert tickets given to supporters of a symphony) do, indeed, involve monopoly aspects. In other instances, the joint production of multiple benefits may involve a technology of supply in which the private output may not be separated from the associated collective output. When, for example, allies purchase conventional armaments, the collective output of deterrence that the armaments provide to all allies cannot be divorced from country-specific outputs arising from deployment decisions. Moreover, the defense armaments are, indeed, purchased on private markets, but that does not eliminate the collective action problem.

2.5.2 Design of Institutional Structures

Theme 3 also stresses the design of institutional structures as a means for overcoming collective action impediments. In particular, Olson indicated that large groups can foster cooperation by organizing themselves in a federal structure with small subgroups. If largeness leads to group latency and suboptimality, then the use of federated cells makes good sense, since individual

---

30. See Cornes and Sandler 1981; Andreoni 1987, 1989, 1990; Sandler and Posnett 1991.
31. On neutrality, see Becker 1974; Bergstrom, Blume, and Varian 1986; Bernheim 1986; Cornes and Sandler 1981, 1985; Warr 1982 and 1983.
32. See, e.g., Booth 1985; Sugden 1982.

action is more readily recognized at the local level. A transaction cost approach, suggested by the seminal book by Williamson (1975), needs to be applied to study the organizational configurations of collective action groups.[33] Clearly, each configuration of a collective structure or group, whether federated or not, implies a different set of transaction costs as well as a different set of collective benefits. If the efficacy of alternative organizational structures is to be ascertained, discrete organizational forms must be compared with one another to identify the structure with the greatest net gains when provision and transaction aspects are considered. Although a federal structure may foster cooperation, collective benefits may be lost, because interactions over the entire collective may be quite limited. Such issues need scrutiny before federal structures are promoted.

Although Olson did not mention other means for overcoming collective failure, many means now exist. A prime candidate involves engineering the technology of supply to eliminate defection as a dominant strategy. Institutions can be designed to create an underlying game structure that fosters cooperation. Many people have studied the effects of institutional design and its resulting game theory structure on the possibility for achieving optimal collective action without resorting to outside authorities.[34] For example, Ostrom (1990) has investigated the emergence of institutional structures that elicit cooperative outcomes in limited-access commons. Libecap (1990) has shown the efficacy of bargaining among participants to promote cooperation in commons where a small number of players repeatedly interact. Olson (1965) is clearly correct that institutions can be designed to circumvent collective action problems. Design principles must eliminate defection as a dominant strategy and promote supporting strategic behavior. With the design of collective action–supporting institutions, the relevancy of cooperative game theory will assume an enhanced importance, as in the theory of clubs.

2.6 Concluding Remarks

This chapter has taken an overview of the three themes developed in *The Logic of Collective Action*. Theme 1 concerns the relationship between group size and collective action; theme 2 involves group composition (symmetry versus asymmetry) and collective action; and theme 3 relates to the means for overcoming collective inaction. Over the course of the chapter, we have seen a number of noteworthy exceptions to Olsonian propositions, such as the exploitation of the large by the small or the inverse relationship between

---

33. See, e.g., Hansmann 1980; Posnett and Sandler 1989; Cauley, Sandler, and Cornes 1986.
34. See Schotter 1980; Ostrom 1990; Taylor 1987; Hardin 1982; Axelrod 1984; Bianco and Bates 1990.

collective provision and group size. These exceptions, although numerous, do not detract from the intellectual contributions of *Logic,* since the most important propositions appear to hold in some of the most relevant scenarios. It is not surprising that, when given the latitude to vary tastes, the technology of publicness, the structure of costs, strategic behavior, and other parameters of the collective action problem, researchers had significant freedom to construct aberrant cases. If Olson's proposition had only applied to uninteresting special cases with few real-world analogues, surely interest in his propositions would have ended long before now. Collective action holds our attention because it is relevant and applicable to a rich array of situations with subtle but important differences.

CHAPTER 3

New Developments in Collective Action

With each passing year, the interest in collective action has grown, both in terms of extending its theoretic foundations and in offering applications. As collective action theory has developed, more formalism has understandably been used. The focus here is to present some of the more important theoretic developments and to indicate how these developments relate to the three basic themes of Olson's original book. To accomplish this purpose, I isolate the basic insights, concepts, and the importance of recent developments in collective action. Since the emphasis is on concepts, elaborate mathematics are avoided except for a few proofs on the neutrality theorem, gathered in the chapter appendix. The interested reader should consult the indicated references for the details of the models.

The chapter has seven subsections. The theory of clubs is reviewed in section 3.1. The importance of the strategic assumption—Nash or something else—is investigated in section 3.2, while the neutrality theorem for pure public goods is analyzed in section 3.3. A brief review of dynamic considerations of collective action is presented in section 3.4. These dynamic aspects open the way for collective action in such game structures as the Prisoner's Dilemma. The influence of uncertainty on collective action is briefly discussed in section 3.5, while a few additional aspects of the technology of public supply are mentioned in section 3.6. Concluding remarks are in section 3.7.

3.1 The Theory of Clubs

A club is a voluntary collective that derives mutual benefits from sharing one or more of the following: production costs, the members' characteristics, or an impure public good characterized by excludable benefits.[1] Such excludable public goods are called club goods. When club goods are shared, emphasis must be placed on the existence of an affordable method of exclusion to keep nonpayers from free riding. If exclusion costs do not *exceed* the efficiency

---

1. The theory of clubs has been surveyed by Sandler and Tschirhart (1980) and Cornes and Sandler (1986). See these surveys for over 200 relevant citations. Also see the recent survey by Scotchmer 1991.

gains from allocating the impure public good in a club arrangement, then the club is a feasible, nonmarket alternative. Exclusion costs are created by barriers used to monitor entry and to collect visitation fees. In a broader sense, exclusion costs may also be incurred by users in terms of queuing costs as they wait to clear barriers.

Club goods include highways, cities, infrastructure, military arsenals, terrorist commando squads, police forces, zoos, museums, golf courses, universities, learned societies, movie theaters, parks, recreation facilities, straits, canals, trauma clinics, and libraries. Many other examples exist. An alliance that shares conventional armaments or a "Star Wars" defense is a club, since noncontributors may have their protection withheld. A fire station offers a club good in the form of fire protection, which can be withheld from noncontributors and is subject to congestion when multiple fires need to be suppressed simultaneously. Satellite communication networks, such as INTELSAT with its geostationary satellites, are club goods. An economic alliance in the form of a common market is another example of a club that uses tariff barriers as a means of distinguishing between members and nonmembers. Many, but not all, supranational organizations can be considered club arrangements, provided that exclusion can be practiced.

Since clubs often share impure public goods whose benefits are subject to rivalry, the notion of crowding or congestion is a crucial consideration. Crowding occurs when one user's utilization of the club good decreases the benefits or the quality of service still available to others. As such, crowding or congestion depends on some measure of utilization, which could include the number of members, the number of visits, or the ratio of members to the number of units provided (i.e., a measure of average utilization). Congestion may take the form of longer waits, slower service, reduced traffic flows, more encounters on nature trails, longer publication delays, higher bacteria counts in swimming pools, higher accident rates (i.e., a more extreme form of encounters), increased noise levels at public performances, interrupted services, or obstructed views. In contrast to impure public goods, pure public goods involve no crowding because the good is nonrival at any utilization level.

In his seminal paper, Buchanan (1965) depicted how voluntary clubs could provide themselves with an impure public good. If members could identify and exclude nonmembers, then tolls (i.e., per-visit fees or membership charges) could internalize or charge for crowding externalities between users, and achieve Pareto optimality without resorting to government intervention. A club is an institutional solution to the collective action problem that internalizes an externality through tolls. Although *Logic* is not typically credited with the development of club theory, the rudiments of club theory can be found in Olson's distinction between *inclusive* and *exclusive* collective goods and groups (1965, chap. 1). An inclusive collective good may be utilized or shared by an unlimited number of individuals without rivalry in consumption in the form of congestion. There is no economic rationale for restricting group size in the case of an inclusive collective good. In contrast, an exclusive collective good cannot be shared by additional consumers without detracting from the derived benefits of the other users. For exclusive goods, group size must be restricted so that rivalry costs are internalized.

Clubs are simply *exclusive groups* in the Olson terminology. Collectives may be inclusive rather than exclusive for two reasons: zero congestion cost or prohibitively high exclusion cost. In the latter case, congestion costs may not lend a motivation to restricting size, since the costs of doing so may not outweigh the gains in efficiency; hence, no barriers are erected. Shopping centers, for example, often provide more parking spaces than needed by customers to accommodate free riders without having to monitor and tow away these nonshoppers. The extra costs of the parking spaces are more economical than providing an exclusion mechanism. As compared with a fully internalized solution, suboptimality remains in the parking example, but it is simply too costly to do anything about.

A number of features of clubs need emphasis. First, membership is voluntary—individuals choose to belong because they view membership as providing a net benefit. In contrast, the consumption choice for a pure public (inclusive) good is not left up to the individual, since exclusion is not possible. Second, the club will attempt to limit membership size; hence, the choice of group size is endogenous and of prime interest. Third, some type of membership fee or per-unit visitation fee must be levied. The latter is preferable when visitations are variable. Fourth, an exclusion mechanism is required.

With a slight modification, Olson's math (see chap. 2) can be extended to incorporate the theory of clubs explicitly. A costless exclusion mechanism is initially assumed, and the population is also assumed identical in terms of tastes and income. Club costs are assumed to be borne solely by the club's members. With homogeneous members, this implies that each of the members covers one n^{th} of the club's costs. When visitation rates are fixed, members' utilization patterns cannot be tailored to individual members' tastes. If everyone is identical, this individualized visitation patterning is not really an issue. In addition, the population is assumed to be partitioned into a set of nonoverlapping clubs, so that there are no excluded individuals—everyone belongs to one of these replicable clubs. Such a configuration of clubs is said to be in the *core*. The core exists if there are no blocking coalitions or subgroups of individuals who could do better by forming a different configuration of clubs. The absence of such a blocking coalition implies that everyone is satisfied with the payoffs assigned to them by the existing partition of individuals into clubs. Hence, the core configuration of clubs is *stable* in the sense that no alternative configuration is in some subset of members' interest. No movement between clubs is observed.

Using Olson's mathematical notation (presented in chap. 2), individual benefits, V_i, are now

$$V_i = V_i(y^i, Q, n) . \tag{3.1}$$

$V_i(\bullet)$ is assumed to be increasing in y^i and Q, and decreasing in n. The latter relationship reflects crowding as the number of sharers increases. To meet sufficiency conditions for an optimum, we assume that $V_i(\bullet)$ is concave. Individual costs or resources, C_i, are

$$C_i = C_i(y^i, Q, n) , \tag{3.2}$$

where C_i is increasing in y^i and Q, and decreasing in n. The latter denotes the equal-sharing-of-cost assumption. Function C_i is also assumed to be convex, so that marginal costs are increasing in the arguments. Differentiating net benefits $(V_i - C_i)$ with respect to y^i, Q, and n yields the following FOCs after simplification.

$$MRS^i_{Qy} = MRT^i_{Qy}, \quad i = 1, \ldots, n \text{ (provision)} , \tag{3.3}$$

$$MRS^i_{ny} = MRT^i_{ny}, \quad i = 1, \ldots, n \text{ (membership)} . \tag{3.4}$$

The provision condition indicates that each member's marginal rate of substitution (MRS) between the club good and the private good must be equated to the member's marginal rate of transformation (MRT) between these goods.[2] Thus, individuals equate their marginal provision benefits with their marginal provision costs. The private good serves as a standard of value.

The novel aspect of club analysis is embodied in equation 3.4, in which optimal group size is obtained when each individual equates his or her MRS between group size and the private good to his or her MRT between the two. In equation 3.4, the marginal benefits derived from having another member is thus equated with the associated marginal costs. These marginal benefits are normally negative owing to crowding, and the corresponding marginal costs are also negative owing to cost reductions derived from cost sharing. As a club increases in size, each member pays a smaller proportion of the provision costs. Three aspects of the club's problem need to be highlighted: (*a*) the

---

2. $MRS^i_{Qy} = (\partial V_i/\partial Q)/(\partial V_i/\partial y^i)$ and $MRT^i_{Qy} = (\partial C_i/\partial Q)/(\partial C_i/\partial y^i)$. Similar expressions hold for MRS^i_{ny} and MRT^i_{ny}.

provision and membership conditions must be *simultaneously* determined, since each expression contains identical variables; (*b*) net benefits are maximized for the representative member, so that average net benefits for the club are maximized; and (*c*) membership fees or tolls are set equal to the right-hand side of equation 3.4, thereby internalizing the congestion externality.

Although Olson (1965) did not explicitly extend his formal model to encompass standard club theory, the principles of club theory were addressed (1965, 30–31, 36–40). The clearest statement is the following.

> When an inclusive collective good is not a pure public good, however, those in the group enjoying the good would not welcome additional members who failed to pay adequate dues. Dues would not be adequate unless they were at least equal in value to the reduction in the consumption of the new entrant. (Olson 1965, 40)

In a letter to Olson, Buchanan acknowledged Olson's independent development of the rudiments of club theory (Olson 1965, 38).

If, at the margin, the club is breaking even in providing the collective good, the sum of the members' marginal costs (ΣMRT^i) must equal the club's marginal costs of provision. That is,

$$\sum_{i=1}^{n} \text{MRT}^i_{Qy} = \text{MRT}_{Qy} \, , \qquad (3.5)$$

where MRT_{Qy} is the club's marginal costs of provision. Equations 3.3 and 3.5 then imply the usual Samuelson provision condition for public goods,

$$\sum_{i=1}^{n} \text{MRS}^i_{Qy} = \text{MRT}_{Qy} \, . \qquad (3.6)$$

Thus, voluntary clubs can achieve Pareto optimality and thus circumvent collective action difficulties if *properly* designed. The key is the exclusion mechanism and the use of congestion-internalizing tolls. The size of the group does not imply greater suboptimality when clubs can internalize externalities and satisfy membership conditions. If the population is too big for an optimally sized club, then multiple clubs can form.

In Buchanan 1965, the club's problem took a slightly different, but equivalent form, in which the representative member maximizes utility,

$$U^i = U^i(y^i, Q, n) \, , \qquad (3.7)$$

where Q is the club good, subject to his or her resource constraint,

$$F^i(y^i, Q, n) = 0 . \tag{3.8}$$

Utility increases with more of the private good and more of the club good, but decreases with more members, owing to crowding (i.e., $\partial U^i/\partial n < 0$). In equation 3.8, resources are expended with an increase in either y^i or Q, but are saved with an increase in group size owing to cost sharing among members. The FOCs of the Buchanan problem are identical in form and interpretation to those in equations 3.3 and 3.4, and, hence, are not repeated. A more stylized replicable club model is

$$\max_{y^i, Q, n} U^i(y^i, Q) \quad \text{subject to } I^i = y^i + [C(Q, n)]/n , \tag{3.9}$$

where I^i is the ith individual's income and $C(\bullet)$ is club costs, which increases with provision and membership. The form of the budget constraint implies equal cost sharing in the club. The influence of membership on club costs (i.e., $\partial C/\partial n > 0$) denotes *marginal crowding costs*. By substituting the budget constraint into the utility function and then finding the FOCs, we have

$$\sum_{i=1}^{n} \mathrm{MRS}^i_{Qy} = MC_Q , \tag{3.10}$$

and

$$C(\bullet)/n = \partial C/\partial n . \tag{3.11}$$

Condition 3.10 is the provision condition that indicates that the sum of the marginal provision benefits of the members equals marginal provision costs ($MC_Q = \partial C/\partial Q$). The membership condition (eq. 3.11) is extremely easy to apply in practice and indicates that per-person club fees equal marginal crowding costs. In other words, the per-person club costs should be minimized, which requires the relevant average costs and marginal costs be equated. The toll is simply C/n. This result, of course, hinges on a number of key assumptions: membership homogeneity, a core solution, and fully financed clubs.

Before considering refinements to club theory, the basic solution in equations 3.3 and 3.4 is illustrated with the help of some simple geometry. To simplify, I assume that the club good is produced under constant returns to scale so that the costs of each extra unit of provision are constant. As before, club costs are equally shared among members. The provision choice is con-

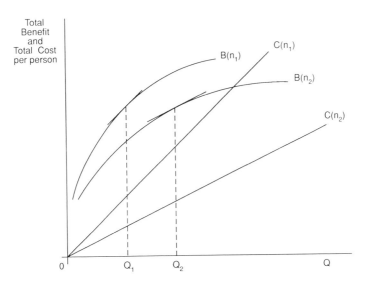

Fig. 3.1. Optimizing provision level for a club

sidered in figure 3.1, where the level of the shared good is on the horizontal axis, and total cost and total benefit per member is on the vertical axis. The $C(n_1)$ curve indicates a member's provision costs for membership size n_1, while the $B(n_1)$ curve is the member's provision benefits for membership size n_1. The shape of the benefit curve reflects diminishing marginal benefits with increased provision. That is, benefits rise with provision, but the rate of increase declines with subsequent increments in Q. Diminishing marginal benefits are consistent with diminishing MRS^i_{Qy}, when the latter represents the marginal benefits in terms of the private good. The linear costs curve out of the origin in figure 3.1 reflects constant returns to scale. For n_1, the optimizing provision level, Q_1, corresponds to the point where the slopes of the two curves are equal, thereby giving the greatest net benefits. If, however, membership were to rise to n_2, then the member's benefit curve shifts down to $B(n_2)$ to account for the loss in total and marginal provision benefits at each provision level owing to increased crowding. The cost curve pivots downward with n_2 as more members share the costs for each facility size. The optimizing provision level is now Q_2, where the slopes of the two curves are equal. The optimums in figure 3.1 correspond to equation 3.3, where MRS^i_{Qy} is the slope of $B(n_j)$ and MRT^i_{Qy} is the slope of $C(n_j)$ for each n_j level. According to figure 3.1, increases in membership size are positively related to the optimizing provision levels; larger memberships would support larger facilities.

In figure 3.2, optimizing membership size is related to different provision levels; hence, the membership condition of equation 3.4 is represented.

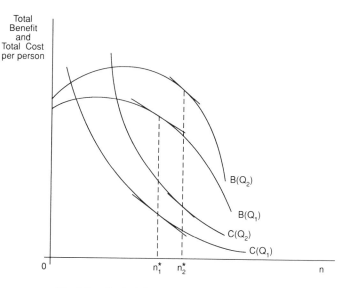

Fig. 3.2. Optimizing membership for a club

Membership is measured on the horizontal axis, and changes in provision levels shift the curves. Per-person benefits and costs are depicted on the vertical axis. For any provision level, say Q_1, the benefits curve shows the benefits per person. Its shape indicates that camaraderie is eventually overpowered by crowding, and, at that point, the benefit curve begins to decline. The cost curves depict the costs per member when a facility of size Q_1 is shared by a varying number of members. Each cost curve in figure 3.2 is a rectangular hyperbola, since costs are equally shared so that the costs per person times the number of members must cover the (unchanged) costs of Q_1 units of the shared good. For Q_1, optimal membership occurs at n_1^*, where the two slopes are equal. Since the slope of $B(Q_1)$ is MRS_{ny}^i, and the slope of $C(Q_1)$ is MRT_{ny}^i, equation 3.4 is satisfied at Q_1. As facility size rises to Q_2, both the costs and benefits curves shift up. The curve of $C(\bullet)$ is likely to become steeper at each n level, while $B(\bullet)$ is apt to become somewhat flatter. The former is due to the greater overall costs to be shared, while the latter is due to reduced marginal crowding costs in larger facilities. If this is the case, then, as figure 3.2 demonstrates, optimizing membership is positively related to facility size. Larger facilities would be supported by larger memberships.

The two partial equilibrium relationships are displayed by the positively sloped "optimum" curves in figure 3.3. The Q-optimum curve comes from figures 3.1 and shows the optimal provision for each n; the n-optimum curve derives from figure 3.2 and depicts the optimal membership for each Q. The linear shapes are for convenience. The relative slopes are required to ensure a

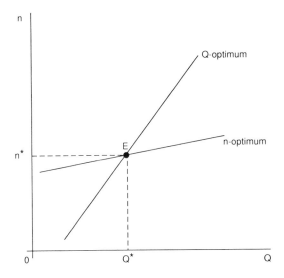

Fig. 3.3. Club equilibrium

stable equilibrium at E, where Q^* and n^* *mutually* satisfy equations 3.3 and 3.4. Figure 3.3 illustrates that the membership and provision level must be chosen simultaneously; a dual decision is required in a club. Neither choice variable can be decided in isolation.

In figure 3.4, the benefit and cost per-person curves for determining memberships are displayed for a *pure* public good. An absence of crowding means that per-person benefits for each facility size is horizontal and, consequently, clubs should be inclusive (since each additional member reduces costs with no loss of benefits). In this case, the n-optimal curve is undefined. If transaction costs, in the form of exclusion costs, are sufficiently great, this can give $C(Q_j)$ such a large negative slope at each membership level that all willing participants need to be included.

3.1.1 Club Theory and the Olsonian Themes

Club theory does not really support the first two Olsonian themes. For theme 1, an increase in club size does not necessarily imply lower provision levels. In fact, club theory hypothesizes that larger memberships will want larger facilities to trade off optimally crowding costs with cost-sharing benefits. Since membership and provision are chosen to satisfy Pareto optimality, an increase in group size does not imply greater suboptimality, especially when replicable clubs can be formed to partition a population of potential members. Because clubs are voluntary and, hence, all members must gain positive net

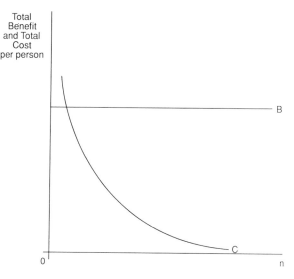

Fig. 3.4.   Inclusive club

benefits from joining, increases in club size need not influence the likelihood of having the club be privileged. Clubs are fully privileged. To get at theme 2 and asymmetry, club theory must be extended to consider heterogeneous members. Such models have shown that no exploitation will occur, provided that members are charged a per-visit fee.[3] Heavier users of the club, whether they be richer or otherwise, pay the same toll per visit, but they pay more in total tolls, since they reveal their preferences with more visits. The club toll scheme internalizes the crowding externality and puts no weight or emphasis on the relative sizes or endowments of the players. Since homogeneous clubs are easier to organize, such clubs are more apt than heterogeneous clubs to be formed. Unlike other types of collectives, membership homogeneity facilitates club formation. Causal empiricism suggests that clubs do tend to attract similar members.

Since clubs are an institutional scheme for circumventing collective action problems, clubs are in keeping with theme 3. The presence of an exclusion mechanism, however, means that costs can be internalized without the need for selective incentives. Alternative institutional forms are utilized in clubs. Clubs can be owned and operated by their members, or can be run by firms to make a profit.[4] Additionally, clubs can be provided by local or central governments. Golf courses, tennis facilities, professional associations, and

3. See Sandler 1984; Sandler and Tschirhart 1984; Scotchmer and Wooders 1987.
4. See Berglas 1976 and 1981; Scotchmer 1985 and 1991.

churches are a few examples of clubs owned and operated by a membership. Movie theaters, trauma clinics, and amusement parks are instances in which a profit-maximizing firm provides the club good. National parks, interstate highway systems, police service, disease control centers, weather services, and fire protection are examples in which a government manages the club. Nonprofit organizations may also provide such club goods as hospitals, ambulance services, and educational facilities.

In the case of profit-maximizing firms, a competitive equilibrium would characterize the club if the population is sufficiently large to support numerous clubs. At an equilibrium, a core is obtained whereby the population is partitioned between replicable clubs and no one is left out.[5] If visits are variable, each member pays a total fee equal to his or her share of total visits times total club costs. If, for example, one-tenth of the visits are attributed to a given member, then his or her total fee is $C/10$. Once an exclusion mechanism is available, the actual ownership arrangement—member owned, firm owned, or government owned—does not make a difference unless legal considerations restrict the latitude of club operations. For example, a government-operated club may have difficulty restricting membership.

The theory of clubs is closely akin to the theory of local public goods, which serves as a foundation of the theory of local public finance. A local jurisdiction (e.g., a county, a township, or a city) provides public goods that are often subject to crowding. Tiebout (1956) viewed individuals as voting-with-their-feet in choosing the jurisdiction whose tax and public good package is most suited to their tastes. In many instances, costs per resident are minimized through the Tiebout arrangement; hence, the stylized club model in equations 3.9 through 3.11 often serves as a foundation for the Tiebout partition result. The local public good model is very similar to the club model, except for the form of payment. Local public goods are usually financed by a tax on land or property values rather than by a toll (Scotchmer 1991).

Clubs also characterize international political economy. Crisis management forces, such as terrorist commando squads, can be dispatched in a club arrangement to member countries, whereby the recipient is charged a user fee for each dispatch. Research and expert groups of scientists are also shared internationally, as are military forces.

3.1.2 Other Considerations in Club Theory

Club theory has been developed in many ways for both homogeneous and heterogeneous populations. Much of this development has focused on the congestion function, which indicates how crowding changes with utilization.

---

5. See Pauly 1967; Berglas 1976; Cornes and Sandler 1986; Scotchmer and Wooders 1987.

Numerous representations for utilization have been used. In a simple form, the congestion function, c, includes the number of members and the size of the shared good.

$$c = c(Q, n), \tag{3.12}$$

where $\partial c/\partial Q < 0$ and $\partial c/\partial n > 0$, so that provision reduces crowding and membership size increases it. In some analyses, congestion costs are incorporated in the club costs function as in the stylized model above, and, hence, are on the constraint side. In other instances, congestion is a detraction from utility and is part of the utility function.

$$U^i = U^i[y^i, c(Q, n)] \, , \tag{3.13}$$

where utility declines with congestion (i.e., $\partial U^i/\partial c$). Buchanan (1965) employed this latter approach and gave the congestion function the form of the identity mapping, so that just Q and n appear. In equation 3.13, the congestion function denotes the technology of public supply that indicates how the public supply is translated into consumption.

This technology of consumption often, but not always, keeps Q in an additive form and introduces an additional argument in terms of utilization. Another common form of this technology of public supply is

$$c = c(Q, nv) \, , \tag{3.14}$$

where v denotes the number of visits of a representative member to the club. If members are heterogeneous, then total utilization becomes Σv^i, in which v^i is the ith member's visitation rate. Other utilization measures have been used (Cornes and Sandler 1986, chap. 11). The form of the congestion function is instrumental in determining: (a) self-financing of clubs by tolls, (b) the optimality of heterogeneous clubs, and (c) the existence and stability of equilibrium.[6]

Multiple clubs, such as the partitioning of nations into alliances, can be analyzed by determining the core for replicable clubs, much as jurisdictions are determined by the Tiebout hypothesis. Nations can "vote-with-their-membership" in different alliances. Past history has, indeed, shown that the configuration of alliances is very fluid. NATO's forty-plus years of stability is a partial exception, but even NATO's membership changed with the addition of Portugal, Turkey, Germany, and Spain. The future will witness nations partitioning themselves into nonoverlapping common markets, such as the

6. See Sandler and Tschirhart 1980.

European Community and the recently proposed Mexico–Canada–United States free trade zone.

Clubs of clubs can also form as a means for coping with random utilization without imposing capacity constraints that require members to be turned away when utilization is particularly heavy (Sterbenz and Sandler 1992). If another club with similar facilities is available and if the utilization patterns of the two clubs are not highly positively correlated, then the memberships of both clubs could be better off by sharing one another's facilities to even out crowding. When, for example, one fire district's equipment and fire fighters are fighting a blaze, the other district's equipment and personnel will respond in the event of another fire in that district. Similar sharing arrangements characterize the dispatching of disaster relief teams, the circulation of books in interlibrary loan arrangements, and the deployment of military forces between allies. When drivers spread their use over alternative routes by listening to radio broadcasts of traffic information, a sharing arrangement is being practiced. Interclub agreements require the use of sharing tolls, or else free riding will surface as one club directs its members to another. With a collective of clubs, membership and provision decisions for the two clubs become intertwined and collective action problems may arise as one club fails to limit memberships or to provide sufficient facilities. Thus, collective action problems may arise when clubs are themselves members of a club.

*3.2. The Strategic Assumption

Logic implicitly assumed Nash behavior, and in recent years, investigators have extended the analysis to other kinds of strategic assumptions. Guttman (1978 and 1987) examined non-Nash behavior in the form of a two-stage matching game in which flat contributions are determined in one stage and matching rates in the other. Each individual's provision level is

$$q^i = a_i + b_i \sum_{j \neq i}^{n} a_j , \qquad (3.15)$$

where a_i is agent i's flat contribution and b_i is his matching rate. Matching behavior, which can be fostered by institutional rules, reduces the effective price of the collective action and leads to increased provision. Federal matching grants to states are an example. A positive conjecture characterizes the strategic interaction. If individuals are identical *and* income effects are absent, then the resulting equilibrium will be Pareto optimal regardless of the number of individuals (Guttman 1978). Group size may, nonetheless, still pose an impediment to collective action, since the feasibility of eliciting matching behavior surely declines with group size, especially if tastes and/or endowments differ.

Cornes and Sandler (1984b and 1986) have formulated a theory of non-Nash behavior based on a nonlinear conjectural variation,

$$d\tilde{Q}^e/dq = b(q/\tilde{Q})^\theta ,$$ (3.16)

where $\tilde{Q}$ denotes spillovers; the e superscript indicates "expected"; b represents a parameter; and θ corresponds to the elasticity of the conjectured response with respect to the relative importance of the agent's contribution. This nonlinear conjectural variation is capable of representing a wide variety of behavior. If individuals are identical, equation 3.16 can be expressed in terms of groups size for symmetric equilibria, since $q/\tilde{Q} = 1/(n - 1)$. Thus, the effect of group size can be analyzed for homogeneous collectives under various strategic scenarios. The model suffers from its static assumption. More sophisticated exercises need to incorporate learning so that conjectures can be updated as information evolves. This requires that uncertainty about the behavior of others be modeled explicitly in an internally consistent fashion, in which the expectations of the group are clearly connected with the expectations of the individuals that comprise the group. Bayes's theorem can be used to update one's priors using information revealed through other players' actions in the preceding periods.

Sugden (1984) developed a theory of collective action based on a notion of reciprocity, whereby individual i meets or exceeds the *minimal* contribution of the rest of the group. Individual i exceeds the minimal effort level if the level that he or she most prefers everyone to make is greater than the minimal effort of others. In essence, moral constraints limit the agent's behavior since he or she cannot take a free ride when others contribute, since he or she must at least match the minimal contribution. Under special circumstances, the reciprocity equilibrium for identical individuals will be analogous to matching behavior (Sugden 1984, 778). In most situations, reciprocity still implies suboptimal provision.

Sugden's theory of reciprocity is quite different than the model based on the weakest link. For the latter, an agent provides his or her optimizing choice of q^i when $q^i \leq \min \mathbf{q}_{-i}$ [where $\min \mathbf{q}_{-i}$ is the minimal component of vector $\mathbf{q}_{-i} = (q^1, \ldots, q^{i-1}, q^{i+1}, \ldots, q^n)$] or else he or she provides $\min \mathbf{q}_{-i}$, depending on whichever is *smaller*. His or her demand for the public good is

$$q^i = \min \{f^i(\bullet), \min \mathbf{q}_{-i}\} ,$$ (3.17)

in which $f^i(\bullet)$ is the demand function of agent i for q^i when $q^i \leq \min \mathbf{q}_{-i}$. Unlike reciprocity, the agent never outdoes the minimal provision with weakest link. Reciprocity is, consequently, expected to have better efficiency properties than the weakest link.

Much still needs to be done to study non-Nash behavior. The effects of asymmetry are especially difficult to analyze when Nash behavior is dropped, since heterogeneous tastes and/or endowments could lead to different learning patterns and, hence, diverse strategic behavior within the group.

3.3 The Neutrality Theorem

The neutrality theorem, which indicates that the Nash-equilibrium provision level for a pure public good is invariant to income redistributions among an unchanged set of contributors, has received much attention since Warr's (1982 and 1983) interest-generating papers. The theorem accounts for the interdependency among contributors and does not require that contributors possess identical tastes. Since the theorem indicates an impediment to the use of an income policy to correct the Pareto-suboptimal Nash equilibrium associated with a pure public good, it is especially noteworthy. If the government were to *tax contributors* to finance more of the public good, then government expenditures on provision would crowd out private contributions on a dollar-for-dollar basis (Roberts 1984). Two alternative proofs of the neutrality theorem are given in the appendix to this chapter.

Although Warr (1982 and 1983) brought the neutrality theorem to the profession's attention, a closely related neutrality result appeared earlier in Becker 1974. Even before Becker, Hirofumi Shibata (1971) came very close to presenting the neutrality theorem when he depicted the Nash equilibrium in his two-person bargaining triangle (1971, 21–22). The Shibata two-person diagram makes it clear that income redistribution cannot affect the Nash equilibrium for a pure public good, provided that both players remain contributors.

In recent years, the bounds to the neutrality theorem have been better drawn. Bergstrom, Blume, and Varian (1986) have proved that neutrality does not hold if the set of contributors is influenced by the redistribution or tax policy. If, therefore, the government raises revenues by taxing noncontributors and then spends these revenues on the public good, Nash-equilibrium provision will rise for a normal good. Tax spillovers that raise revenues by taxing people outside the benefit range of a collective good can, consequently, augment collective provision. But such a policy is unlikely to be Pareto optimal, inasmuch as those who are taxed are worse off when they finance a good that they do not consume. The dependence of neutrality on an unchanged set of contributors also implies that *large* redistributions between contributors may indeed have a nonneutral influence by altering the set of contributors. Small redistributions that imply an "internal" solution (thereby maintaining the set of contributors) have no impact on provision. When neutrality *holds*, group asymmetry has no influence on *total* provision levels since *small* redistributions from the small (poor) to the large (rich), while shifting burdens onto the large, will not affect provision. Larger redistributions are, however, another matter and would be in keeping with Olson's exploitation hypothesis. With asymmetric contributors, the extent of the redistribution need not be too great before the smallest players are pushed to a corner, in which they no longer contribute. Once this occurs and the set of contributors changes, neutrality is lost.

Another series of articles have demonstrated that neutrality does not extend to joint products or selective incentives.[7] Thus, Olson's original emphasis on these selective incentives as a policy tool appears to have been well placed. A redistributive incomes policy that taxes those with the greatest derived private benefits from the collective action will increase collective provision, since these individuals are still motivated to contribute to get private benefits that are not provided by government provision. In other words, tax-financed public benefits are unlikely to crowd out the contributions of privately motivated individuals. Altering selective incentives can be an effective tool for engineering greater collective action.

If strategic assumptions other than Nash are invoked, then the neutrality theorem and its pessimism with respect to income policy may not hold. For example, an institutional arrangement that induces positive conjectures, as in the case of matching behavior, need not abide by neutrality when the conjectural variation is *variable and dependent* on the amount of the individual's contribution. When, however, the conjectured response of spillovers to one's own contribution is a nonzero constant, neutrality still holds (Dasgupta and Itaya 1991; Sandler and Posnett 1991). If, for example, the matching rate is a constant amount of contributions, as is true for many federal matching grants to states, then neutrality would hold if a redistributive income policy is applied to the states. Institutional design obviously matters. Bruce (1990) has also demonstrated that leader-follower behavior, in which the leader uses the follower's reaction path as its constraint,[8] also abides by neutrality. (The proof of neutrality for leader and follower is shown in the appendix.) Since leader-follower equilibria are likely to be asymmetric, with the follower doing much of the contributing, relatively small redistributions may be sufficient to induce a corner solution in which the number of contributors changes. Neutrality no longer holds at such corners; hence, leader-follower neutrality may not be very robust.

---

7. See Cornes and Sandler 1981 and 1984a; Andreoni 1987, 1989, 1990.

8. The conjectural variation is the slope of the follower's Nash reaction path. If this path is negatively sloped, then collective provision is even less than that of Nash behavior (see chap. 2). Neutrality is, therefore, especially bothersome.

Neutrality also hinges on the technology of public supply; the summation technology is a crucial ingredient in the establishment of neutrality. Vicary (1990) showed that neutrality may not apply to weakest-link technology when income is redistributed from the rich to the poor. At a weakest-link equilibrium, each contributor will match contributions. If, say, everyones' tastes are the same and utility-maximizing contributions are increasing in income, then the poorest individual's contribution will be matched by everyone. Thus, income-equalizing redistributions will then increase the poorest individual's income and contribution and, with it, everyone else's matching contribution. In this example, equality-enhancing redistribution is an effective collective action strategy. Group homogeneity needs to be encouraged. The opposite redistribution applies to the best shot, where inequality and enhanced asymmetry are apt to promote collective action. For the best shot, the largest or richest individual is the sole contributor when all goods are normal. Since scientific breakthroughs (e.g., the discovery of a Star Wars defense, or a cancer cure) is a best-shot technology, a government's policy of unequal support of research institutions and universities makes good sense. Asymmetry is needed for technologies like the best shot. Countries need their Harvards, Oxfords, and Australian National Universities to get off the best shot. Equal support of all institutions may not lead to the best shot being fired.

Since many collective action problems involve joint products, impure public goods, and diverse technologies of public supply, neutrality may not hold and, hence, there is clearly room for income policy. Future work must investigate how to design Pareto-improving income redistributions for collective action. It is not enough to know how to increase collective action, since action that is coerced or engineered may not improve everyone's welfare. Policies that increase equilibrium provision by taxing noncontributors (who do not desire the collective good) are not Pareto improving.

3.4 Dynamic Considerations

Logic considered collective action problems in a static, timeless environment. Single-shot, simultaneous-move games can be an adequate abstract description of such environments. In the real world, agents often interact repeatedly (e.g., members of Congress in a logrolling situation, nations in a military alliance, countries along a polluted waterway, western states in the United States facing seasonal threats of fires, and individuals contributing to a public good needing replenishment). When repeated interactions are allowed, the set of Nash equilibrium strategies may be very large. The Folk theorem of repeated games indicates that any individually rational strategy can be an equilibrium (McMillan 1986, 14–16).

Consider a two-person collective action problem with payoffs corresponding to the Prisoner's Dilemma. In a single play, the Nash equilibrium consists of each agent playing his or her dominant strategy of defecting. If, instead, the game is repeated an infinite number of times and the discount rate is not too great, then a strategy of Tit-for-Tat is also a Nash equilibrium.[9] Tit-for-Tat corresponds to choosing the cooperative strategy in the first round and then matching the opponent's choice in the preceding round. Another Nash-equilibrium strategy involves cooperating in the first play and cooperating in subsequent plays so long as the opponent cooperated in the previous round. Once the other player defects, then the strategy requires the player to defect thereafter. Threat-backed cooperative strategies are equilibria, since short-run gains from defection may be less than long-run losses as threats are executed. If, however, discount takes are low, so that future benefits are greatly disfavored over immediate benefits, then short-run gains from defection may exceed long-run losses, and defection may still dominate. With repeated interactions, the single-shot game prediction may no longer apply. More subtle considerations may be required. The outcome of collective action depends on whether the game is repeated a finite or an infinite number of times and whether there is complete or incomplete information about the players' types. Simple relationships concerning group size and composition are not possible to draw for general scenarios.

To illustrate the Tit-for-Tat Nash equilibrium for a repeated Prisoner's Dilemma, we modify a normal game representation (from Ordeshook 1986). In figure 3.5, the Prisoner's Dilemma, public good game of figure 2.6 for two agents is extended to a repeated game framework in which the game is played an infinite number of times. These payoffs in the single-play Prisoner's Dilemma are (4,4) for mutual cooperation, (0,0) for mutual defection, and $(-1,5)$ and $(5,-1)$ for single defection. Each agent is permitted three intertemporal strategies:[10] (1) Tit-for-Tat, (2) cooperation on every round, and (3) defection on every round. The discount rate is r, which is a fraction less than one. If both players choose Tit-for-Tat, then each cooperates on the first and all subsequent rounds, and receives a payoff of 4 on every round for a present value of $4/(1 - r)$.[11] Similar payoffs characterize cells b, d, and e, in which mutual cooperation occurs on every round. If, however, the first agent uses Tit-for-Tat, while the second uses defection, then the first player receives -1 in the first round and 0 thereafter, and the second player receives 5 in the first round and 0 thereafter. This follows because after the first round, the Tit-

---

9. See especially Ordeshook 1986, 442–48; Axelrod 1984.

10. This assumption is a convenience, since an infinite number of possible strategies are possible. These three are sufficient to illustrate the point that a cooperative strategy may be a Nash equilibrium.

11. This follows because $(1 - r)^{-1} = 1 + r + r^2 + r^3 + \dots$. The discount factor and the interest rate, i, are related since $r = (1 + i)^{-1}$; hence $4/(1 - r) = 4 + (4/i)$.

		2	
	T-f-T	C	D
T-f-T	*a* $\frac{4}{1-r}, \frac{4}{1-r}$	*b* $\frac{4}{1-r}, \frac{4}{1-r}$	*c* -1,5
1 C	*d* $\frac{4}{1-r}, \frac{4}{1-r}$	*e* $\frac{4}{1-r}, \frac{4}{1-r}$	*f* $\frac{-1}{1-r}, \frac{5}{1-r}$
D	*g* 5,-1	*h* $\frac{5}{1-r}, \frac{-1}{1-r}$	*i* 0,0

Fig. 3.5. Repeated Prisoner's Dilemma; r = discount rate. Strategies are: T-f-T = Tit-for-Tat—cooperate on first trial; then match the opponent's choice in preceding trial. C = cooperate in perpetuity. D = defect in perpetuity.

for-Tat strategy requires player 1 to match the opponent's repeated defections. The payoffs in cell g have a similar interpretation, but with the players' roles switched. When player 1 uses cooperation and player 2 employs defection throughout the rounds, player 1 receives -1 in every round, whereas player 2 receives 5 in every round. The present value of these perpetual payoffs are, respectively, $-1/(1-r)$ and $5/(1-r)$ in cell f. A similar situation characterizes cell h, but with roles switched. Mutual defection on every round in cell i yields 0 payoffs to each agent.

Nash equilibria correspond to cells a and i, provided that $4/(1-r) > 5$, or that future benefits are not discounted too heavily (i.e., $1/[1-r]$ is not too small). If, in figure 3.5, agent 1 plays Tit-for-Tat, the best response of agent 2 is to play Tit-for-Tat. Only cells a and i are pure Nash equilibria. The mutual Tit-for-Tat Nash equilibrium Pareto dominates the mutual defection equilibrium, and has much to recommend it. Tit-for-Tat strategies consistently outperformed other strategies in computer simulations (Axelrod 1984).

Figure 3.6 shows repeated versions for the Chicken and Assurance 1 games when each agent again has three strategies. The Chicken game (fig. 3.6a) corresponds to the payoff matrix of figure 2.6c, in which a penalty of $-x$ is imposed for mutual defection. The payoffs in the nine cells can be

2

T-f-T	T-f-T	C	D
T-f-T	*a* $\dfrac{4}{1-r}, \dfrac{4}{1-r}$	*b* $\dfrac{4}{1-r}, \dfrac{4}{1-r}$	*c* $-1-\dfrac{xr}{1-r}, 5-\dfrac{xr}{1-r}$
1 C	*d* $\dfrac{4}{1-r}, \dfrac{4}{1-r}$	*e* $\dfrac{4}{1-r}, \dfrac{4}{1-r}$	*f* $\dfrac{-1}{1-r}, \dfrac{5}{1-r}$
D	*g* $5-\dfrac{xr}{1-r}, -1-\dfrac{xr}{1-r}$	*h* $\dfrac{5}{1-r}, \dfrac{-1}{1-r}$	*i* $\dfrac{-x}{1-r}, \dfrac{-x}{1-r}$

a. Chicken

2

T-f-T	T-f-T	C	D
T-f-T	*a* $\dfrac{4}{1-r}, \dfrac{4}{1-r}$	*b* $\dfrac{4}{1-r}, \dfrac{4}{1-r}$	*c* $-3,-3$
1 C	*d* $\dfrac{4}{1-r}, \dfrac{4}{1-r}$	*e* $\dfrac{4}{1-r}, \dfrac{4}{1-r}$	*f* $\dfrac{-3}{1-r}, \dfrac{-3}{1-r}$
D	*g* $-3\ -3$	*h* $\dfrac{-3}{1-r}, \dfrac{-3}{1-r}$	*i* $0,0$

b. Assurance 1

Fig. 3.6. Other repeated games; *r* = discount rate

computed quite easily. In cell *c*, for example, the players receive $(-1,5)$ in period 1. Thereafter, both defect and receive $-x$ in all subsequent rounds with a present value of $-xr/ (1-r)$. Nash equilibria correspond to cells *a, h,* and *f*. The reader should compute the remaining cells. The Tit-for-Tat strategy is again a Nash equilibrium. Cells *h* and *f* are also Nash equilibria, since it is in some player's interests to avoid the mutual defection outcome even if he or she must be the perpetual sucker (Chicken). Some collective action occurs in this stylized game even when extended to a large number of players.

In figure 3.6b, the Assurance 1 game of figure 2.6e is extended to the simple, repeated-game scenario. Nash equilibria correspond to cells *a, b, d, e,* and *i*. Any combination of Tit-for-Tat and cooperation is an equilibrium strategy pair. Clearly, an infinite repeated game framework can possess many cooperative outcomes. The absence of collective action is no longer the necessary outcome even for bothersome Prisoner's Dilemmas.

Knowledge about the game's length is crucial when analyzing collective action problems in repeated-game frameworks. If a Prisoner's Dilemma is repeated a finite number of times with complete information, then the Nash equilibrium is to defect in each round. Such games are solved backward. In the final period, defection is the dominant strategy. Given that defection occurs in the last period, the dominant strategy in the next-to-last period is also to defect. So it goes for *all* preceding periods. Institutional arrangements that do not limit the number of interactions between the players and, thereby, allow for perpetual interactions may promote the adoption of a cooperative strategy. Dominant noncooperative strategies will, however, be played in every period when the game is viewed as finite in length.

In recent years, much attention has been paid to the notion of Nash equilibria in a repeated-game framework. We have already seen that many Nash equilibria may exist in a repeated-game framework. Concepts such as subgame perfect and sequential equilibria have been developed to cull equilibria strategies with noncredible threats.[12] A subgame consists of a game beginning at a node of a game tree and extending to all subsequent nodes so that no information set of a player is broken up.[13] A finite game in extensive form is given in figure 3.7, where agent 1 moves first, then agent 2, and finally agent 1. The payoffs are indicated at the four possible endpoints, while the three possible subgames are indicated by the square brackets. The subgame perfect equilibrium, which yields a Nash equilibrium on every component subgame, corresponds to agent 1 playing a_2 and agent 2 playing b_1 in figure 3.7. This follows by moving up the tree to solve the game. For sub-

---

12. See, e.g. Selten 1975; Kreps and Wilson 1982.
13. An information set consists of all of the possible nodes that a person could be at when it is his or her turn to move. In fig. 3.7, all information sets consist of a single node.

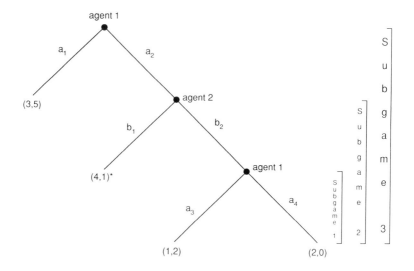

Fig. 3.7. Identification of subgames

game 1, player 1 would play a_4 to maximize his or her payoff; hence, in subgame 2, player 2 plays b_1 for a payoff of 1, since playing b_2 would eventually give him or her only 0. For subgame 3, player 1 plays a_2 since he or she assumes that agent 2 will follow with b_1. Playing a_2 gives him or her a payoff of 4 instead of 3. If this same game is represented by a 3 × 2 normal form matrix, the Nash equilibria are the following sequence of strategies: (1) a_1 followed by b_2 with payoff (3,5), or (2) a_2 followed by b_1 with payoff (4,1). I have used a refinement to remove the first Nash equilibrium.

Uncertainty may also characterize the type of opponent that an agent is playing against (e.g., tough or weak, or high or low collective good demander). The introduction of this type of uncertainty also requires that the Nash equilibrium concept be refined to remove noncredible threats. When uncertainty is present, finite length games may end in cooperation and collective action. Once again, the extensive form of the game must be consulted to judge between Nash equilibria, since the normal form does not provide sufficient information.

To understand this last point, consider the simple game in figure 3.8, depicted in both extensive and normal forms. Player 2 moves first and can go either left or right. A move to the left ends the game with the resulting payoffs (2,0). If, however, player 2 moves right, then player 1 can counter with up or down. The Nash subgame perfect equilibrium is for agent 2 to move right and

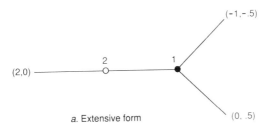

a. Extensive form

Agent 2

		Left	Right
		a	*b*
Up		2,0	-1,-.5
Agent 1		*c*	*d*
Down		2,0	0,.5

b. Normal form

Fig. 3.8. Weak chain

for agent 1 to then move down. Player 1 gets 0, but player 2 gets his or her best payoff of .5. In figure 3.8b, the 2 × 2 matrix displays the game in normal form. Two Nash equilibria are evident in cells *a* and *d*. The Nash equilibrium in cell *a* involves agent 1 carrying out a threat (to play up) that hurts him or her more than not carrying it out. By solving the game backward, we eliminate this noncredible equilibrium from consideration. If this game is played a finite number of times, then agent 2 moves right and agent 1 moves down in each period.

A standard storyline for this game is the chain store paradox in which agent 2 is a small entrant to the market and agent 1 is a large chain store. The small store can enter (move right) or not enter (move left). If the small store enters, the chain store can fight (move up) or acquiesce (move down). The subgame perfect equilibrium in figure 3.8 corresponds to the small store entering and the chain acquiescing. The payoffs listed are for a "weak" chain, one without the stomach to fight and unconcerned about its reputation for weakness. With this weakness, the chain store would be challenged in all of its markets as the game is repeated with other small challengers.

The game shown in figure 3.9a depicts the same game for a strong chain that is better off fighting and preserving its reputation than acquiescing. In this case, the perfect equilibrium is for agent 2 not to enter, since entry means a certain fight and a loss of -0.5 for agent 2. Hence, the Nash equilibrium now implies a fight. In figure 3.9b, a situation of asymmetric information applies, since agent 2 does not know whether he or she faces a strong or weak chain. Thus, two payoffs are possible when agent 1 fights or acquiesces. Equilibria for a repeated game now depends on how the uninformed player attempts to intuit the type of opponent that he or she faces. A rule for updating information is then needed. The more often player 1 fights, the more likely agent 2 is to believe that he or she faces a strong chain. I leave further discussion of these equilibria to other sources and simply note that, when information is incomplete, numerous solution concepts are available.

In many collective action situations, the agent knows his or her own type but may not know whether the other player has large or small demands for the public good. Intertemporal strategies for repeated collective action problems may lead to cooperation over time even when a finite number of plays is involved if sufficient uncertainty characterizes the problem. The rules of the game (e.g., the sequence of plays), the nature of the information asymmetry, and the learning dynamics of the players are considerations that, in addition to group size and composition, are important in understanding collection action in repeated frameworks.[14]

In chapter 2, other game forms were shown to apply to collective action problems. Each game form may possess a large set of Nash equilibria when played repeatedly. A game such as Chicken with high penalties for mutual defection has a great likelihood of some public good being provided in the equilibrium. Other games, such as the Battle of the Sexes, may permit greater cooperation in repeated frameworks than in a single shot when communication between players is permitted and mixed strategies are permitted (Farrell 1987). The Assurance games are also apt to foster cooperative outcomes in repeated plays. Although the collective action problem does not vanish in a dynamic scenario, even troublesome such games as the Prisoner's Dilemma may have favorable outcomes in some cases when long-term defection losses are large.

---

14. See Gardner and Ostrom 1991; Andreoni 1988b.

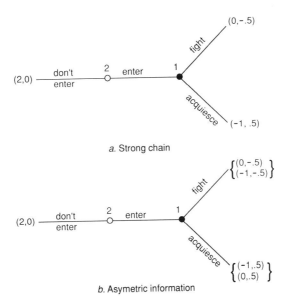

a. Strong chain

b. Asymetric information

Fig. 3.9.   Chain store game

To illustrate a dynamic voluntary contribution game, I draw on recent work by Bagnoli and Lipman (1989) and Bagnoli and McKee (1991) that illustrates not only the perfect equilibria concept, whereby nonsensible Nash equilibria are deleted, but also the crucial importance of the institutional rules. Their storyline is close to, but different than, the minimum contributing set and the nonrefundable discrete contribution scenarios previously discussed. In repeated plays, a set of individuals is asked to contribute to a public good that is only provided when a certain cost, say 50, is met or exceeded. If this threshold cost is exceeded, the extra contributions are kept; if, however, contributions are insufficient, then the money is *returned* to the players. Bagnoli and McKee (1991, 351) gave as an example the case where the faculty of Oregon hired a lobbyist to represent their collective interests in the legislature. In case the lobbyist's salary was not met, the money would be returned. The allowance of a refund can promote collective action. Individuals know the following: the number of other individuals, their wealth, the valuations of the individuals, and the threshold for provision.

The refund game has many Nash equilibria. In fact, any set of contributions summing to exactly 50 is a Nash equilibrium, provided that each individual can afford his or her pledge. Thus, in a four-person case, the contribution sets (25/2, 25/2, 25/2, 25/2) and (0, 9, 16, 25) are equilibria. Other equilibria include (0, 0, 0, 0) and any contribution pattern "summing to less than fifty dollars and having the property that the sum would still be less than fifty if any one person chose to contribute his or her entire valuation, is a Nash equilibrium" (Bagnoli and McKee 1991, 355; a few words have been changed in this quote to fit the example).

Clearly, the notion of a Nash equilibrium, while eliminating excessive contributions, does not limit equilibria very much. A vector of excessive contributions is not a Nash equilibrium, since a decrease in contributions, up to the overpayment, would get the collective action provided and leave everyone better off. If, say, the contribution set is (0, 9, 16, 25) and everyone pays less than or equal to his or her valuation of the collective action, then none of the contributors would want to reduce payments, since then the action is not provided and he or she is worse off. Hence, all payment sets totaling 50 are Nash equilibria. In a similar manner, we can establish that all payment contributions less than 50, even if any one person contributed his or her entire valuation, is a Nash equilibrium.

To cull nonsensible equilibria, we use Selten's (1975) notion of a *trembling-hand perfect equilibrium,* in which, among the undominated equilibria, the players choose their best reply to the strategy that he or she believes the other agents will play with and without a slight miscalculation or "tremble." In the previous refund game, the perfect equilibria are those in which the contributions total 50 and include feasible (affordable) payments. Consider the case where players 2, 3, and 4 contribute 8, 16, and 25, respectively. Since such a payment configuration is possible (through a tremble), player 1 should not pay zero. If player 1's payment does not make a difference, then the money is refunded. In fact, all payoff arrangements that are affordable and that total less than 50 are nonsensible since some player can do better by contributing. Bagnoli and Lipman (1989) prove that the set of perfect equilibria includes the Pareto optimal set where each player pays his or her true valuation.[15]

The refundable game implies perfect equilibria in which Pareto optimality is achieved regardless of the number of players. For these perfect equilibria, *all* contributors are pivotal, because the sum of their contributions exactly equals the cost (Bagnoli and McKee 1991, 357). In an experimental situation, Bagnoli and McKee (1991) found that the subjects, indeed, gravitated to the perfect equilibria where contributions just financed the collective action. Large groups, however, took longer to get there. Again we see that institutional design can make all the difference.

In a recent article, Fershtman and Nitzan (1991) investigated the private provision of a pure public good in a dynamic framework in which the good can be continuously varied. Thus, the choice is not discrete in terms of either

---

15. This proof relies on separable utility functions and the absence of income effects.

the number of units provided or some threshold target of contributions. In the Fershtman-Nitzan exercise, an individual derives nonrival and nonexcludable benefits from a *stock* level of a public good, accumulated over time. This stock can be enhanced in each period provided that the addition to the stock exceeds the amount that depreciates. This model represents public investment in infrastructure. Free riding is now a messier problem, since a current contributor can free ride on anticipated current and future contributions of others. The accumulated stock also provides a free-ride incentive.

3.5 Uncertainty in a Static Framework

Agents are not always well informed when making collective action decisions. In recent years, researchers have investigated the influence of various kinds of uncertainty on collective action using a static framework. For example, uncertainty may arise with discrete contributions in which a minimal number (amount) of contributors (contributions) is needed to provide the good.[16] If contributions are nonrefundable, then contributors must consider the various contingencies and their likelihoods. Individual choice in this nonrefundable discrete contribution case depends on the rationality assumption or objective imputed to the individuals (Frohlich and Oppenheimer 1978, 53–63). Three possible rationality assumptions are minimax, minimize regret, and maximize expected utility. Minimax has the individual maximizing his or her security level (i.e., one's lowest possible payoff) by choosing the *best* of the worse outcomes associated with the strategies. In a nonrefundable contribution scenario, this is likely to lead the individual to withhold his or her contribution so that the agent does not risk contributing when insufficient numbers of others contribute. Minimax is not conducive to collective action. Minimizing regret, in contrast, is conducive to collective action because the greatest regret results when an agent's failure to contribute keeps the collective action, with its net positive payoff, from occurring. Finally, maximizing expected utility gives a more moderate prediction concerning collective action than either minimax or minimizing regret. Most treatments of continuous contributions use this latter objective. Uncertainty may, in addition, characterize the amount of spillovers (Sandler, Sterbenz, and Posnett 1987; Shogren, 1987 and 1990; Kim 1991), the price of the collective good (Gradstein, Nitzan, and Slutsky 1988a), or the endowments of the contributors (Gradstein, Nitzan, and Slutsky 1988b). This literature has investigated whether risk-averse individuals are more apt to contribute in the face of uncertainty. Also, the suboptimality of uncertainty has been compared with that of certainty. Different cases have been distinguished based on the convexity of the marginal utility function, decreasing absolute risk aversion, and

---

16. Austen-Smith 1981; Frohlich and Oppenheimer 1978.

other considerations. Although special cases have been found in which uncertainty can ameliorate the collective action problem, the introduction of uncertainty does not, in general, reduce uncertainty in collective action problems.[17] In a striking case, Nitzan and Romano (1990) demonstrated that sufficient uncertainty on the cost side can worsen Nash equilibrium outcomes in discrete, public good scenarios.

The introduction of uncertainty yields a plethora of cases and few general results. Clear-cut relationships between group size and collective rationality and/or group asymmetry and collective irrationality are especially difficult to establish when uncertainty is present.

3.6 The Technology of Public Supply

Throughout the first three chapters, the technology of public supply is seen to be a key consideration in the analysis of collective action. The concept is behind the form of the congestion function in the theory of clubs, the validity of the neutrality theorem, the underlying game structure, and the structure of the joint product relationship. Slight variations in the specification of this technology can yield alterations in the model structure, outcome, and normative implications. A fairly general specification of this technology is the joint product case, previously specified in chapter 2. In the case of fixed proportions, this technology indicates that each unit, q, of the collective good provides γ units of a private output, x, and δ units of a pure public benefit, z. For individual i, this technology implies

$$x^i = \gamma q^i \, , \qquad (3.18)$$

and

$$z^i = \delta q^i \, . \qquad (3.19)$$

If the public output abides by summation (i.e., $Z = \Sigma z^i$) and the technological coefficients do not differ between people, then the i agent's utility function is

$$U^i = U^i\left(y^i, \, \gamma q^i, \, \sum_{i=1}^{n} \delta q^i \right) \qquad (3.20)$$

A special case of equation 3.20 is Andreoni's (1989 and 1990) warm-glow model in which contributing to charity yields personal pleasure, q^i, and

---

17. See, e.g., Sandler and Sterbenz 1990; Sandler, Sterbenz, and Posnett 1987; Shogren 1990.

adds to the overall level of the public good, since $Q = \Sigma q^i$. The Andreoni warm glow is a special case of the joint product model provided that $\gamma = \delta = 1$. Although the technology of warm glow only differs from the pure public good model by the presence of q^i as an additional argument in the utility function, this difference is sufficient to break neutrality and allow for an income policy. Moreover, the extent of suboptimality *may* be vastly curtailed in the warm-glow model. The Olsonian themes regarding group size and composition may not hold with this slight change in technology when the private influence is especially strong.

The variety of joint product technologies available is virtually limitless. For example, a collective action may yield *multiple* public and private outputs. Fixed proportions can be replaced with variable proportions. In the case of multiple outputs, the public outputs may be purely or impurely public. If impurely public outputs are present and exclusion can be practiced, then a club arrangement can charge tolls to cover congestion and levy other charges for the members' specific private benefits.

The adoption of institutional rules may, itself, have an influence on the technology of publicness. Thus, those rules that promote technologies in keeping with collective action are most desirable.

3.7 Concluding Remarks

New developments in collective action have been many and varied. In this chapter, a few of the noteworthy extensions, including the theory of clubs, the strategic assumption, the neutrality theorem, dynamic behavior, uncertainty, and the technology of public supply, have been highlighted. The theory of clubs is especially noteworthy because it suggests that collective action can be accomplished, in many instances, without a government. The neutrality theorem indicates that simple solutions that do not account for the general equilibrium aspects of a collective action problem may prove ineffective. Income redistribution and tax policies, when applied to a group of contributors, will have complex interactions that must be acknowledged.

APPENDIX

3.A.1 Alternative Proof 1 for the Neutrality Theorem

The Nash problem corresponds to

$$\max_{y^i, q^i} \{U^i (y^i, q^i + \tilde{Q}^i) \mid I^i = y^i + pq^i\},$$

in which $\tilde{Q}^i = \sum_{j \neq i} q^j$, I^i is the agent's income, p is the per-unit price of q, and 1 is the per-unit price of the private good. The other symbols have been defined in the text. Individuals are not assumed to be identical. A Nash equilibrium corresponds to the simultaneous satisfaction of the following FOCs,

$$\pi^i_Q(I^i - pq^i, q^i + \tilde{Q}^i) = p, \quad i = 1, \ldots, n \tag{1}$$

in which $\pi^i_Q(\bullet)$ is the ith agent marginal rate of substitution between the public good and the private good. These FOCs follow from the above optimization. Taking a total differential of equation 1, while holding p constant, gives

$$\pi^i_{Qy}(dI^i - pdq^i) + \pi^i_{QQ} \, dq^i + \pi^i_{QQ} \, d\tilde{Q}^i = 0, \quad i = 1, \ldots, n \tag{2}$$

in which

$$\pi^i_{Qy} = \partial \pi^i_Q / \partial(I^i + pq^i) \quad \text{and} \quad \pi^i_{QQ} = \partial \pi^i_Q / \partial Q.$$

We then substitute $d\tilde{Q}^i = dQ^N - dq^i$ into equation 2 and solve for dq^i to yield:

$$dq^i = dI^i/p + [\pi^i_{QQ}/p\pi^i_{Qy}]dQ^N, \quad i = 1, \ldots, n . \tag{3}$$

We next sum equation 3 over i and solve for dQ^N to give

$$dQ^N = k \sum_i dI^i/p , \tag{4}$$

in which

$$k = \left[1 - \sum_i \left(\pi^i_{QQ}/p\pi^i_{Qy} \right) \right]^{-1} \quad \text{and} \quad dQ^N = \sum_i dq^i .$$

Neutrality follows immediately, since income redistribution implies $\sum_i dI^i = 0$, which, by equation 4, indicates that $dQ^N = 0$. Q.E.D.

3.A.2 Alternative Proof 2 for the Neutrality Theorem

The second proof follows the methodology in Bruce 1990. To simplify the presentation, we assume just two agents—i and j. Furthermore, all prices are normalized. The ith agent's problem is

$$\max_{Q, y^i} \{U^i(y^i, q^i + q^j) | I^i + q^j = y^i + Q\} ,$$

where q^j has been added to both sides of the budget constraint. The quantity $I^i + q^j$ is known as full income, F^i (Bergstrom, Blume, and Varian 1986). The individual is depicted as choosing total contributions, Q, for the group. If $Q > q^j$, then the ith agent's demand or reaction function can be written as

$$q^i = f^i(I^i + q^j) - q^j. \tag{5}$$

Interchanging i and j gives the demand function for agent j in terms of full income, $I^j + q^i$, and spillins, q^i. To derive dq^i and dq^j, we totally differentiate equation 5 and its counterpart for agent j and solve simultaneously to obtain

$$dq^i = [f^i_F dI^i - f^i_F(1 - f^j_F)dI^j]/\nabla , \tag{6}$$

and

$$dq^j = [f^j_F dI^j - f^j_F(1 - f^i_F)dI^i]/\nabla , \tag{7}$$

in which

$$\nabla = f^i_F + f^j_F - f^i_F f^j_F > 0 \quad \text{and} \quad f^i_F = \partial f^i / \partial(I^i + q^j) .$$

Adding equations 6 and 7 yields

$$dQ = (f^i_F f^j_F / \nabla)\sum_i dI^i , \tag{8}$$

which implies $dQ = 0$ when $\sum_i dI^i = 0$. Q.E.D.

3.A.3. A Proof of Neutrality for Stackelberg Leader-Follower Behavior

We assume that the leader is agent j and the follower is agent i. The leader maximizes his or her utility subject to the follower's Nash reaction path. Thus, the leader solves the problem

$$\max_{q^j} U^j[I^j - q^j, f^i(I^i + q^j)] , \tag{9}$$

in which y^j is in terms of j's budget constraint, all prices are normalized to one, and $f^i(\bullet)$ is the follower's full-income reaction function as in equation 5. The follower maximizes utility subject to the leader's choice of q^j; that is, the follower solves

$$\max_{q^i} U^i(I^i - q^i, q^i + q^j) \tag{10}$$

with q^j exogenous. The FOCs for equations 9 and 10 are

$$-U_y^j[I^j - q^j, f^i(I^i + q^j)] + f_F^i(\bullet)U_Q^j[I^j - q^j, f^i(I^i + q^j)] = 0 , \tag{11}$$

and

$$-U_y^i(I^i - q^i, q^i + q^j) + U_Q^i(I^i - q^i, q^i + q^j) = 0 , \tag{12}$$

respectively. If income is redistributed so that $dI^i = -dI^j$, then a total differentiation of equations 11 and 12 would show that $dQ = dq^i + dq^j = 0$. This follows because the differential of equation 11 implies that $dI^j = dq^j$ for an income redistribution, while the differential of equation 12 implies that $dI^j = -dq^i$. Hence, each participant directs his or her income change solely into the public good and the total level of Q is unchanged since $dI^i + dI^j = 0$.   Q.E.D.

A graphic proof can be devised using the Cornes-Sandler diagram along the same lines used to establish neutrality for Nash behavior (Cornes and Sandler 1986, 86, fig. 5.7). By displacing the origin of the diagram along a 45-degree line, income is redistributed between the leader and follower. In the process, neither the follower's reaction path nor the leader's tangency with this path is affected on the new, displaced axes. A 45-degree line through the (displaced) leader-follower equilibrium, S, would correspond to the same total Q as before the redistribution. The neutrality, of course, requires that neither player stops contributing after the redistribution.

CHAPTER 4

Applications

Perhaps the greatest achievement of collective action theory has been its wide-ranging application to major fields of economics. In *Logic,* Olson investigated a host of applications that included the behavior of oligopolies, labor unions, political lobbies, and farm collectives. The Marxist theory of state and class was also illuminated with the principles of collective action by Olson (1965, 98–110). Rather than review and extend Olson's applications, I intend to strike out on my own and deal with a different and broader set of applications. Some overlap between applications exists, since labor unions and political lobbies are also studied here.

This chapter illustrates the concepts developed in chapters 1 through 3. In particular, I intend to show that certain key features characterize those instances in which collective action appears to be effective. First, the existence of jointly produced private benefits and excludable public benefits is an important ingredient. When these private and excludable public benefits are a large proportion of the total benefits derived from a collective activity, private efforts or club arrangements work quite well without much prodding. Thus, for example, the fostering of private benefits by charities and/or military alliances is commonly observed. If, on the other hand, the collective action is primarily purely public, then Olson's concerns, as embodied in his themes, hold. In consequence, group size inhibits efficiency, and the large is exploited by the small. Second, the technology of public supply, by which individual efforts are aggregated to give total levels of collective action, is a crucial consideration. When a summation technology applies so that each individual's contribution to the collective activity is perfectly substitutable, Olson's concerns are again very relevant. Institutional structures are more effective when based upon a technology of public supply, such as weakest link, that is more conducive to collective action.

By analyzing numerous examples, I am also able to illustrate the applicability of such concepts as the neutrality theorem, club theory, and the varied means used to design "collective action friendly" institutions. Except for a few applications marked by asterisks, the discussion is kept free of technical details. Space does not permit a full analysis of each of the applications presented. In consequence, choices must be made in terms of emphasis and coverage. To assist the reader's further study of these applications, key references are either given in the text or in footnotes.

4.1 Historical Examples

In controlling plagues, fighting pollution, overthrowing repressive regimes, or deterring a common enemy, nations throughout history have faced collective action contingencies. The Delian League of Classical Greece serves as an apt example of a military alliance between city-states in which free riding was a problem.[1] The league was formed in 478 B.C. during a period in which Athens and Sparta almost single-handedly repulsed invasions from Persia. Because Greece is very compact, the Athenians and Spartans could not afford to concede the Persians a foothold anywhere in the Aegean. Small Greek cities in the region realized that Athens and Sparta could not exclude them from protection, whether they helped to contribute to their own defense or not. In consequence, defense benefits were nonexcludable. Moreover, the removal of the Persian threat provided nonrival benefits to the city-states of the Aegean. Many small Greek city-states thus refused to help repel the Persians, mainly because of the rational incentives to free ride on a defense arrangement with nearly pure public outputs. Smaller cities also did not want to risk fighting on the losing side. Even though benefits were nonrival, Athens and Sparta were, understandably, concerned about getting the other city-states to contribute so that they did not have to foot the bill alone. For a time, the large were exploited by the small in the Olsonian tradition.

The Delian League solved this public good problem in the Olsonian style with a simple selective incentive: coercion, including violence. Noncooperative city-states were threatened with invasion and/or punishment. Each member of the league was required to take a permanent oath of loyalty, which included making annual contributions to the treasury of the league in Delos. Some cities (e.g., Eubeoa in 472 B.C.) were forced to join; a greater number attempted to secede once the Persians were defeated, but were forcibly prevented (e.g., Naxos in 467 B.C.; Thasos in 462 B.C.). In 431 B.C., the Peloponnesian War broke out between Athens and Sparta over the control of the Aegean and ended in 404 B.C. with the victory of Sparta.

As Athens and Sparta became enemies and the Persian threat waned, the league gradually became an instrument of Athenian imperialism, providing (in the view of allied cities) more of a private than a public good (e.g., imposing Athenian settlers and democratic regimes, and moving the alliance's

---

1. The first two historical examples were developed by John A. C. Conybeare and appeared in an earlier draft of a paper dealing with the Triple Alliance and Triple Entente, two pre–World War I alliances (see Conybeare and Sandler 1989 and 1990).

treasury to Athens), which increased the incentives for allies to defect. As disaffection mounted, Athens became increasingly harsh in maintaining the alliance. When the island of Melos refused to join the alliance in 415 B.C., Athenian forces executed the men and sold the women and children into slavery.

Thucydides' (1970) account of the Peloponnesian War abounds with reference to public good problems. Pericles, an Athenian leader, urged a strong stand against Sparta on the grounds that Sparta and her allies had a major collective action problem.

> . . . they cannot fight a war against a power unlike themselves, so long as they have no central deliberative authority to produce quick decisive action, when they all have equal votes, though they all come from different nationalities and everyone of these is concerned with its own interests—the usual result of which is that nothing gets done at all. . . . It never occurs to any of them that the apathy of one will damage the interest of all. Instead each state thinks that the responsibility for its future belongs to someone else, and so, while everyone has the same idea privately, no one notices that from a general point of view things are downhill. (Thucydides 1970, 93)

A second historical example is due to Adam Smith, who believed that Britain, like Athens, was exploited by free riders in times of military crisis. Wars with Spain (1739–48) and France (1756–63) cost £120 million (tripling the national debt) and were fought for the security of North American colonies that contributed neither revenue nor military forces to the effort. "If any of the provinces of the British empire," Smith concluded, "cannot be made to contribute towards the support of the whole empire, it is surely time that Britain should free herself from the expense of defending those provinces" (1976, 2:486). Britain, unlike Athens, could afford to withdraw from the provision of international public goods not directly connected with the maintenance of domestic sovereignty. This follows because the threat posed by Spain and France to the colonies did not present a direct danger to the British Isles, thousands of miles away.

These two examples suggest that alliance public or collective goods are not unique to the contemporary world. Athens could not defend itself against the Persians without simultaneously defending small free riders. Britain voluntarily provided a public defense good to its colonies, in the belief (mistaken, according to Adam Smith) that the empire provided indirect side-payments in terms of resource pools and markets that compensated for the public good provision. The only aspect of historical alliances that may, at first, seem unique is the use of coercive selective incentives, but recent actions by the United States in fostering the alliance for Operation Desert Storm (e.g., the forgiveness of billions of dollars of Egyptian debt, the shipment of Patriot missiles to Israel, and veiled threats of future actions by the U.S. Congress regarding foreign aid and troop deployments) indicate that selective incentives are still used. Like modern alliances, historical alliances share defense activities with private, impurely public, and purely public benefits.

A host of eighteenth- and nineteenth-century alliances shared arsenals that yielded joint products of varying degrees of publicness. In an interesting paper, Thies (1987) examined two alliances (the Triple Alliance and the Triple Entente) begun prior to World War I and a number of post–World War I alliances that include the Anglo-French (1924–38), the Franco-Polish (1926– 38), the Franco-Czech (1930–38), and the Franco-Belgian (1920–36). These alliances relied upon conventional armaments (e.g., tanks, artillery, foot soldiers) that are subject to partial rivalry as a given size armed force is spread over a longer front. Increased fortification at one place along the front meant less fortification elsewhere. Moreover, the deployment decision by the providing ally could exclude some regions or allies from protection. Conventional armaments also yield purely public deterrence since such armaments threaten an aggressor with the possibility of retaliation. This threat is nonrival and may, as in the case of the Athenian and Spartan confrontation with the Persians, be nonexcludable between allies. Although conventional armaments give forth a host of benefits of varying degrees of publicness, a significant proportion of their benefits are private (benefiting the deploying nation alone) or else excludable between allies. The existence of these private and excludable benefits meant that benefits could be withheld and, hence, free riding could be limited. (A fuller discussion of this point is provided in the next section.) Predictably, in very few instances did these historical alliances display the disproportionate burden-sharing behavior associated with the pure public good paradigm of defense (Thies 1987). In a follow-up study, Conybeare and Sandler (1990) found little evidence of free riding in the Triple Alliance (Germany, Austria-Hungary, and Italy) and the Triple Entente (United Kingdom, France, and Russia) during 1880–1914. The sole exceptions were France and Russia, whose geographical position on either side of the enemy allowed for some substitution of forces and, consequently, free riding between the two fronts.

As a final historical example of collective action, the containment of plagues and diseases serves as an appropriate example. Since plagues and diseases transgress national boundaries, one nation's public health problem becomes that of another through the migration of population, airborne viruses, and the transportation of pests. The bubonic plague, a bacterium-based disease carried by fleas from infected rats, decimated parts of Europe and

Africa on a number of different occasions. The migration of infected rats in the holds of ships spread the disease far and wide. In times prior to vaccines and other health measures, nations attempted to protect their own citizens and those of other nations by isolating themselves. Forbes indicates that

> the origins of international cooperation in public health are to be found in the response of nations to the threat of epidemic disease. Throughout history nations and communities adopted various prophylactic measures by which they attempted to isolate themselves against the importation of pestilence, plague, and disease. An early prophylactic measure was the cordon sanitaire enforced by a military blockage of an infected area. A less comprehensive form of population isolation—quarantine—was introduced in the fourteenth century when Venice adopted a forty-day (*quaranta*) isolation period that applied to incoming persons and goods. Between the fourteenth and nineteenth centuries quarantine measures were widely adopted throughout the world as nearly all countries instituted unilateral and largely uncoordinated regulations to control the international diffusion of disease. (Forbes 1980, 116)

Although a quarantine or cordon sanitaire conferred public benefits by controlling the spread of the disease to other nations, independent national actions were also taken because such measures also protected the nation's population against new exposures to the disease-bearing agents. That is, significant nation-specific or private benefits motivated these acts of containment. As Forbes (1980) noted, frequent and prolonged quarantines created other collective action concerns as communication and commercial links were temporarily severed. A concern for these other collective action problems led to new forms of cooperation, culminating in the creation of the World Health Organization (WHO) in 1948. WHO sought to foster the treatment, containment, eradication, and tracking of diseases that threatened the world community.

4.2 Military Alliances: The Case of NATO

Defense has long been viewed as a pure public good with nonexcludable and nonrival benefits. However, when defense is shared between nations in an alliance, the pure publicness of defense expenditures may be doubted, since for some defense outputs the providing ally may be able to withhold benefits from allies so that exclusion may be practiced. If the actual deployment of the weapon system impacts or safeguards *only* the area receiving protection, then benefits may also be partially rival. In a recent contribution, Goff and Tollison

(1990) argued that defense benefits within a nation may also impact and protect regions differently, thereby fostering impure public benefits even within a nation.

To distinguish purely public, impurely public, and private defense benefits, various authors have developed a joint product analysis of military alliances.[2] The joint product model views an alliance arsenal as fulfilling at least three general functions: (1) deterrence, (2) damage limitation or protection, and (3) private or nation-specific goals. Deterrence forestalls an attack by an opposing alliance by threatening a sufficiently costly punishment to any would-be aggressor. To be effective, deterrence must be based on a credible threat that is swift and automatic. If the threat does not appear to be automatic, then a would-be aggressor may discount the threat and act. Deterrence is nonrival because a threat can protect additional nations and/or populations without diminishing the benefits to those already protected, provided that the threat is credible and the promised punishment is sufficiently devastating. Deterrence will fail whenever there is serious doubt about execution on behalf of those threatened, as Iraq's failure to withdraw from Kuwait sadly illustrates. Nonexcludability may or may not characterize deterrence. When a nation's people, property, territory, or airspace must be compromised in any enemy attack directed against another ally, the providing nation cannot withhold retaliation on behalf of its ally and deterrence is, indeed, nonexcludable. Suppose that nation A hosts the troops, citizens, or direct investment of ally B, then an enemy invasion of the host ally A ensures collateral damage to the interests of ally B; in consequence, ally B cannot withhold a retaliatory pledge made on behalf of ally A. In other cases, geographic considerations (e.g., the Persian threat to the Aegean) cause allies to face common threats that make deterrence nonexcludable. For example, a nuclear attack on the Republic of Ireland (Canada) would, due to fallout, misses, and wind direction, kill millions in the United Kingdom (United States). Obviously, the United Kingdom (United States) could not deny its neighbor deterrent protection.

Defense outputs are impurely public between allies when their benefits are either partially rival or else partially excludable by the providing nations. Conventional forces and arsenals yield both deterrence and damage-limiting protection, needed when deterrence fails and conflict begins. Although the deterrence benefits are purely public, damage-limiting protection is subject to consumption rivalry in the form of force thinning as a fixed arsenal is spread to defend a longer perimeter or a greater surface area. In other words, the deployment of conventional forces to limit damage does not afford equal protection to all allies. Moreover, increasing the concentration of troops along

---

2. See Sandler and Cauley 1975; Sandler 1977; Murdoch and Sandler 1982 and 1984; Sandler and Forbes 1980. Also see Boyer 1989; Gonzales and Mehay 1990 and 1991; McGuire 1990.

one ally's border may increase the vulnerability of another ally's border owing to rivalry. Since deployment decisions can exclude one or more allies, conventional armaments possess partially excludable benefits. The possibility of exclusion and the presence of thinning or congestion costs imply that a club arrangement can be used, in part, to allocate defenses within a conventional alliance. As such, an optimal size for the alliance could be determined to adjust cost sharing and thinning considerations, at the margin, with respect to an entrant. The presence of purely public deterrence means that some free riding will be present even under a club arrangement. If, however, the alliance primarily shares purely public deterrence, as *may* have been the case for the North Atlantic Treaty Organization (NATO) in the late 1940s and 1950s, then a club arrangement cannot be implemented. When purely public benefits are the primary output derived from an arsenal by the allies, there is no need to restrict alliance membership. Most important, free riding should be prevalent with an exploitation of the large ally by the small.

Conventional forces can also be used by allies to pursue country-specific private benefits (e.g., protecting coastal waters, engineering civil projects, thwarting terrorist threats, curbing domestic unrest, pursuing nationalistic goals, and providing disaster relief). Although such country-specific benefits are *private between allies,* these benefits are *public within an ally.* Thus, at the national level, collective action is required, but, at the international (alliance) level, allies need not cooperate to achieve efficiency with respect to country-specific benefits, since market principles can be applied to allocate resources accordingly. For instance, a nation cannot rely on a neighbor or ally for protection of, say, its ocean resources without entering a contractual arrangement that is in both parties' interests. As the share of private and/or excludable benefits from an alliance arsenal increases, market or clublike arrangements can be pursued more fully. In consequence, the extent of free riding is inversely related to the proportion of private and/or excludable defense outputs derived from the arsenal. Alliances that depend on conventional forces are more apt to share burdens according to the proportion of benefits received by the allies. In contrast, strategic nuclear forces are less likely to serve country-specific defense needs and are also less apt to contain rivalrous benefits. Since such strategic forces possess a small proportion of private and excludable benefits, these forces are most apt to be associated with the free-rider problem highlighted by Olson and Zeckhauser (1966).

NATO was formed in 1949 as an offset to Soviet domination of Eastern Europe. The original alliance included Belgium, Canada, Denmark, France, Iceland, Italy, Luxembourg, the Netherlands, Norway, Portugal, the United Kingdom, and the United States. Greece and Turkey joined NATO in 1952; West Germany in 1955; and Spain in 1982. Thus, the alliance has grown to sixteen allies.

Until the mid-1960s, NATO relied on its strategic arsenal to deter the Soviet use of conventional forces in Western Europe, since NATO's conventional forces were outnumbered by Soviet tanks and ground troops. Moreover, the U.S. threat to retaliate on behalf of its NATO allies was credible during this period, inasmuch as the Soviet Union had not yet developed a retaliatory strike force. Consequently, the United States had little to fear from using its strategic arsenal, as shown by President Kennedy's aggressive stance during the Cuban missile crisis. Once the Soviet strike force had been deployed in the last half of the 1960s, the credibility of the U.S. retaliatory threat was diminished. The stationing of U.S. troops along the central front and at European airfields, U.S. investments in Europe, and a shared cultural heritage gave some credence to the commitment of the U.S. pledge. Nevertheless, some Europeans had their doubts.

By the early 1970s, many developments had altered the public/private mix of defense benefits derived by NATO and, hence, the possibility for free riding. Important events included the Soviet nuclear arsenal buildup, the deployment in the 1960s and 1970s of a small nuclear strategic deterrent by Britain and France, and the increased importance placed on conventional weapons. This last development took place throughout the last half of the 1960s and the early 1970s as the NATO alliance changed its emphasis from a strategy of mutual assured destruction deterrence (MAD), based on nuclear annihilation, to that of flexible response. This latter doctrine permits NATO to respond in different ways to a Warsaw Pact challenge; conventional forces, tactical nuclear forces, or strategic force may be used and, in the latter case, a missile exchange may be limited or complete. With the flexible response doctrine, the European allies must be prepared to defend themselves against conventional aggression in the European theater. Any ally that sits back and does not increase its military preparedness could invite aggression, since an opposing alliance might have a better opportunity to gain an advantage in a conventional foray on that ally's soil.

In the 1980s, the Reagan buildup emphasized weapon procurement over operations and maintenance. The strategic weapons' share of the budget increased for the three nuclear allies—the United States, France, and the United Kingdom—thereby increasing the relative share of the NATO budget going to weapons with a greater degree of publicness (Hansen, Murdoch, and Sandler 1990). Consider the case of the United States. In the five years prior to 1983, the strategic procurement component of the U.S. defense budget averaged 1.82 percent of the total. In the subsequent five years, it averaged 3.92 percent of the total, clearly marking a new emphasis on strategic procurement.

Two popular burden-sharing measures are now presented to take a retrospective view of NATO since 1955. In table 4.1, an ally's share of total NATO military expenditures is calculated. From 1965 to 1970, the over-

TABLE 4.1. NATO Defense Burdens, in Percentages, by Country, for Various Years

	1955	1960	1965	1970	1975	1980	1985	1987
U.S.	77.1	73.2	71.2	74.5	58.3	56.2	62.5	69.9
Canada	3.0	2.6	2.2	1.9	1.7	1.8	1.9	2.0
Belgium	0.6	0.6	0.7	0.7	1.4	1.5	1.1	0.8
Denmark	0.3	0.3	0.4	0.4	0.6	0.6	0.5	0.4
France	5.3	6.3	6.3	5.8	9.1	10.3	8.6	7.4
West Germany	2.7	5.4	7.0	5.9	10.6	10.4	8.3	5.7
Greece	0.2	0.3	0.3	0.5	1.0	0.9	0.9	0.6
Italy	1.4	2.1	2.5	2.4	3.2	3.7	3.4	3.5
Luxembourg	0.0	0.0	0.0	0.0	0.0	0.0	0.0	0.2
Netherlands	0.7	0.9	1.1	1.1	2.0	2.1	1.6	1.3
Norway	0.3	0.3	0.4	0.4	0.6	0.7	0.6	0.6
Portugal	0.1	0.2	0.4	0.4	0.5	0.3	0.2	0.2
Turkey	0.3	0.5	0.6	0.6	1.2	1.0	1.0	0.7
United Kingdom	7.8	7.2	7.0	5.6	9.8	10.4	9.3	6.9

Source: Stockholm International Peace Research Institute, *World Armaments and Disarmament: SIPRI Yearbook,* various years.

Note: Military expenditures divided by the total NATO military expenditures multiplied by 100. Military expenditures are expressed in 1980 prices using GDP price deflators for each country, and converted to U.S. dollars using 1980 exchange rates. Spain was left out of the sample because it joined NATO after 1980; Iceland was left out because it has no military expenditure. Columns may not sum to 100 due to rounding errors.

whelming defense burden was placed on the United States, with the United Kingdom, France, and West Germany sharing much of the residual. This pattern conforms well to the exploitation hypothesis that the large allies would shoulder the defense burden of the smaller ones owing to NATO's reliance on MAD and relatively pure public strategic weapons.

In Table 4.2, a second burden measure—the proportion of GDP spent on defense—shows much the same pattern for ten NATO allies: the United States, the United Kingdom, and France devoted by far the largest shares of GDP to defense. Six allies have been left out of the sample. Portugal, Luxembourg, and Iceland were excluded because their defense expenditures were so small. Spain only joined NATO in 1982. After the late 1970s, Greece and Turkey defense figures were unreliable, owing to their territorial dispute over Cyprus. This dispute meant that neither Greece nor Turkey wanted its foe to know the extent of its defense expenditures. In recent years, both nations allocated about 6 percent of GDP to defense due, in part, to their territorial dispute.

By the mid-1970s, the doctrine of flexible response, with its emphasis on conventional armaments, had taken hold and had achieved the predicted impact of reducing free riding and shifting more of the burden for NATO to the

TABLE 4.2. Military Expenditures as a Percentage of GDP (by country for various years)

	United States	France	West Germany	United Kingdom	Belgium	Netherlands	Denmark	Norway	Italy	Canada
1961	9.18	6.30	3.97	6.29	3.26	4.56	2.61	3.01	2.90	4.25
1963	8.84	5.64	5.21	6.16	3.42	4.47	3.04	3.59	3.10	3.66
1965	7.56	5.19	4.33	5.87	3.16	4.00	2.83	3.75	3.10	2.94
1967	9.51	5.11	3.61	5.67	3.13	3.95	2.66	3.51	2.91	2.90
1969	8.69	4.52	3.61	4.94	2.95	3.62	2.46	3.60	2.53	2.34
1971	6.85	4.00	3.39	4.87	2.83	3.27	2.44	3.39	2.70	2.22
1973	5.83	3.80	3.48	4.75	2.75	3.10	2.04	3.13	2.60	1.92
1975	5.75	3.85	3.66	4.86	3.02	3.29	2.44	3.39	2.48	1.86
1977	5.14	3.83	3.36	4.69	3.14	3.37	2.27	3.10	2.39	1.89
1979	5.12	3.88	3.26	4.41	3.26	3.20	2.32	3.09	2.39	1.73
1981	5.83	4.10	3.39	4.71	3.44	3.20	2.53	2.89	2.11	1.73
1983	6.50	4.12	3.37	5.16	3.24	3.19	2.45	3.08	2.27	2.11
1985	6.65	3.97	3.20	5.13	2.98	3.10	2.15	3.09	2.28	2.13
1987	6.45	3.92	3.06	4.70	2.92	3.03	2.10	3.19	2.22	2.04

Sources: Military Expenditures from Stockholm International Peace Research Institute, *World Armaments and Disarmament*: SIPRI Yearbook, various years. GDP from *International Monetary Fund Financial Statistics Yearbook*.

Europeans. In table 4.1, the U.S. share of NATO defense spending dropped from an average value well over 70.0 percent to 58.3 percent. The rest of the allies, except Canada, began assuming a greater defense burden in the mid-1970s. As shown in table 4.2, the United States, France, the United Kingdom, and West Germany devoted a smaller percentage of GDP to defense after 1975 as compared with the 1960s, while the smaller allies, except the Netherlands, maintained GDP percentages. This pattern of GDP burdens is behind the dramatic reallocation displayed in Table 4.1. Apparently, the new strategic doctrine accomplished what two decades of arm twisting could not— a shifting of the defense burden from one side of the Atlantic to the other.

As expected, another reversal of burdens took place in the 1980s during the Reagan buildup, with its emphasis on strategic weapons. As shown in table 4.1, the U.S. share of the NATO burden increased in the 1980s. Of the next three largest allies, the two nuclear allies decreased their burdens less than the nonnuclear ally (West Germany). Similar patterns appear in table 4.2.

Sandler and Forbes (1980, table 2) provided a test of the exploitation hypothesis using NATO data for the 1960s to the mid-1970s. These authors used an ally's GDP to proxy its economic size and the percentage of GDP spent on defense to proxy its defense burden. If Olson's exploitation hypothesis held, then these two measures should be correlated so that larger allies assumed greater defense burdens. In particular, Sandler and Forbes computed the Kendall rank correlation between an ally's GDP and its percentage of GDP spent on defense. In keeping with the exploitation hypothesis, there is a significant correlation until 1966, thereby implying that the large allies shouldered the burden of NATO until about the start of flexible response. Thereafter, other factors, such as the distribution of benefits between allies, appeared to drive defense expenditure patterns.

The analysis of NATO indicates that the mix of pure public, impure public, and private benefits in a collective is not immutable. A change in strategic doctrine, the development of new technology (e.g., the deployment of laser-guided munitions in the early 1970s), and alterations in diplomacy can alter the mix of public/private benefits in NATO and, with it, the way in which burdens are shared. The development of Star War's technology (see chap. 6), the integration of Western Europe by 1992, and the deployment of a new generation of strategic weapons by the medium-sized nuclear allies could have a profound effect on the way future burdens are shared in NATO.

Until now, the literature on military alliances has treated the technology of public supply as either summation or weighted sum (see McGuire 1990). The type of weapons shared and the kind of war anticipated may require a different type of technology of supply than those used to date. In the case of a conventional war, the weakest fortification along a front may ultimately determine the overall defense of the alliance. As such, Hirshleifer's (1983) weakest link technology would apply. In the case of an alliance reliant on a strategic nuclear deterrent or a Star War's umbrella, the best shot technology may be most appropriate. Weakest link tends to attenuate the free-rider problem, while best shot tends to exacerbate it. Future work should attempt to test for the best underlying technology for the NATO alliance during various stages of its history. Normative conclusions could then be drawn from the test results.

4.3 Foreign Aid

Foreign aid poses a collective action problem for the international community. Many developing nations must rely on other nations to provide them with resources and cash to finance public investment projects. By increasing the well-being of a recipient nation, foreign aid serves as an input that produces an output that is both nonexcludable and nonrival to all nations with an interest in the recipient's well-being. That is, the recipient's well-being, produced in part by foreign aid, enters potential donors' utility functions and is nonrival between donors. Improvements in the well-being of a recipient nation are easy to spot and, hence, offer nonexcludable benefits to all would-be donors. Foreign aid may also provide jointly produced benefits to a donor that is private between nations but public within the donor nation. When the donor derives an advantage from its gift of aid and this advantage is not shared with others, private benefits motivate giving, much as private aspects stimulate allies' defense expenditures.

If foreign aid is untied, aggregate aid to a recipient represents a fungible resource, since the source of the contribution is immaterial. In consequence, a summation technology of supply applies; the recipient's well-being is dependent on the sum of aid received from others. Suboptimality in the supply of foreign aid is then to be expected, owing to standard pure public good considerations. Suppose that all potential donors have the same tastes but different endowments. Further suppose that a recipient's well-being is a normal good in the utility function of would-be donors, then the demand for giving will be positively related to the donors' income. Wealthier nations would have a greater desire to give, so that the richest nations will bear the burden of foreign aid. A clear asymmetry arises and Olson's exploitation hypothesis applies. Some potential donors may contribute nothing, relying instead on the foreign aid given by the wealthier nations. Foreign aid levels would then be suboptimal and there would be a need for some policy initiated at the supranational level. The manner used to finance foreign aid at the supranational level becomes a crucial consideration owing to the neutrality theorem. If an international agency (e.g., the U.S. Agency for International Development [AID], or the World Bank) supplements a recipient's foreign aid from revenues *collected from donor nations,* then foreign aid at the supranational level would crowd out foreign aid from donors on a dollar-for-dollar basis. This then implies that such agencies must seek their funding from nondonor countries if they intend to increase foreign aid by their action. Any shock to the international system, such as sharp oil price increases, that redistribute income among the set of donor nations may yield no net change in foreign aid even if the gainers have a higher propensity to contribute. This neutrality result can be upset if the redistribution of income, no matter how it is engineered, alters the *set* of contributors. When foreign aid yields pure public benefits to the donors, proposals put forward by third world countries to redistribute income to the underdeveloped world by taxing the resources of the wealthier nations may be self-defeating, since such taxes might reduce voluntary foreign aid.

In many instances, foreign aid may yield both a purely public benefit to the set of donors and country-specific private benefits. Donor-specific private benefits may arise owing to a donor's relative location to the recipient. If, say, a recipient country is positioned strategically vis-à-vis a donor nation, aid-assisted growth may augment the recipient's political stability, which, in turn, fosters the donor's own security. More-distant donors may not receive any security benefits. Private benefits may also arise from tying foreign aid to certain stipulations that are advantageous to the donor. For example, foreign aid may carry the condition that the donor can maintain military bases on the recipient's territory (e.g., U.S. bases in the Philippines). When foreign aid possesses both private and public benefits for donor nations, the neutrality theorem does not necessarily apply and crowding out may not be a problem. A carefully engineered redistribution or tax scheme (see, e.g., Andreoni 1989; Sandler and Posnett 1991) could increase overall giving if international agencies were to tap donors who derive relatively greater private benefits from foreign aid for resources.

Within recipient nations, bureaucrats and crooked leaders will be tempted to divert foreign aid to serve their own betterment. This corruption creates a collective bad offset to the collective good derived from giving. If humanitarian aid is used to support military adventurism, then the aid might even put donors at risk. An enforcement mechanism, which is itself a collective action problem among donor nations, is needed to ensure that the money and resources are used as intended, to relieve poverty. Hence, there is a need for on-site inspections and procedures to monitor distribution patterns for foreign aid.

4.4 Charities

Although foreign aid and charities share some important analogies, there are a number of crucial differences. First, charities invariably involve large numbers of donors, whereas foreign aid at the nation-state level often concerns bilateral agreements. At times, multiple countries may come to the rescue of a country confronting famine (e.g., Ethiopia in the 1980s) or catastrophe, but, nevertheless, the number of participating countries typically is not very large. In contrast, charities draw donors from the general population and, consequently, donors may number in the millions. Second, charities can garner funding from multiple levels of government (e.g., state, local, and central) and can engage in commercial activities to supplement revenue sources. In recent years, there has been a tremendous growth in nonprofit institutions that raise revenues in the form of donations, fees, investment income, rents, sales, and government grants, so as to provide charitable outputs (Hansmann 1980; Weisbrod 1988). In the United States, 4.4 percent of national income originated from productive activities in the nonprofit sector in 1985 (Weisbrod 1988, 172). Third, charities have developed novel forms of institutional structures to circumvent the collective action problem by making their activities more attractive to donors. Fourth, charities can often take advantage of favorable tax treatments to lower the effective cost of giving. The latter accounts for the true opportunity cost, in terms of foregone resources, needed by the donor to increase the output of the charity by $1. A rise in the tax deductibility of charitable giving lowers this price to donors, while increases in fund-raising and administrative expenditures on the part of the charity lowers the charity final output and, hence, raises the cost of giving.

The large number of contributors associated with many charities raises a conundrum. If charities are providing a pure public good in their philanthropic activities, and if a large number of donors are relied upon for contributions, then the group should be latent and, hence, not form. In fact, Sugden (1982) provided an interesting demonstration that the pure public good theory of philanthropy is inconsistent with the existence of large fund-raising charities (large in terms of income and the number of donors), when taken together with available evidence concerning the income elasticity of charitable giving. Yet fund-raising charities exist. Charities collect billions of dollars annually in the United States. In 1985, the 150,000 charities registered in England and Wales received a total income in excess of £12.5 billion or 4 percent of gross national product (Posnett 1987). Clearly, the standard wisdom, drawn from conventional theories of pure public goods, does not apply to charities. But why?

Apparently, the answer lies both in a failure of charities to provide a pure public good and in the charity's ability to design an institutional structure that manages to circumvent standard free-riding concerns. The pure public good theory of philanthropy rests on three primary assumptions: (1) the output of charitable activity produces benefits that are nonrival and that may, in principle, be enjoyed equally by contributor and noncontributor alike; (2) each individual holds a zero (Nash) conjecture regarding the effect of his or her own contribution on the contributions of others; and (3) individuals behave in such a way as to maximize utility. In choosing among possible assumption violations, Sugden's preferred candidate is utility maximization.

If one interprets "utility" in the classical Benthamite way, as a psychological experience of pleasure, it is not a matter of logical necessity that an individual should seek to maximize his own utility. For example, a public-spirited act utilitarian might instead seek to maximize the sum of utilities for all people in society. Another person might be a rule utilitarian following those rules that, if generally followed, would maximize the sum of utilities. A third person might act on the Kantian principle of following those rules that he could will to be general laws. (Sugden 1982, 349).

Most other researchers have turned to the violation of assumption 1—the pure publicness assumption—for an explanation of observed behavior concerning charities. As such, charities are viewed as providing an activity that has pure public and private outputs. In other words, people are motivated, in part, to contribute owing to excludable benefits that are not available from the general contributions of others.

Table 4.3, taken from Posnett and Sandler 1986 (219), indicates income sources for eight of the largest charities in Britain in 1983. Fees and subscriptions constitute sizable income sources for the National Trust, Dr. Barnado's, and the Salvation Army. In the case of the National Trust, fees are collected to permit visits to the trust's sites—a clear private benefit is conferred to visitors. Dr. Barnado's, for example, receives fees from local authorities as payment for children placed in its care, and uses surpluses to finance its care of other children. Direct trading, involving the sale of private goods, is a significant revenue source for Oxfam; in total, it accounted for 39.1 percent of its income. Voluntary contributions, in the form of donations and legacies, account for approximately 50 percent of the income of the charities listed in table 4.3. Weisbrod (1988, 197, table C.4) indicated that nonprofits in the United States depended on service fees and other income for approximately 50 percent of their receipts in 1980. Nonprofits, such as educational and research institutions, received almost 80 percent of their income from sources other than private giving or the government.

Charities are able to compete against the for-profit sector in the sale of private goods owing to cost advantages. These may arise from favorable tax treatment that exempt direct trading from corporation taxes when certain requirements are met (see Posnett and Sandler 1986, 215–16). Moreover, charities can reduce costs through the use of voluntary labor and exemptions

TABLE 4.3. Proportion of Total 1983 Income by Source for Major Fund-Raising Charities in Great Britain (in percentages)

Charity	Fund-Raising and Donations	Legacies	Fees and Subscriptions	Rent and Investment	Trading	Grants from Statutory Authorities	Grants from other Charities	Other Income
National Trust	—[a]	—[a]	33.5	26.7	3.8	6.1	6.3	6.3
Dr. Barnardo's	19.1	20.7	45.9	7.0	7.3	—	6.3	—
Salvation Army	14.7	21.9	39.7	21.1	—	0.4	2.0	0.2
Imperial Cancer Research Fund	14.4	60.0	—	24.1	0.7	—	—	0.3
Oxfam	32.1	6.8	—	1.4	39.1	10.3	9.3	1.0
Cancer Research Campaign	29.5	62.5	—	7.4	0.7	—	—	—
Royal National Lifeboat Inst.	29.8	46.9	6.4	4.7	4.6	—	—	7.6
Save the Children Fund	—[b]	—[b]	—	3.8	2.9	22.4	—	2.8
Percent of aggregate income of all charities listed	24.3	23.9	21.0	14.6	6.8	4.2	2.7	2.5

Source: Annual Accounts; data compiled by John Posnett, University of York.
[a]The National Trust generated 17.2 percent of its income from a combination of fund-raising and endowment.
[b]The Save the Children Fund generated 68.1 percent of its income from a combination of fund-raising and endowment.

from minimum wage laws. In some situations, charities have monopoly power, as in the sale of visitation rights to historical sites by the National Trust. The presence of these private benefits means that alternative funding sources, as provided by private trading or government grants, need not crowd out private donations in a dollar-for-dollar fashion, since the neutrality theorem is not applicable.[3] In a study of British charities, Posnett and Sandler (1989) found little or no evidence of any crowding out. This result is consistent with results reported by Abrams and Schmitz (1978) and Clotfelter (1985) in which crowding out was nowhere near a dollar-for-dollar basis. Moreover, autonomous income (rents, investment income, and fees) was a *net* addition to contributions with no crowding out (Posnett and Sandler 1986, table 4).

The design of institutional structures to deal with collective action aspects of charity fund-raising has been recognized since *Logic*, where Olson (1965, 62–63) mentioned the use of federated structures to limit group size. For example, the United Fund and Easter Seals organize much of their fundraising drives at a local level, where peer group pressures are more effective. Furthermore, in the case of the United Fund, revenues are used to support local charities so that benefits have the greatest potential impact on contributors. When organized at the local level, individuals may be more willing to contribute due to a system of rewards (e.g., status or prestige) and punishments (e.g., stigma), valued by a sufficiently large number of individuals to make the group viable. This type of induced cooperation is more likely in a relatively small group, in which the costs of detecting noncooperative behavior are low and the value of rewards is high due to close social interaction.

Since donors cannot control how their money is used by the charity, an important asymmetric information problem exists between uninformed donors and well-informed organizations. This problem is especially acute for organizations that depend on voluntary contributions from a large number of donors, since donors may have little incentive to become knowledgeable about activities of the charities that they support, especially if their contributions are modest. To limit transaction costs and to assure donors that funds go to stated purposes, large public fund-raising organizations limit the degree of trustee discretion. In contrast, charities that depend on a few donors who may themselves serve on the board of trustees are expected to have a high degree of trustee discretion. Thus, sources of income may help shape a charity's organizational form in terms of trustee discretion. A study by Posnett and Sandler (1988) provides evidence consistent with this hypothesis.

---

3. See, e.g., Cornes and Sandler 1981 and 1984a; Andreoni 1987, 1989, 1990; Posnett and Sandler 1986, 1988, 1989; Steinberg 1986 and 1987.

4.5 Growth of Nations

In 1982, Olson published *The Rise and Decline of Nations*, in which he spelled out some macroeconomic implications of *Logic*. Prior to the publication of *The Rise and Decline of Nations*, most of the principles of collective action had been applied to microeconomic issues concerning the allocation of resources by individuals and firms. Olson (1982) argued that a nation's political stability allows for the emergence of (mostly small) special-interest groups that vie for a nation's income and resources. In stable nations, the number of such groups grows with time. The agenda of these "distributional" coalitions is to redistribute income to their members through lobbying activities. Thus, farmers ask for price support programs, emerging firms request tariff protection against foreign competition, senior citizens lobby for improved medical insurance, and environmental groups demand an end to offshore drilling. Since many coalitions are small in relationship to the population, they are *not* concerned with the social and transaction costs that their actions impose on the economy. Olson reasoned that a small coalition would experience only a tiny fraction of the efficiency losses associated with the price distortions resulting from their redistributive policies. If, say, the coalition consists of one-millionth of the population, then, on average, only this fraction of the efficiency loss is borne by the coalition. The remainder of the burden is spread over the entire population. If, however, the coalition's gain from the redistribution exceeds this fraction-weighted loss, then the coalition will continue its redistributive activity. Societies that accumulate relatively large numbers of these redistributional coalitions are especially prone to losses of efficiency that impede growth. In contrast, large coalitions are more apt to curb inefficient activities, since their share of the loss in efficiency is greater and, consequently, is likely to outweigh redistributional benefits at a lower activity level. Since large groups are often more difficult to organize than small ones, the general population that pays for the benefits received by small coalitions is usually not able to lobby against these special interests.

In mature societies, significant social costs could arise as coalitions distort prices, slow the adoption of new technologies, or inhibit the reallocation of resources to new, growth-promoting sectors. A nation's growth was, therefore, predicted by Olson (1982) to suffer from such coalitions. Since these coalitions increase as a nation ages, younger nations (states) were predicted to have better growth performance than older nations (states). This provocative hypothesis indicates that macroeconomic issues may also depend, in part, on collective action considerations. Moreover, collective action may, at times, harm rather than promote social welfare.

There have been numerous attempts to test Olson's hypothesis; noteworthy examples include Olson 1982; Choi 1983; Murrell 1983; and Vedder and Gallaway 1986. Most tests involve regressions in which the dependent variable is some growth measure (e.g., growth in per capita income) and the independent variables include an age indicator for the state or nation. The studies cited previously have found a significant negative relationship between growth and the nation's age, consistent with Olson's hypothesis. Many of the tests are, however, very simplistic and do not consider alternative hypotheses that could explain growth differences between nations.

Vedder and Gallaway (1986) introduced a host of additional independent variables into the regression that included tax measures, union membership, public assistance measures, and economic activity indices (e.g., agriculture and mineral). By accounting for more factors, their study attempted to ascertain whether other alternatives could explain the personal income growth in forty-eight U.S. states during 1970–82. Their results strongly supported Olson's hypothesis: the state's age and its membership in distributional coalitions are negative determinants of growth. The inclusion of distributional coalitions per se is important in lending support to Olson's hypothesis. Future econometric studies must examine the influence of the extent and behavior of interest groups over time on the growth of income.

Surely more work on the aggregate impact of special-interest groups on economic growth is needed. The influence of special-interest groups in developing nations is of particular interest, since wasteful activities could siphon off much-needed resources from support for infrastructure projects.

*4.6 Labor Unions

Olson devoted chapter 3 of *Logic* to depicting labor unions as a collective action problem, in which union members share the collective goods of higher wages and other nonpecuniary fringe benefits associated with a union shop. Olson reasoned that either membership must be compulsory or else selective incentives must be provided to motivate laborers to join. If the union cannot motivate laborers to support the union, then workers have incentives to free ride on union accomplishments. Union action to establish a closed shop, whereby only union members can be hired, is an attempt to make union-provided collective actions excludable.

In two contributions, Booth (1984 and 1985) has reexamined whether workers may be motivated to join without compulsory actions. Following Akerlof's (1980) theory of social custom, Booth (1985) showed that codes of behavior may motivate workers to join unions even in the absence of an enforcement mechanism. Booth (1985) made the benefits derived from the union wage, w, both nonrival and nonexcludable to all workers in the industry, but viewed reputation, r, as an *excludable* benefit only acquired by union members. Reputation is an increasing concave function of the proportion of the labor force, M, belonging to the union. This membership proportion varies between 0 (no members) and 1 (every worker in the industry is a union member). Union members receive utility,

$$U^{in} = U^{in}[r(M), w - s] , \qquad (4.1)$$

in which the superscript *in* denotes a member and s is the membership fee,

$$s = a + (b/M) , \qquad (4.2)$$

which includes a fixed component, a, and a variable component b/M that falls with union membership size. Nonunion workers receive

$$U^{out} = U^{out}(0, w) , \qquad (4.3)$$

in which superscript *out* depicts a nonunion worker. Since reputation can only be acquired by union membership, reputation for nonunion members is 0. An individual is motivated to join whenever net benefits from membership exist, so that

$$U^{in}[r(M), w - a - (b/M)] - U^{out}(0, w) > 0 . \qquad (4.4)$$

Booth (1985, 257–60) demonstrated, via the intermediate value theorem,[4] that stable equilibria can exist at the "corners," where $M = 0,1$, as long as everyone is identical and the difference depicted in equation 4.4 equals 0 for some $M \in (0,1)$. According to Booth, the stable equilibrium at $M = 1$ violates the free-rider tendency since everyone chooses to join. But this equilibrium is very much in keeping with Olson's view of collective action problems, inasmuch as reputation is, in essence, a selective private incentive produced jointly due to social custom with the purely public wage component. Without this excludable, jointly produced union benefit, membership would, indeed, be zero as Olson and Booth recognize. Jointly produced outputs can motivate, provided that they are excludable. These motivating benefits may, however, be rival, nonrival, or partially rival. Booth's analysis is reminiscent of club theory.

---

4. The intermediate value theorem states that if a continuous function is defined over a closed interval $[a,b]$, and if the values of the function at the endpoints of this interval are not equal (i.e., $f(a) \neq f(b)$), then for every real number r between $f(a)$ and $f(b)$ there exists an x in the domain (a,b) such that the value of the function at this x is r (i.e., $f(x) = r$).

4.7 International Responses to Terrorism

Since the late 1960s, the international community has experienced an ever-increasing threat of terrorism. Terrorism is the premeditated use, or threat of use, of extranormal violence or force to gain a political objective through intimidation or fear. Although terrorist motivations vary widely between groups (e.g., nationalism, separatism, nihilism, issue-specific concern), terrorist tactics are similar and include hostage taking, bombings, assassinations, and hoaxes. Transnational terrorism concerns terrorist activities involving terrorists or government participants from two or more nations. Incidents originating in one nation and terminating in another, such as a skyjacking, are transnational, as are incidents involving demands made of an agent in a nation other than the one hosting the incident. Terrorist events that include victims, terrorists, or the institutions of two or more nations are considered transnational. These transnational terrorist incidents can be associated with numerous collective action problems between countries due to externalities, since, for example, the deterrence decision in one targeted nation conveys benefits and costs to other potential targets. Benefits result when one nation's actions reduce the threat for other nations, while costs arise when a nation's actions force the terrorists elsewhere. The latter situation is known as a transferable externality and is analogous to the situation where neighborhoods that stand up to crack dealers induce these dealers to set up shop elsewhere. All neighborhoods (nations) must take a united stance, and this is a difficult collective action to accomplish.

If a set of nations are targeted by a state that sponsors terrorism (e.g., Iraq, Iran, Syria), then any retaliatory response on the part of one nation would confer nonexcludable and nonrival benefits to the other *targeted* nations. Situations may arise in which the *net* benefits from retaliation to the retaliator are negative (i.e., retaliatory costs exceed the nation's derived benefits) when the nation is the sole retaliator. If, however, net benefits are positive when two or more nations retaliate, then a Prisoner's Dilemma game, as shown in figures 2.1, 2.6, and 2.8, applies and no nation may go it alone. Unless the payoff from the status quo of not retaliating is sufficiently negative (so that a Chicken game applies), no nation may provide a retaliatory response. When, however, a state sponsor selectively targets some nation's people and property (e.g., the people and property of the United States and Israel), benefits derived from retaliation may be sufficiently great to warrant a unilateral response, even though the full costs are shouldered by the sole retaliator. In the case of the Libyan raid on April 15, 1986, the Reagan administration obviously viewed these net benefits as positive. For state-sponsored terrorism, the retaliation dilemma raises many of the issues (e.g., group asymmetry and suboptimality) that Olson mentioned in *Logic*.

Lee (1988) raised the further possibility that some nations may hurt the collective interests of the group in ways worse than free riding. Lee (1988) developed the notion of "paid riding," whereby an agent "sells" the public good of terrorism deterrence that the efforts of others attempt to create. Paid riding occurs when a country offers terrorists a sanctuary if the terrorists promise restraint on the host country's soil. The paid-rider option dominates the free-rider option of doing nothing. By selling or reducing the public good, the paid rider reduces the incentive of the retaliator to act, since the level of deterrence that its actions would achieve is partially undone by the paid rider. Thus, the retaliator's net benefits are even less than with free riders and may imply that the group is no longer privileged.

A collective action problem may also characterize nations' deterrence expenditure decisions to curb attacks when confronting terrorists that operate on two or more nations' soil. If each nation decides its deterrence independently, then each may allocate *too many* resources to inducing terrorists to switch where they stage their events. This follows because the nations do not account for the negative transference externality (by inducing terrorists to operate on another nation's soil) that these deterrence choices create for others. If nations were to share intelligence concerning the group's true preferences for attacking alternative targets, then the overdeterrence outcome would be aggravated as nations are better able to calculate what it takes to make the terrorists go elsewhere. Piecemeal policy, in which intelligence (but not deterrence) decisions are shared, may make the cooperating nations worse off. Both intelligence sharing and deterrence decisions pose collective action concerns. Neither decision can be handled in isolation because each is interdependent, so that the problem of second best applies. A grand strategy for coordinating policy on both fronts is required to reach Pareto optimality.

The creation of a transnational commando squad that could be shared on a per-incident basis denotes another collective action aspect of antiterrorism policy. Currently, many nations maintain their own commando units to deal with terrorist incidents (e.g., the United States, Egypt, Israel, the United Kingdom, Italy, Germany, France, Switzerland, Belgium, Denmark, the Netherlands, Norway, Austria, and Indonesia). For nations confronted with only domestic terrorism, the creation of one's own commando unit makes sense; however, for nations threatened by transnational incidents, many of which may occur on foreign soil, a transnational unit, deployed throughout the world's trouble spots, has much to offer. The existence of so many identical commando units represents much duplication of effort and wasted resources that could be channeled, in part, toward setting up a transnational squad. Such a squad would be used more frequently, thus providing its members with greater experience. Commando units deployed in the home country may not be able to reach the incident in time (e.g., the U.S. Delta Force did not get to Cyprus in time to help with the June 14, 1985, hijacking of TWA flight 847). Moreover, surprise and secrecy are compromised when units have to be dispatched from distant bases.

Since the dispatching of the squad can be withheld and since, moreover, a nation's use of the squad can be monitored, a club arrangement can be used to finance the operation by charging nations user fees on a per-incident basis. Countries faced with more incidents would pay more in total tolls or user fees.

Lest the reader think that all collective actions are beneficial, one must remember that terrorism is itself a collective action performed by the members of a group. Terrorists use a wide variety of tactics to achieve their collective goal, which may or may not reflect the interests of society at large.

*4.8 Problems of the Commons

An apt example of a collective action problem is the commons in which a scarce resource is owned collectively by a set of agents. Common property examples include fisheries, oil pools, hunting grounds, deep-sea mineral beds, orbital bands in geostationary space, and radio-wave frequencies. The analysis of the commons demonstrates the overexploitation of the scarce fixed resource, in which the *average product* of the variable input, not its *marginal product*, is equated to the input's rental rate when access is free and the set of exploiters large. Overexploitation is relevant to a commons in both a static, steady-state framework and a dynamic analysis. To maintain simplicity, I present a static analysis.

Consider a set of exploiters consisting of a given number of profit-maximizing firms, each having free access to an exogenously fixed common property resource such as a fishing ground. Each firm combines the common property resource with a single private input, a fishing vessel, to produce an output of fish. With the size of the commons fixed, the total output or catch, C, depends solely on the size of the total fishing fleet, R, which represents effort on behalf of exploiters. The production function is

$$C = F(R) , \tag{4.5}$$

which is increasing and strictly concave (i.e., $F'(R) > 0$ and $F''(R) < 0$). Other sources of supply for fish are assumed so that the price of the catch is exogenously fixed at unity. Vessels are also assumed to be sold on competitive markets at a price of p per vessel.

To illustrate a commons problem with many of the Olsonian themes, I further assume a "pure" homogeneous commons where fish are evenly distributed throughout the fishing grounds, so that each vessel hauls in the same catch. This assumption allows the catch, c, of each firm to equal its *share* of total effort times the total catch:

$$c = [r/R]F(R) = [r/(r + \tilde{R})]F(r + \tilde{R}) ,   (4.6)$$

in which r is the firm's number of vessels and $\tilde{R}$ is the aggregate fleet for the other firms in the commons. Obviously, the total fleet in the commons, R, equals $r + \tilde{R}$. Each exploiter's benefit equals its value of catch, which, in turn, is a fraction of the total value derived from the commons. This representation is analogous to the Olsonian depiction of a collective action problem.

The Pareto-optimal solution for the commons is found by choosing the aggregate fleet size that maximizes total profit, π, for the set of exploiters.[5]

$$\pi(R) = F(R) - pR .   (4.7)$$

The optimizing fleet size, R^*, for the commons is uniquely determined by the FOC, $F'(R) = p$, which is independent of the distribution of vessels among the exploiters. The fleet's marginal product must be equated to the variable input's price. This is the allocation of effort resulting from competitive exploitation in the presence of well-defined property rights.

The Nash equilibrium corresponds to the profit-maximizing choice of r on the part of the individual firms.

$$\max_{r} \{[r/(r + \tilde{R})]F(r + \tilde{R}) - pr\} ,$$

in which $\tilde{R}$ is an exogenous parameter owing to Nash behavior. The associated FOCs can be written as

$$p = (r/R)F'(R) + (\tilde{R}/R)[F(R)/R]   (4.8)$$

after some manipulations. At a symmetric equilibrium involving n exploiters, we have $r/R = 1/n$ and $\tilde{R}/R = (n - 1)/n$, which means that equation 4.8 can be expressed as

$$p = (1/n)F'(R) + [(n - 1)/n]F(R)/R .   (4.9)$$

---

5. Profit maximization is equivalent to maximizing the sum of producer and consumer surplus in this stylized problem.

In equation 4.9, the price of a vessel is equated to a weighted sum of its marginal and average product. If $n = 1$, price equals marginal product and Pareto optimality is obtained; if, instead, $n \rightarrow \infty$, price converges to average product and profits approach zero. In the latter case, the full tragedy of the commons is experienced.

A comparison of the Nash fleet, R^N, for the commons that satisfies equation 4.8 with the Pareto-optimal fleet, R^*, shows an overexploitation in which $R^N > R^*$ when $n > 1$. Since R^* is independent of the number of exploiters, while R^N increases as n increases reaching the R corresponding to $p = F(R)/R$ in the limit, the ratio R^N/R^* becomes larger as n rises (Cornes and Sandler 1986, 128–31). In consequence, inefficiency does worsen as n increases, consistent with theme 1 of *Logic*. If the sizes of the exploiters are unequal, then a clear asymmetry can be shown in which effort and, hence, exploitation are positively correlated to fleet size in a pure commons. Small firms are crowded out of the commons by larger firms with mightier fleets. In consequence, the small is exploited by the large—the reverse of the usual exploitation theme.

Equation 4.9 indicates that the Nash equilibrium lies between the Pareto-optimal solution and the zero-rent equilibrium, R^O, associated with unlimited access so that $R^O > R^N > R^*$. As such, the Nash equilibrium depicted above can be viewed as that of a limited-access commons if exploitation is prior to the point at which $p = F(R)/R$. Profits need not be zero in the Nash equilibrium. With long-run considerations, entry will be pushed until profits, net of entry fees, are zero.

In an interesting series of experiments, Walker, Gardner, and Ostrom (1990) tested this theory of the commons. Each subject was allowed to allocate tokens to a private good market and a commons market. In the latter, the subject's return declined with increased allocations by others. A summation technology characterized the payoff function and a player's payoff depended on his or her share of the total tokens allocated to the commons. Group size was maintained at eight; thus, the influence of group size was not investigated. These experiments showed that the Nash equilibrium best characterized the subjects.

If the commons were less pure, so that fish were not evenly distributed, allowing some fishing spots to be more productive than others, then firms may derive private benefits by positioning their fleets over these bountiful areas. The presence of these firm-specific private benefits can serve to lessen inefficiency. Symmetry of effort may also be lost if firms differ according to technology. Although *Logic*'s characterization of collective action problems is clearly analogous to the pure commons problem, less-stylized models may yield results at odds with the Olsonian themes. As in the case of public goods,

Assurance and other game structures may be more appropriate for some commons problems.

Until now, the output is assumed to be sold in a competitive market so that the price of fish has been treated as a constant normalized at a value of 1. An interesting second-best problem arises when the output of the commons is sold in an imperfectly competitive market in which the price of fish, P, is a function of the total catch so that the representative firm's profit is

$$\pi = \{[P(C)C/R - p]r\} \, , \tag{4.10}$$

in a pure commons. Since demand inelasticity due to monopoly power leads to overconservation (i.e., a lessening of the tragedy of the commons), while an increase in the number of exploiting firms typically leads to underconservation, a finite number of firms for a commons can be found corresponding to a social or Pareto optimum (Cornes, Mason, and Sandler 1986). One distortion can serve to offset or ameliorate another, thereby limiting the need for outside intervention to correct for the collective action failure. At a symmetric equilibrium where everyone behaves identically, the Nash equilibrium associated with equation 4.10 would yield a Pareto optimum for the following number of exploiters.[6]

$$n^* = 1 + \epsilon_C/[(\epsilon_C - 1)\epsilon_D] \, , \tag{4.11}$$

where ϵ_C is the elasticity of input productivity (i.e., $\epsilon_C = RF'[R]/C$) and ϵ_D is the price elasticity of market demand. Since the ϵ_C lies between zero and one, n^* equals or exceeds one.

Equation 4.11 depicts a number of possibilities. If market demand is perfectly elastic, then equation 4.11 implies the conventional wisdom: a single firm must exploit the commons to achieve a social optimum. For a given elasticity of input productivity, equation 4.11 indicates that the more inelastic market demand is, the greater the number of firms in the commons should be if a social optimum is to be achieved. This follows because the increase in market imperfection leads to a greater degree of conservation as firms restrict output, thereby taking advantage of buyers' unresponsiveness to price. Hence, more exploiters can be admitted to the commons, since the resulting increase in exploitation is needed to offset the conservation associated with monopoly power. Holding market demand elasticity fixed allows us to focus on the influence of input-side distortions by varying ϵ_C. In equation 4.11, as ϵ_C nears one, n^* approaches infinity, implying that free access is desirable. If $\epsilon_C = 1$, then average and marginal products are equal; hence, equating aver-

---

6. For a derivation, see Cornes, Mason, and Sandler 1986, 642–45.

age product to the real rental rate leads to no input-size distortion. As diminishing returns increase and ϵ_C approaches zero, the commons problem intensifies and n^* must be restricted.

Sandler and Sterbenz (1990) have extended the pure commons model to cases where harvest uncertainty is present so that effort, in terms of the variable input (vessels), may be associated with different catch levels due to random stock considerations (e.g., uncertain migratory patterns). To capture stock uncertainty, the aggregate catch is now

$$C = Z(R)\bar{X}_o v , \tag{4.12}$$

where $\bar{X}_o$ is the mean initial stock and v is a nonnegative random variable with a mean of one. With an uncertain stock, the representative, risk-averse firm now solves the following problem.[7]

$$\max_{(r)} \int_0^\beta U(\pi^*)g(v)\, dv ,$$

in which $\pi^* = (r/R)Z(R)\bar{X}_o v - pr$, $g(v)$ is the probability density function. Expected utility corresponds to this integral. If the FOC for this problem is investigated, uncertainty is seen to reduce the exploitation of the commons for a fixed number of risk-averse firms when compared with certainty (Sandler and Sterbenz 1990, 159). As a result of risk aversion, uncertainty is undesirable for the firms. In this pure commons model, total uncertainty is fixed for the commons; but the uncertainty faced by each exploiter depends on its *share* of the exploitation efforts in the commons. By reducing its fleet, a risk-averse firm is therefore attempting to limit its own uncertainty. In doing so, the collective action problem known as the tragedy of the commons is ameliorated. This amelioration also characterizes the long-run equilibrium as well as some stylized, noncompetitive cases with risk-neutral and risk-averse exploiters.

The underdeveloped world appears especially prone to commons problems. A relevant example is the gathering of firewood for fuel that has laid waste to forests throughout the developing world. When monsoons come, the loss of the forests means widespread flooding, famine, and pestilence. Within many developing nations, the property rights to the forests are allocated on a free access basis. In other cases, the forests that protect a lowland nation (e.g., Bangladesh) are found in upland nations with no incentives to consider the hardships that their exploitation can cause another nation. Commons

---

7. A risk-averse agent will not except an actuarially fair bet. Such agents insure against risk.

problems are more prevalent in the developing world, since the means for assigning and enforcing property rights are at a more primitive stage than in the developed world. The Law of the Sea Treaty, for example, gave the rights to the seabed resources within 200 miles to coastal nations in an effort to overcome the commons problem by making $n = 1$. Developing countries are apt to suffer under this arrangement for two reasons. First, these nations do not have the resources or technology to enforce their 200-mile rights, thus leaving them vulnerable to exploiters from within and outside the country. Second, the wealth of the deep seabeds, located beyond 200 miles, can be taken by those developed countries with the technology to do so. Similar problems arise with respect to polar and outer space resources.

Some of the most-pressing problems confronting mankind (e.g., ozone depletion, carbon dioxide buildup, and acid rain) arise because the atmosphere and airsheds are open-access commons (see chap. 6). The buildup of carbon dioxide is especially difficult to deal with, since some nations stand to gain as the earth heats up. These potential gainers have perverse incentives that make global warming a potential windfall. The best chance for mankind to deal with this problem may be now, when uncertainty with respect to gainers and losers is still present. Once gainers can be identified, they have a strong incentive to work against collective interests.

Institutional arrangements are, in some instances, needed to control over-exploitation in the commons (see Ostrom 1990). The use of contracting has been examined as a means for controlling overexploitation. For fisheries, Johnson and Libecap (1982) have shown that contracts are difficult to formulate and enforce when heterogeneity characterizes the exploiters. In other words, pure commons with identical agents are easier to control with contracts. This result is in keeping with theme 2 of *Logic* concerning asymmetries. For oil fields in Oklahoma and Texas, Libecap and Wiggins (1982) demonstrated empirically that the concentration of ownership facilitated contractual arrangements in agreement with theme 1 of *Logic*.

Sanctions can also be used to limit exploitation. Since these sanctions are themselves a collective benefit to the exploiter, their funding and provision pose additional difficulties. In addition, the certainty of enforcement is important. If, for example, exploiters do not believe that their activities can be monitored sufficiently, the threat of sanctions may not have much effect. Thus, the certainty of enforcement is a crucial concern. The imposition of sanctions could alter the game structure from that of Prisoner's Dilemma to that of fully privileged.

In a renewable resource commons, the problem of extinctions is ever-present. Uncontrolled exploitation could sufficiently deplete populations so that the species becomes extinct, as in the case of the passenger pigeon. In some instances, as extinction is approached, the payoffs for overexploitation may turn so negative that the dominant strategy may become cooperation. Thus, the game structure may change from that of Prisoner's Dilemma to that of Assurance, provided that players are properly informed about the resource status. The latter is, however, sometimes not known until it is too late.

4.9 Strategic Trade Policy

Collective action problems are also relevant in the study of international trade. If perfect competition and nonincreasing returns to scale prevail so that the terms of trade cannot be influenced by a nation's actions, then the theory of comparative advantage indicates that social welfare can be maximized under a regime of free trade. Although it is in the collective interest of all nations to promote free trade, a defector may achieve individual gains at the expense of the collective by imposing protectionist policies (e.g., tariffs or quotas). Since each nation may experience a payoff matrix in which the imposition of a tariff is a dominant strategy, a classic Prisoner's Dilemma may apply and distorting tariffs may characterize the entire trading community. The study of an optimal tariff involves the choice of the Nash equilibrium tariff, whereby the externality imposed on others is ignored. More sophisticated players may anticipate one another's strategies, leading to nonzero conjectures. Asymmetries in information may support leader-follower behavior, whereby the follower moves first and the leader then chooses its tariff using the follower's Nash reaction path as its relevant constraint. Distributional aspects can be greatly influenced by the strategic assumption.

In the last few decades, trade economists have extended the theory of free trade to include increasing returns to scale and imperfect competition (Krugman 1987). The latter qualification is especially significant in terms of collective action, since imperfect competition raises a completely new set of justifications, whereby protectionist policies can yield nation-specific benefits at the expense of the international community. Strategic trade policy "holds that government policy can tilt the terms of oligopolistic competition to shift excess returns from foreign to domestic firms" (Krugman 1987, 134). Industries that generate knowledge externalities (e.g., computer, aerospace) that can benefit the entire economy of the protectionist are the prime candidates for subsidies and/or other distortions that enable these industries to gain a foothold in the international market. Krugman (1987, 135–37) demonstrated with a simple 2 × 2 matrix how, in the absence of a subsidy, competition between Airbus and Boeing would yield a Coordination game with two pure-strategy Nash equilibria, in which one of the two firms controls the market. If, however, a sufficient European subsidy is given to Airbus, then there is only one pure-strategy Nash equilibrium, with Airbus in control. Trade restricting policies, whether based on strategic considerations or otherwise, will lead to retaliation and could plunge the international community into another era of protectionism, where all suffer. The problem with this new analysis of strategic trade policy concerns its use of an atemporal model to analyze an intertemporal problem—the adoption of new technologies. The atemporal model does not allow reputation costs, associated with repeated games, to be included. Although clear short-term benefits can come from strategic trade policies as put forward by Krugman, long-term costs may outweigh these gains as trading partners retaliate and impose other restrictions on one another. A second problem with strategic trade policy is its partial equilibrium nature, with its focus on a single activity. Other activities may be affected through forward (output) and backward (input) linkages to the protection proposed; second-best considerations are relevant.

Protectionist lobbies create a collective bad that can lead to widespread harm as trade wars get started. In the end, people buy more-limited market baskets at inflated prices. Inasmuch as protectionist lobbies are often small in relation to the general population, lobbies have an organizing advantage over the people who are harmed by protectionist policies.

4.10 Principal-Agent Analysis

In recent years, economists have developed agency theory to design an optimal contractual arrangement between a principal and an agent when asymmetric information prevails.[8] In a firm, the principal is the owner or manager, while the agents are the workers; in a government, the principal is the electorate, while the agents are the elected officials; and in a union, the principal is the union membership, while the agents are the union leaders. Asymmetric information is germane when a principal can view the final outcome (e.g., an output level, a provision level of the public good) but is unable to observe the agent's actual action. This situation would prevail when an exogenous risk factor intervenes in the output or provision process so that the agent's effort is no longer uniquely tied to each outcome. Rather, a distribution of outcomes is associated with each effort level. Information is one-sided because the agent, and not the principal, knows the agent's true effort. This asymmetric information leads to a moral hazard problem, insofar as the agent may take advantage of the principal's ignorance as an excuse to supply suboptimal levels of effort. Agent-principal difficulties can be minimized if the principal can design a contract or payment schedule for agent efforts that induces the agent to supply a fuller effort level. An entire schedule relating outcomes to payment must be chosen to maximize the principal's welfare subject to incentive-compatible and individual rationality constraints. Incentive compatible constraints ac-

---

8. See, e.g., Ross 1973; Stiglitz 1974; MacDonald 1984.

count for the agent's optimizing responses (in terms of FOCs) derived in the first step of the procedure, while an individual rationality constraint ensures that agents' welfare is no less with the contract than in alternative employment opportunities. Such contracts often involve the sharing of risk between the principal and the agent, unless the latter is extremely risk averse. If a first-best result cannot be achieved by the contract, then agency costs arise in terms of losses associated with second-best contracts.

Although there are many general representations for the agent-principal problem, the analysis is sufficiently complex for even single-agent, single-principal problems to preclude exact or closed-form solutions for the optimal payment schedule. Unlike the standard optimization problem in which a scalar value is chosen for a single-level problem, principal-agent analysis involves the choice of an entire function (i.e., a payment schedule) for a multilevel problem. At least two levels are required, since optimizing the principal's welfare must be consistent with the first level, which involves the agent's welfare maximization.

At least two relevant aspects of the principal-agent analysis apply to the theory of collective action. The first involves the number of agents, while the second concerns the use of nonmarket institutions to correct collective action failures. In regard to the first, Holmstrom (1982) and Rasmusen (1987) have noted a free-rider problem common in teams when individual effort is unobservable. The difficulty that Holmstrom recognized is a classic collective action problem that limits individual efforts, induced by payment schedules. With identical workers, each shirker loses pay equal to only $1/n$ (where n is the team size) of his or her reduced effort, but gains in the efforts of others. For linear payment schemes, individual effort decreases in proportion to the team size. The larger the team, the more inefficient individual effort. Thus, the first theme of *Logic* is fully supported (Cauley and Sandler 1991). In fact, the problem displayed by Holmstrom (1982) is mathematically identical to the commons problem discussed in section 4.8. When the team confronts a fixed amount of uncertainty, an increase in team size may have positive influences that offset, to some extent, free riding. If multiple, risk-averse agents are involved, an increase in team size makes the risk premium for agents fall by a factor of $(1/n)^2$ due to risk spreading (Cauley and Sandler 1991). Because an increase in team size is a double-edged sword due to negative free-riding influences and positive risk-spreading influences, an optimally sized collective could be determined to balance these forces at the margin.

To circumvent the free-rider problem, nonlinear payment schedules are proposed that, like preference-revelation mechanisms, make each agent face the social choice problem of the team through the use of sidepayments. This can be accomplished by withholding rewards to each agent unless Pareto-optimizing levels of output are achieved, so that the existence of even a single shirker would cause harm to all team members. Many variations of this theme are possible (Rasmusen 1987).

A second aspect of the principal-agent problem that concerns collective action has to do with theme 3 of *Logic,* in which mechanisms are designed to overcome suboptimality. Public policy itself poses a principal-agent problem, since the agent (e.g., an elected official or bureaucrat) has more information regarding their efforts and the random states of nature than the principal for whom they serve. Thus, the provision of a pure public good by a government may not improve efficiency greatly unless an incentive mechanism is put into place to motivate elected officials. Since this mechanism is costly, transaction costs in the form of agency costs must be considered when determining whether a nonmarket structure should be instituted to provide the collective good.

A more basic information problem confronts these nonmarket institutions that may still exist even though the principal is properly motivated by an incentive scheme. That is, the principal must still ascertain the preferences of his or her constituency so as to determine the provision level of the collective good. Hence, a properly functioning, nonmarket institutional structure requires well-informed agents who are sufficiently motivated to satisfy the (revealed) preferences of the constituency. This is a tall order.

4.11 International Organizations

Thus far, two international organizations—military alliances and the World Health Organization—have been mentioned as a means for confronting collective action problems. Many other international organizations have come into existence due to collective action considerations. A few examples include the United Nations (UN), INTELSAT, the Common Market, Interpol, pollution pacts, and the European Space Agency. The UN tries to promote world peace (a pure public good), while pursuing a host of other humanitarian goals (e.g., curbing world hunger). INTELSAT links more than eighty nations in an external communication network made up of geostationary satellites that carry over two-thirds of all transoceanic messages. The Common Market promotes free trade among the member nations, while affording protective barriers to nonmember products. The promotion of trade within the trading bloc provides a pure public good in terms of efficiency gains to the members. Interpol is a transnational police linkage that facilitates the sharing of intelligence with respect to criminal activity of a transnational character (e.g., terrorism or drug running). Pollution pacts, such as the Baltic Pact, give a pure public good to their members in the form of a cleaner environment (see, e.g., Hoel 1991). Finally, the European Space Agency allows the countries of Western Europe to pool markets and resources to achieve sufficient scale economies in the development of launch capabilities, space colonization, and space exploration.

When the analysis is at the supranational level, participants may include nation-states, whose interests are represented by policymakers. In international organizations, participants may include both governments and private corporations, as in the case of INTELSAT. Clearly, principal-agent considerations, discussed previously, abound in international organizations due to the additional supranational level. Unless policymakers are given the proper incentive schedule, they may not pursue the goals of their constituent principals, which are often the nation's population. At the agent level, cooperation must be fostered by the institutional arrangement so that net gains can be achieved beyond the noncooperative equilibrium.

Transaction costs are a crucial consideration for supranational structures because sizable expenditures of fixed costs for communication, infrastructure, and administration are required. Variable transaction costs arise as the structure or institution is utilized to decide policies. Unless a sufficient number of policies are enacted, the transaction costs per policy may be too high due to these fixed costs, so that the international organization cannot achieve sufficient benefits to match or exceed transaction costs. When these fixed transaction costs are too high to warrant the establishment of the supranational linkage, a nonconvexity in the transaction set exists. Since many inputs (e.g., communication networks, infrastructure, administrative staff) can be used for a host of different activities, these inputs are public in the sense that they enter the production function of several policy outputs simultaneously. The presence of public inputs is a sufficient condition (Baumol, Panzar, and Willig 1988, 75–77) for economies of scope, which exist when

$$C(q_1, q_2) < C(q_1, 0) + C(0, q_2) \qquad (4.13)$$

holds. In equation 4.13, the cost, $C(q_1, q_2)$, of providing both q_1 of activity 1 and q_2 of activity 2 in a single institution is cheaper than the total cost of providing the two activities in separate institutions.

If economies of scope truly characterize international organizations, then these institutions should provide multiple collective goods. This, indeed, appears to be the case. The NATO alliance, for example, not only provides deterrence, but also polices illicit drug trade, improves highway safety throughout Europe, and facilitates scientific research. The UN engages in a wide range of peace-promoting, educational, philanthropic, and scientific pursuits. Common markets not only foster free trade, but promote technology development and transfer among members. The pursuit of these multiple benefits may be an important means for circumventing transaction set nonconvexities by spreading fixed costs over a diverse set of activities.

The appearance of economies of scope makes it more difficult to determine an optimal group size when club goods are shared by these institutions. This follows because economies of scale with respect to the membership size for one activity may have little relationship to economies of scope when multiple outputs with diverse congestion functions are involved. Thus, the introduction of economies of scope requires us to redefine the optimal membership when excludable collective goods are shared by international organizations or other types of clubs (Sandler and Tschirhart 1991).

Another issue concerns the nature of the supranational linkage. Should participating nations be tightly or loosely joined? In a tight link, the participating nations sacrifice their autonomy to the collective, while in a loose link, the participants do their own thing with little consultation or coordination with their counterparts. A structure such as NATO, in which less than one percent of its expenditure is commonly funded, is a loose structure (Sandler and Forbes 1980, 432, table 1). Moreover, NATO allies use a unanimous voting rule that also serves to keep the structure loose. Collectives that share activities with a large proportion of excludable benefits, as may be the case in NATO since the late 1960s, need not coordinate activities closely to take advantage of efficiency gains. Surely the nature of the collective good as well as transaction costs are behind the optimal architecture of an international organization.

*4.12 Rent-Seeking Behavior

Another example of collective action is the activity of rent seeking, in which agents or a collective expend resources to obtain a return that results in no net addition of output to society. Tollison (1982, 578) states that "rent seeking is the expenditure of scarce resources to capture an artificially created transfer." Distributional coalitions, such as those behind Olson's *Rise and Decline of Nations,* are rent seekers because they spend resources in trying to obtain a greater piece of the economic pie without adding to the size of the pie through their activities. As such, rent seeking denotes an economically wasteful activity and is an example of how the pursuit of collective gains can lead to losses at an aggregate level.

The notion of rent seeking was first put forward by Tullock (1967) when he argued that the waste of monopoly included more than the traditional deadweight triangular loss (also see Krueger 1974; Posner 1975). Figure 4.1 illustrates Tullock's analysis for the monopoly case, in which a linear demand curve and its marginal revenue curve (dashed line MR) are displayed. If marginal cost is horizontal and if costs are independent of market structure, then the monopoly charges P_m and sells Q_m, while the perfect competitive industry charges P_c and produces Q_c. The deadweight loss is equal to the area

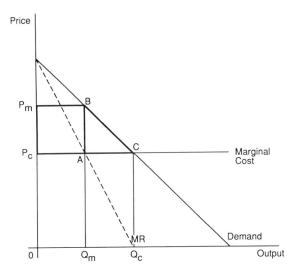

Fig. 4.1. Rent seeking for a monopoly

of triangle *ABC*, whereas monopoly profit is the area of rectangle $P_c P_m BA$. Tullock considers this profit area as a potential source of additional social loss through rent seeking. *Potential entrants* or competitors may induce the monopolist to expend resources up to area $P_c P_m BA$ to protect its rent. When competitive rent seeking occurs, society loses not only *ABC*, but also $P_c P_m BA$. Tullock (1980) has shown that when groups or individuals compete for a rent in a noncompetitive tournament arrangement, each will carry its rent-seeking activity until marginal costs equal the marginal return from rent seeking. In the Tullock model, marginal adjustments in bids are allowed, since the likelihood of winning equals the rent seeker's expenditure on the tournament as a proportion of the total expended by all rent seekers. Tullock (1980) demonstrated that, in total, rent seeking captures only half of the rectangle when only two players compete.

Applebaum and Katz (1986) have extended Tullock's tournament result to include not only the prize, but also the deadweight loss from rent seeking. Among other results, these authors demonstrated that total rent seeking increases with the size of the rent (prize) and the deadweight loss, and it decreases with the number of competing groups when a symmetric equilibrium is assumed. Tullock (1980) has examined situations in which there is overexploitation of the rent-seeking rectangle. A classic collective action problem then results, since everyone could be better off by not rent seeking.

Katz, Nitzan, and Rosenberg (1990) altered Tullock's 1980 model to the case where two groups of different sizes pursue rents by lobbying a government for public goods. Group 1 with n members lobbies for public good x that benefits *each* member by αR dollars with $0 < \alpha < 1$; group 2 with m members lobbies for public good y that benefits each member also by αR dollars. For each group, once the good is provided, the per-person ex-post benefit is independent of group size. Furthermore, benefits are not based on a summation technology. Following Tullock, the likelihood of success (ϕ) for groups 1 and 2 are

$$\phi_1 = \sum_{i=1}^{n} x_i \Big/ \left(\sum_{i=1}^{n} x_i + \sum_{i=1}^{m} y_i \right) , \tag{4.14}$$

and

$$\phi_2 = 1 - \phi_1 = \sum_{i=1}^{m} y_i \Big/ \left(\sum_{i=1}^{n} x_i + \sum_{i=1}^{m} y_i \right) ,$$

where x_i is the contribution of the ith member of group 1 and y_i is the contribution of the ith member of group 2. With risk neutrality, the expected utility of individual i in group 1 is

$$U_i = \phi_1(\alpha R - x_i) + \phi_2(-x_i) , \tag{4.15}$$

which is equivalent to

$$U_i = \phi_1 \alpha R - x_i . \tag{4.16}$$

The optimal x_i for each member of group 1 must satisfy the following FOC at a symmetric equilibrium where $x_i = x$ for every i and $y_j = y$ for every j:

$$my/(nx + my)^2 = (\alpha R)^{-1} . \tag{4.17}$$

By an analogous set of steps, the FOC for a group 2 member is

$$nx/(nx + my)^2 = (\alpha R)^{-1} . \tag{4.18}$$

If the respective sides of equations 4.17 and 4.18 are added together and the result simplified, we get an expression for total rent seeking,

$$nx + my = \alpha R/2 , \tag{4.19}$$

for the symmetric Nash equilibrium. This finding is reminiscent of Tullock's (1980) result. In equation 4.19, total rent seeking is only 50 percent of the per-person rent-seeking benefits.

Equation 4.19 is neutral to the distribution of individuals between the groups. This result is in contrast to theme 1 of *Logic* and arises due to the technology of public supply. To pursue this finding, we follow the methodology of Katz, Nitzan, and Rosenberg (1990, 52–53), and divide equation 4.17 by equation 4.18 to yield

$$my = nx \; , \tag{4.20}$$

or that total rent seeking is equal between groups so that success probabilities are one half. For each group, equations 4.20, 4.18, and 4.17 imply

$$x = \alpha R / 4n \; , \tag{4.21}$$

and

$$y = \alpha R / 4m \; . \tag{4.22}$$

By these equations, we see that an increase in group size decreases *individual* rent-seeking efforts since $\partial x / \partial n = -\alpha R / 4n^2$ and $\partial y / \partial m = -\alpha R / 4m^2$. Owing to symmetry, total contributions decrease by $\alpha R / 4n$ and $\alpha R / 4m$ in the two groups, respectively. This decrease is *exactly offset* by the entrant's contribution as seen in equations 4.21 and 4.22; hence, group size is *immaterial* to the equilibrium. Obviously, other technologies of supply other than the one considered here could make group size a more important determinant of relative rent-seeking activities between groups. Group heterogeneity may also affect the role played by relative group size. Thresholds or discrete aspects of group support could also alter the influence of group size in competing, rent-seeking collectives.

A second potential instance of rent seeking is depicted in figure 4.2, where an externality associated with the output is corrected with the use of a quota or output standard of q^*. Marginal private cost is depicted by line MPC, while marginal external cost is denoted by line MEC. For each level of output, both a private and an external cost are incurred. The latter is experienced by third parties in the population. To find the marginal social cost (MSC) line, we sum the MPC and MEC lines vertically at each output level. The demand curve for the outputs is schedule *D*. With no government intervention, output is at q^o, and MSB is less than MSC. The imposition of a quota at level q^* where MSC = MSB assists producers and externally affected third parties at

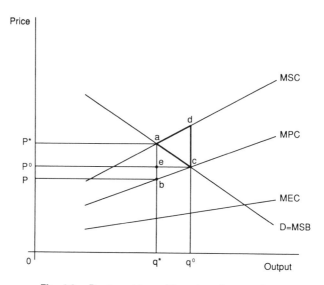

Fig. 4.2. Rent seeking with external correction

the expense of consumers. In figure 4.2, consumers lose area P^0P^*ae of consumer surplus. Producers gain the difference between area P^0P^*ae and area bec of producer surplus, while third parties gain (or avoid) area $badc$. All together, the quota leads to a deadweight loss of area adc.

Since producers can actually gain from a quota, they might lobby the government for this kind of intervention as opposed to a per-unit Pigouvian tax of ab at output level q^*. With such a tax, producers lose area PP^0cb, while consumers' and third parties' welfare is unchanged as compared to the standard. In contrast, the government gains PP^*ab in tax revenues. Although the deadweight loss is still area adc so that efficiency considerations have not changed, distributional changes will induce rent-seeking activities on the part of producers. These activities could add to the inefficiency by as much as area PP^*ab. Such lobbying efforts could explain why standards are indeed more prevalent than taxes.

4.13 Economies of Scale, Economies of Scope, and Collective Action

This subsection is concerned with cost considerations that can promote collective action. In chapter 2, we discovered (by way of examples) that the technology of collective supply, institutional structures, and the strategic assumption are important in determining the underlying game structure. The Prisoner's Dilemma does not need to characterize the game structure for collective action problems. I now demonstrate that cost considerations can influence the underlying game structure.

Economies of scale that involve a decrease in average cost can give a game structure in which mutual cooperation is among the Nash equilibria, as illustrated by the following example. Suppose that two players can each contribute one unit of the public good. Suppose further that if two units are produced in the same production process, then each unit costs $4. If, however, a single unit is produced, then its cost is $6. Scale economies are present since per-unit costs decrease when production is done cooperatively in a single plant. If *each* unit produced yields $5 in benefits to contributor and noncontributor alike, then the matrix shown in figure 4.3a indicates the net payoffs to the two players, with player 1's payoff listed first. When both cooperate in contributing and production, they each gain 10 (= 2 × 5) at a cost of 4 for a net payoff of 6. If only one player contributes, then the contributor gains a net payoff of -1, since benefits of 5 come at a cost of 6 due to the absence of scale economies at one unit of output. The noncontributor can then free ride on the contributor for a gain of 5 without any cost. The payoff structure shown in figure 4.3a is somewhat reminiscent of the Assurance 1 game shown in figure 2.6e, since the Nash equilibria are the same in pure strategies.

There is no dominant strategy for the game shown in figure 4.3a. In pure strategies, Nash equilibria correspond to cells *a* and *d,* where both players cooperate or defect. Unlike the Prisoner's Dilemma, defection is not a dominant strategy. If, moreover, player 1 (2) cooperates, it is then in player 2's (1's) interest to cooperate whenever scale economies reduce per-unit costs below the per-unit benefit. As in the Assurance game, contracts are self-enforcing; if player 1 cooperates, then player 2 gains by cooperating. In an *n*-person game, these economies of scale can reduce the incentives for free riding as group size increases and per-unit costs fall further. Many clubs find their motivation in these economies of scale. In essence, exclusion is practiced with respect to cost savings, since an agent must contribute to gain the cost saving. Economies of scale imply decreasing average costs that, in turn, imply strictly subadditive costs:[9]

$$C\left(\sum_{i=1}^{n} q^i \right) < \sum_{i=1}^{n} C(q^i) , \tag{4.23}$$

---

9. If we let

$$q = \sum_{i=1}^{n} q^i ,$$

2
Cooperate   Defect

	a	b
Cooperate	6,6	-1,5
1		
	c	d
Defect	5,-1	0,0

a. Economies of scale

2
Cooperate   Defect

	a	b
Cooperate	4,4	-1,5
1	c	d
Defect	5,-1	0,0

2
Cooperate   Defect

	a	b
Cooperate	12,12	2,10
1	c	d
Defect	10,2	0,0

b. Economies of scope and
a single activity

c. Economies of scope and
a double activity

Fig. 4.3. Potential effects of economies of scale and economies of scope on game structures in 2 × 2 games

where n is the number of contributors, q^i is the number of units contributed by the ith agent, and $C(\bullet)$ denotes costs. Equation 4.23 indicates that the cost of producing the total number of units in one facility is less than the sum of the costs of producing q^i units in separate facilities. In this equation, cost sub-additivity applies since $C(2) < 2C(1)$.

then $q > q^i > 0$ if $(q^1, \ldots, q^n)$ is a nontrivial division of q. By decreasing average cost, we have

$$C(q)/q < C(q^i)/q^i ,$$

so that

$$(q^i/q)C(q) < C(q^i) .$$

In many public good situations (including the provision of infrastructure), economies of scale exist and costs are subadditive, thereby making collective action advantageous. This advantage may occur within a nation when a project serves multiple jurisdictions, or between nations when a project serves many nations. If the output of a production process is based on volume, while costs are based on surface area, then scale economies are likely. Scale economies may be obtained without collective production provided that both parties buy from the same producer, whose average costs are declining.

The presence of scale economies as a motivation for collective action is well known. I merely emphasize that these economies may alter the game from that of the Prisoner's Dilemma to one more in keeping with collective action.

The number of activities undertaken by the collective may also be an important determinant of the feasibility of collective action. To illustrate, we consider a case of economies of scope as depicted in equation 4.13, where the costs of providing two activities is cheaper than the sum of the stand-alone costs of providing them separately. Suppose that the costs of providing *each* unit of collective activity one or two is $6, while the cost of providing a unit of *both* activities is $8. Further suppose that each unit of either activity gives *each* of the two players $5 in benefits. In figure 4.3, the matrix shown in figure 4.3b indicates the net payoffs for the provision of either activity alone. A classic case of the Prisoner's Dilemma applies for either activity provided alone, since the per-person benefit is less than the per-person cost. In consequence, neither activity is undertaken.

If, however, both activities are provided, then the payoffs shown in figure 4.3c apply. For cell *a*, both players provide a unit of both activities at a per-person cost of $8 and a per-person benefit of $20. Gross benefits are $20 since each player gains 5 from each of the two units of the two activities; net payoffs are, consequently, $12. The other payoffs are computed similarly. In cell *b*, for example, player 1 cooperates by providing a unit of both activities at a cost of 8 with benefits of 10 to both players. With both activities provided, the existence of economies of scope makes the game fully privileged with cooperation as the dominant strategy. Thus, the presence of economies of scope may mean that more than one activity must be done by the group to elicit collective action. The latter may only be desirable for some combinations of activities.

Summing both sides, we get

$$\sum_{i=1}^{n} C(q^i) > \sum_{i=1}^{n} (q^i/q)C(q) = C(q).$$

*4.14 Public Inputs and Infrastructure

An input is public or collective when it enters two or more firms' production functions.[10] If the input is nonexcludable and perfectly indivisible between firms, then the input is purely public. Public inputs may enter two or more firms' production functions (e.g., industry-specific knowledge or research findings), or they may enter two or more production functions with respect to different industries or products (e.g., highways used for a number of different products). The latter situation may give rise to economies of scope and may justify a firm or an organization providing multiple products.

The existence of public inputs is quite prevalent in the real world and is behind a host of collective action problems. Scientific findings, for example, are not final consumption goods, but intermediate inputs used to produce final commodities. Similarly, an arsenal, held by an alliance or a nation, is an intermediate input that produces security, which is a final consumption good. These final goods may themselves be private or public. Thus, a rich set of possibilities exists. Infrastructure may be used to yield output for firms, in which the final commodity (i.e., the firms' outputs) is private between the users of the public input.

Many possible models can be constructed. I present a simple representation. Suppose that a single primary factor, labor, is utilized by n firms to produce a private consumption good, q. The ith firm produces q^i according to the following well-behaved, twice-continuously differentiable production function.

$$q^i = f_i(L_i, r), \quad i = 1, \ldots, n , \tag{4.24}$$

where L_i is the labor used by firm i and r is a public intermediate good. The production function is increasing in both inputs and, moreover, is assumed to be strictly concave. The public input is itself produced by labor under constant returns to scale:

$$r = f_r(L_r) . \tag{4.25}$$

In equation 4.25, production of r is positively related to the input of labor (L_r), and the average productivity of labor (r/L_r) equals the marginal productivity

---

10. Public inputs are examined by de Gorter and Zilberman 1990; Groves and Loeb 1975; Henderson 1974; Hillman 1978; Kaizuku 1965; Kohli 1985; Manning, Markusen, and McMillan 1985; Martin, Zacharias, and Lange 1990; McMillan 1979b; Mohring 1970; Negishi 1973; Sandmo 1972, 1973.

(df_r/dL_r) due to constant returns to scale. The model is completed by the labor distribution constraint,

$$L = \sum_{i=1}^{n} L_i + L_r , \tag{4.26}$$

which indicates that the fixed supply of labor, L, is allocated between the production of the private consumption good and the production of the public input. In the former case, production processes (one for each firm) may draw labor. Although r enters each firm's production function, a single production process is relevant, since, once produced, r is utilized by all n firms due to the publicness assumption.

The Pareto-optimal requirement for efficient input supply is derived by maximizing any firm's output subject to the constancy of the other $n - 1$ firms' outputs and to the labor distribution constraint. In the appendix to this chapter, I derive the Pareto-optimal condition:

$$\sum_{i=1}^{n} \frac{(\partial f_i/\partial r)}{(\partial f_i/\partial L_i)} = \frac{1}{df_r/dL_r} , \tag{4.27}$$

which states that the *sum* of the ratios of marginal productivities between the public input and the primary input *equals* the reciprocal of the marginal productivity of labor in producing the public input. In equation 4.27, the left-hand side depicts the marginal benefits derived by the entire industry from an additional unit of the public input, while the right-hand side denotes the marginal costs, in terms of additional labor, associated with an additional unit of the public input. Since the industry consists of n firms, the marginal benefits must be aggregated over the entire industry. These marginal benefits correspond to the marginal productivities of r, normalized by the marginal productivity of L_i in producing good q^i. As such, equation 4.27 is reminiscent of the Samuelsonian sum of MRSs = MRT condition.

The analysis can be complicated in many ways. First, the input, r, may be public both within and between industries. This complication by itself would show up as a change in the summation indices, so that all affected firms' marginal productivity ratios are included. A double summation over firms within an industry and over industries may be required. Second, the number of public inputs may be increased beyond one. This extension would require a set of conditions like equation 4.27, one for each public input (Manning, Markusen, and McMillan 1985, 235). Third, additional primary inputs could be included. In this case, each pair of primary inputs would require their ratio of marginal products to equal the input price ratio for all firms using both inputs. Fourth, congestion may characterize the public input, so that the utilization of the input reduces its level. This can be modeled by making r depend on primary inputs and some measure of public input utilization. When congestion is present, group size becomes an important variable to be determined along with input allocation. Toll arrangements for users of the public input can "internalize" or adjust for crowding costs through user charges. In other words, a club arrangement can be instituted. Fifth, the public input may be used to produce a public consumption good. Publicness would then involve firms at the input stage and consumers at the output stage. Market failures may consequently be double tiered.

Financing the public input may prove especially problematic. We first examine financing possibilities for a single pure public input case as modeled above. Following McMillan (1979b) and Sandmo (1972), I sketch a tax-based scheme under the best possible scenario, in which each firm pays a Lindahl-type tax price based on its derived marginal productivity from the public input. The ith firm would attempt to maximize profits, π_i:

$$\pi_i = p_i f_i(L_i, r) - wL_i - t_i \,, \tag{4.28}$$

where t_i is its tax share and p_i is the price of the private consumption output. If the public input industry is assumed to have zero profit wherein tax revenue just covers expenditures, we have

$$\sum_{i=1}^{n} t_i = wL_r \,, \tag{4.29}$$

in which w is the wage rate for labor. With constant returns characterizing $f_r(\bullet)$, the proper per-unit tax price is

$$t_i^*/r^* = p_i(\partial f_i/\partial r), \quad i = 1, \ldots, n \,. \tag{4.30}$$

In equation 4.30, the ith firm pays a per-unit public input tax price equal to its marginal value product associated with the public input. As shown in the appendix to this chapter, this tax price meets the efficiency condition in equation 4.27.

Although a marginal productivity pricing scheme is a theoretical possibility, it is unlikely to be feasible in large industries unless a central authority can compute the public input's marginal productivities for each of the firms. The profit function in equation 4.28 can be rewritten as

$$\pi_i = \pi_i \left(L_i, t_i, t_i + \sum_{j \neq i} t_j \right) \tag{4.31}$$

with the use of equation 4.29 (see McMillan 1979b, 89). The Nash equilibrium choice of t_i, associated with maximizing profits, would achieve the following set of equations:

$$\frac{\partial f_i / \partial r}{\partial f_i / \partial L_i} = \frac{1}{df_r / dL_r}, \quad i = 1, \ldots, n, \tag{4.32}$$

in which each firm ignores the benefits that its tax contribution to the public input confers on others (see equation 4.27). In consequence, too little of the public input is provided—a standard collective action result.

There are, however, some reasons to be more hopeful with respect to public inputs in contrast to public goods. Public inputs may, at times, involve a small number of firms. In such cases, mergers may occur due to scale economies and/or scope economies resulting from the public input. If, say, three firms are affected by a public input, then a three-way merger motivates the conglomerate firm to account for all relevant marginal productivities associated with resources allocated to input r when making allocation decisions.

Since firms in a public input situation must interact repeatedly, a repeated game scenario is particularly relevant (McMillan 1979b, 91–97). If the game's end point is uncertain and/or if the player's time-horizon is infinitely long, then a cooperative solution may be an appropriate Nash equilibrium, provided that the discount rate is not too high.

In essence, the public input problem is a generalization of the commons problem. For the latter, a fixed (often nature-determined) input is public to a set of exploiters, who do not have to pay for the input's use. Moreover, the fixed input is subject to congestion that reduces the input's productivity. In the more general case considered here, the public input need not be fixed and may be augmented through production. For public inputs, crowding may, but need not, occur. If the number of firms is sufficiently small and/or interactions are repeated indefinitely, cooperation may evolve for public inputs, as in the commons. The analogy with the commons is important, because of the wide range of institutional structures that have developed to manage the latter (see, especially, Ostrom 1990). Many of these institutional arrangements could work for public inputs.

An important institutional solution, short of merger, is contracting between firms. If firms face repeated interactions among one another with respect to a public input, a contract by "convention" may result, in which each firm adheres to cooperative behavior (see Hardin 1982 for an excellent analysis of contract by convention). Such conventions are feasible when either the game structure does not have a dominant (single-shot) defection strategy or else a cooperative Nash equilibrium exists in the repeated game framework. For public inputs, resolution by contract is most likely when the number of firms is small. If, however, a central authority representing the firms' interests (e.g., a producer association) comes into existence, contracting is possible even in a large-number scenario. An interesting real-world example is generic advertising in industries characterized by numerous firms. Generic advertising is a public input because it increases the profit of all firms in the industry and is itself produced by primary factors.[11] The beef-, pork-, milk-, and orange-producing industries engage in generic advertising to increase sales and profits of member firms. In these four cases, a producer association taxes its firms to finance the advertising campaign. Obviously, it is in no single firm's interest to engage in its own advertising campaign due to product homogeneity and its small share of any likely gain.

The technology of supply can come into play in at least two different ways—through the production function for the private consumption good, $f_i(\bullet)$, and through the production function for the public input, $f_r(\bullet)$. Henderson (1974), Manning, Markusen, and McMillan (1985), and Martin, Zacharias, and Lange (1990) have analyzed the importance of the form of $f_i(\bullet)$. To illustrate some important technologies, we now assume that each q^i is produced with a vector of m primary inputs, denoted by $\mathbf{x}^i = (x^i_1, \ldots, x^i_m)$, and a single public input so that

$$q^i = f_i(\mathbf{x}^i, r) . \tag{4.33}$$

An important form for equation 4.33 is

$$q^i = g(r)\tilde{f}_i(\mathbf{x}^i) , \tag{4.34}$$

where $f_i(\bullet)$ is multiplicatively separable in the two inputs and $f_i(\bullet)$ and $\tilde{f}_i(\bullet)$ are assumed linearly homogeneous in only the primary inputs. Thus, a doubling of the components of $\mathbf{x}^i$ doubles output for a fixed level of the public input. Increasing returns to scale are present because doubling all inputs (including the public input) would consequently more than double output.

The production technology in equation 4.34 leads to a financing problem when a Lindahl-pricing scheme is utilized, because insufficient revenues are collected. Problems of self-financing are always associated with increasing returns to scale because marginal cost–based financing, such as Lindahl pricing, does not collect enough due to the marginal cost being less than average

---

11. For competitive industries, see the recent treatment in Stegeman 1991.

cost. In fact, returns to scale occur when the ratio of marginal costs to average costs is less than one. This problem can be circumvented in a second-best manner by adding a full-financing constraint requiring the sum of tax revenues to cover the resource costs of the public input. The resulting tax scheme is called Ramsey pricing and is dependent on output shares of the firms and elasticity of supply considerations.

Another possible form for equation 4.33 is

$$q^i = f_i[k_1(x_1^i, r), \ldots, k_m(x_m^i, r)] , \qquad (4.35)$$

in which the public input augments the factor productivity of each primary input so that $\partial k_j / \partial r > 0$ but $\partial k_j / \partial r \neq \partial k_s / \partial r$ so that the augmentation need not be neutral or equivalent between inputs, as in equation 4.34. Obviously, many different scenarios are possible and each can have different implications for self-financing and incentives for collective action.

4.15 Concluding Remarks

This chapter has indicated the rich array of applications associated with the theory of collective action. Each of the subsections could, itself, be expanded into a chapter in its own right, since each application has a significant body of literature with many related topics of interest. My intent has been to introduce the reader to the large number of applications available. Numerous other applications, not considered, exist, including the control of pollution, the pursuit of scientific discovery, the adoption of advanced technologies, and the modification of weather. Hence, the applications here are merely representative. Further applications are considered in chapters 5 and 6, where empirical studies and modern-day contingencies are investigated.

APPENDIX

4.A.1 Derivation of Optimality Condition 4.27

The Lagrangian is

$$\mathcal{L} = f_1[L_1, f_r(L_r)] + \sum_{j \neq i}^{n} \lambda_j \{f_j[L_j, f_r(L_r)] - \bar{q}_j\}$$
$$+ \sigma \left(L - \sum_{i=1}^{n} L_i - L_r \right) , \qquad (1)$$

where $\bar{q}_j$ is the fixed level for the jth firm's output of the private consumption good. Maximizing equation 1 with respect to L_1, L_j, and L_r gives the following FOCs.

$$L_1: f_{11} - \sigma = 0 , \tag{2}$$

$$L_j: \lambda_j f_{jj} - \sigma = 0 , \tag{3}$$

$$L_r: f_{1r}(df_r/dL_r) + \sum_{j \neq 1} \lambda_j f_{jr}(df_r/dL_r) - \sigma = 0 , \tag{4}$$

where $f_{11} = \partial f_1/\partial L_1$, $f_{1r} = \partial f_1/\partial r$, $f_{jj} = \partial f_j/\partial L_j$, and $f_{jr} = \partial f_j/\partial r$. First we use equations 2 and 3 to express σ in terms of f_{11} and $\lambda_j f_{jj}$. Second, both sides of equation 4 are divided by σ and df_r/dL_r to yield

$$f_{1r}/\sigma + \sum_{j \neq 1} \lambda_j f_{jr}/\sigma = 1/(df_r/dL_r) . \tag{5}$$

Using the expressions for σ, derived with equations 2 and 3, in equation 5, we immediately transform equation 5 into equation 4.27.

4.A.2 Full Financing of the Efficiency Condition

We next intend to show that

$$t_i^*/r^* = p_i(\partial f_i/\partial r) , \tag{6}$$

for $i = 1, \ldots , n$ implies equation 4.27. We first sum both sides of equation 6 over the firms to yield

$$\sum_{i=1}^{n} t_i^*/r^* = \sum_{i=1}^{n} p_i(\partial f_i/\partial r) . \tag{7}$$

If labor is used efficiently in producing q^i, then

$$w = p_i f_{ii}, \quad i = 1, \ldots , n , \tag{8}$$

which follows from a maximization of profits in equation 4.28 with respect to L_i while treating r and t_i as parameters. Rewriting equation 8 as $p_i = w/f_{ii}$ and substituting for p_i in equation 7, we get

$$\Sigma t_i^*/(wr) = \Sigma f_{ir}/f_{ii} , \tag{9}$$

where indices of summation are suppressed. By the zero-profit condition of equation 4.29, equation 9 becomes

$$L_r/r = \Sigma f_{ir}/f_{ii} , \tag{10}$$

which is equation 4.27 since $L_r/r = (df_r/dL_r)^{-1}$ by constant returns.

CHAPTER 5

Empirical Developments

This chapter extends the study of applications a step further by reviewing econometric procedures that lend themselves to direct and indirect tests of the three themes and recent theoretical developments. Some issues (e.g., neutrality, the influence of institutional structures, and the exploitation hypothesis) are directly testable, others (e.g., suboptimality) are indirectly testable, and still others (e.g., the influence of group size on the likelihood of being privileged) are not testable. The intention here is to motivate and display test procedures, rather than to present actual tests. In many places, I refer the reader to the literature in which actual tests have been performed for military alliances,[1] agricultural research collectives,[2] and local jurisdictions.[3] Since my intent is to give the reader a general overview and intuitive understanding of relevant empirical exercises, I limit (where possible) the discussion of theoretical or econometric details. The interested reader should consult the literature for further details. Although the discussion is in terms of a generic collective good, the analysis applies to a wide range of examples, including police protection, health care, fire suppression, education, health services, research findings, defense provision, pollution removal, and parks.

Since the publication of *Logic,* much of the empirical investigation of collective action has focused on the estimation of the demand for collective or public goods. At the outset, a distinction must be drawn between the demand for a private good and the demand for a collective good. A demand function for a private good is derived from a framework whereby an individual maximizes utility subject to a linear budget constraint. The derived demand relationship depends on the individual's income, prices, and taste characteristics. Individual demands are aggregated, at each price, to yield a market demand curve. In the case of collective goods, a utility maximization framework is again used, but the nature of the agent may change because individuals, states, organizations, or nations may be the relevant demander. Most important, the exogenous parameters of the problem follow from the

1. See, e.g., Olson and Zeckhauser 1966; Smith 1981; Murdoch and Sandler 1984; Sandler and Murdoch 1990; Gonzales and Mehay 1991.

2. See, e.g., Khanna, Huffman, and Sandler 1990; Khanna 1991.

3. See, e.g., Borcherding and Deacon 1972; Bergstrom and Goodman 1973; Deacon 1978; Denzau and Grier 1984; Inman 1978; Pommerehne 1978.

budget constraint and the collective action interaction. The latter interaction shows up as a *spillover* or *spillin*, which refers to the amount of the collective good received from the actions of the other agents. In consequence, the contributions of others to the good appear in the demand function for public goods.

At least two procedures have been used to derive and test for the demand for collective goods. The first is the oligarchy approach, in which a decision maker (or group of decision makers) chooses the level of the collective good in an attempt to promote or maximize the well-being of his or her (or their) constituency. This approach implicitly identifies the decision maker's utility or welfare function as reflecting the interests of those whom he or she represents, and is most appropriate for a representative democracy (Pommerehne 1978). When the oligarchy maximizes its utility, the constituency's utility is also assumed to be maximized. The oligarchy approach is no different in practice from an individual choosing his or her private contribution (subscription) to a public good. Both the oligarchy model and the individual subscriptions model imply the same essential arguments in the demand function. Of course, the nature of such variables as income or price will depend on the *identity* of the optimizer—for example, a governmental oligarchy's income is the tax revenue collected, while an individual's income is his or her earnings. The nature of the exogenous variable hinges on who is doing the maximizing.

A second paradigm is the median voter model where the demand for the collective good is that of the median voter (identified by median income). In a direct democracy, the median voter's choice is decisive when issues are unidimensional, an odd number of votes are cast, and a pairwise majority-rule comparison of issues is made (Mueller 1989, 66–67, 189–93). Issues are unidimensional when all of the alternatives can be measured along a single spectrum—for example, the level of expenditure.

The remainder of the chapter consists of five sections. In section 5.1, a procedure is devised for distinguishing between pure public good and joint product models. This procedure also provides a test for the neutrality theorem. Section 5.2 presents a method for determining the allocative process of a collective. In particular, Nash behavior is empirically distinguished from cooperative Lindahl behavior. In doing so, the underlying game structure is identified. A procedure for differentiating between the median voter and oligarchy models is discussed in section 5.3. The need for additional tests is indicated in section 5.4, and concluding remarks are contained in section 5.5.

5.1 Procedure 1: Testing Pure Public Good Versus Joint Product Models

The nature of the agent must always be specified before deriving a demand function for a collective good. If agents are individuals, then a private provision model for the collective action, as presented in chapters 2 and 3, is appropriate. If, however, the agents are nations, then the decision maker within each agent must be identified. For illustrative purposes, we assume that nations are the agents that must determine how much to contribute to the provision of a collective good. Military alliances and pollution pacts are apt examples. The allocation of funds to agricultural research by states within the United States is another example. For each agent, an oligarchy (e.g., an elected leader and his or her chosen advisors, a state legislative committee) makes the decision. Decision-making oligarchies are, consequently, viewed as deciding collective good contributions assuming Nash behavior, whereby each oligarchy responds optimally to the best response of the other nation's oligarchies.

5.1.1 Pure Public Good Model

The first model assumes the existence of a pure private good, y, and a pure public good, Q, which provides benefits to n agents, each of whom contributes q^i units of the pure public good. As shown in chapter 2, the Nash subscriptions model depicts each agent as choosing the private and public good expenditures to maximize utility subject to a budget constraint and to the prevailing public good contributions of the other agents,

$$\tilde{Q}^i = \sum_{j \neq i} q^j \ .$$

The agent therefore maximizes

$$U^i = U^i(y^i, Q^i) \ , \tag{5.1}$$

subject to the level of $\tilde{Q}^i$ and to his or her budget or resource constraint,

$$p_y y^i + p q^i = I^i \ , \tag{5.2}$$

where p_y is the price of the private good, p is the price of the public good, and I is the agent's utility. In equation 5.1, the public good equals the agent's own provision of the public good plus that of the other agents; that is $Q^i = q^i + \tilde{Q}^i$. If, say, the agent is a government, then income might be tax receipts and y denotes publicly provided private goods. When the value of spillins, $p\tilde{Q}^i$, is added to both sides of the budget constraint, the ith agent's subscriptions problem becomes

$$\underset{y^i,\, Q^i}{\text{maximize}} \ \{U^i(y^i, Q^i) \mid p_y y^i + p Q^i = I^i + p\tilde{Q}^i\} \ , \tag{5.3}$$

in which each agent views himself or herself as choosing the total public good provision level subject to a budget constraint that incorporates the value of spillins (Bergstrom, Blume, and Varian 1986). Equation 5.3 is set notation for indicating that the ith agent maximizes his or her utility subject to the spillin-augmented budget constraint. The problem depicted in equation 5.3 is called a "full-income approach" since both income and the value of spillins (i.e., $p\bar{Q}^i$) are included in the agent's endowments or earnings.

In equation 5.3, I implicitly assume that $Q^i > \bar{Q}^i$ so that each agent makes a net positive contribution to the public good. Using standard procedures,[4] the problem in equation 5.3 can be transformed to imply the following demand functions:

$$y^i = y^i(F^i, p_y, p) , \tag{5.4}$$

and

$$Q^i = Q^i(F^i, p_y, p) , \tag{5.5}$$

for each agent, where F^i denotes full income,[5] $I^i + p\bar{Q}^i$. A Nash equilibrium is obtained when each agent desires an allocation (y^e, Q^e) such that equations 5.4 and 5.5 are simultaneously satisfied, *and $Q^e = Q^i$* for each i. The appearance of full income in the demand functions for the pure public good is indicative of the neutrality theorem. This follows because an increase in money income has the same influence as an equal increase in the value of spillins. Furthermore, the full income term sets collective good demand apart from private good demand, where spillovers have no role to play when there are no collective goods being purchased. Equation 5.5 implies that offsetting changes in income and the value of spillins, as is the case for interior solutions to the pure public good subscriptions model, would leave an agent's demand for the total amount of the public good unchanged. Only the sum $I^i + p\bar{Q}^i$ matters.

Equation 5.5 represents a system of demand equations with an equation for each agent. To estimate equaton 5.5 for a set of agents, an equilibrium must be assumed in which the left-hand side term is equal for all agents. The

---

4. Standard procedures require deriving the FOCs of eq. 5.3. These conditions are both necessary and sufficient if the utility function is quasi-concave. If the associated bordered Hessian determinant is further restricted to be strictly positive, then the implicit function theorem would allow these FOCs to be solved implicitly for y^i and Q^i, as in eqs. 5.4 and 5.5.

5. Full income appears in the demand function for the private good due to the interdependence of the private good and pure public good demand vis-à-vis the budget constraint. If only private goods were being purchased, money income, I^i, not full income, would appear in the private good demand function.

interaction between the agents means that an estimation of the system in equation 5.5 must account for simultaneity (Sandler and Murdoch 1990). This issue is addressed further when demand functions are compared.

5.1.2 Joint Product Model

In the case of joint products (see secs. 2.5 and 3.6), each unit of the collective good, q, provides a private output, x, and a pure public output, z. The agent's joint product relationships are

$$x^i = f_i(q^i) , \tag{5.6}$$

and

$$z^i = g_i(q^i) , \tag{5.7}$$

where the technology functions are strictly increasing and concave. In total, each agent consumes

$$Z = z^i + \tilde{Z}^i \tag{5.8}$$

of the derived public output in which

$$\tilde{Z}^i = \sum_{j \neq i} z^j .$$

The ith agent's utility function is

$$U^i = U^i(y^i, x^i, z^i + \tilde{Z}^i) , \tag{5.9}$$

and his or her budget constraint is

$$p_y y^i + pq^i = I^i , \tag{5.10}$$

where p is the unit price of the collective input. In the appendix to this chapter, I demonstrate how this problem implies demand functions for the collective good of the following form:

$$Q^i = Q^i(F^i, p_y, p, \tilde{Q}^i), \quad i = 1, \ldots, n . \tag{5.11}$$

A Nash equilibrium is achieved when each of the agents desires an allocation such that equation 5.11 is satisfied, and $Q^e = Q^i$ for all i. If the collective good is an input that produces both a pure public and private output, an agent's equilibrium demand is a function of its full income, the price of the collective good, the price of the private good, and the exogenously determined spillins. An agent's demand for the collective good is affected in two ways by an increase in the other agents' spending on the collective good: indirectly through full income (since spillins are part of full income) and directly through spillins. Because of this latter influence, a change in spillins influences the *mix* between private and pure public outputs as no private benefits are gained from $\tilde{Q}^i$. The appearance of $\tilde{Q}^i$ in system 5.11 implies that the neutrality theorem does not extend to joint products; a redistribution of income can affect the Nash equilibrium choice for the aggregate level of the collective good, since $\tilde{Q}^i$ is affected. Offsetting changes in the sum $I^i + p\tilde{Q}^i$ would no longer leave the demand for the collective activity unchanged.

5.1.3 A Nested Test Procedure

A comparison of equations 5.5 and 5.11 indicates that these equation systems differ by the appearance of an additional $\tilde{Q}^i$ term in equation 5.11. Suppose that a log-linear specification is utilized to express equations 5.5 and 5.11 for testing purposes. Under these circumstances, the following estimating equation system can be used to test equations 5.5 and 5.11.

$$\ln Q^i = \beta_{i0} + \beta_{i1}\ln F^i + \beta_{i2}\ln \tilde{Q}^i + \beta_{i3}\ln p + \epsilon_i, \qquad (5.12)$$

$$i = 1, \ldots, n,$$

where the β_{ij}'s are unknown parameters, p denotes the relative prices, and the ϵ_i's are error terms. In equation 5.12, the Nash pure public good model can be obtained by setting $\beta_{i2} = 0$; hence, the significance level of β_{i2} provides a nested test for distinguishing between the pure public good and the joint product model.[6]

A number of remarks regarding the regression equations implied by equation 5.12 are in order. First, with time-series data, the error terms may be correlated between periods. If this is the case, then an autocorrelation parameter must be estimated and used to correct the estimations. Second, full income and spillins are likely to be correlated with the error term, since spillins constitute part of full income so that a simultaneity problem occurs. To properly identify the equation, the researcher must use a two-stage least squares procedure in which the exogenous variables are employed as instrumental vari-

---

6. When two equations differ by one additional independent variable—e.g., $y = f(x)$ and $y = g(x, z)$—a nested test can be performed by examining the significance level of the z-coefficient. If it is insignificant, $y = f(x)$ applies; otherwise, $y = g(x, z)$ applies.

ables (Sandler and Murdoch 1990). In equation 5.12, full income and spillins must first be estimated in terms of the set of exogenous variables—the constant terms, the prices, and the set of income variables (the I^i's). These estimated variables are then used to identify ln Q on the second stage of the procedure. Third, representations other than log linear can be used to express equation 5.12. For instance, linear and nonlinear representations may be appropriate; alternative forms can be judged by statistical criteria.

The most important feature of equation 5.12 is that it provides a simple procedure for discriminating between pure public and joint product models. In doing so, the appropriateness of the neutrality assumption is ascertained as an important by-product. A comparison between the two models also provides some indirect and circumstantial evidence for the exploitation hypothesis and suboptimality. If joint products are known to be present, then the theory implies that the private joint products provide incentives for agents to contribute to the collective good. In consequence, free riding and suboptimality should be curtailed in comparison to a pure public good scenario. Moreover, contributions are tied more closely to benefits received and, hence, need not imply exploitation of the large by the small. A suggested test of this hypothesis is offered in section 5.1.4.

5.1.4 A Review of Recent Tests

When tested with real-world data, two studies have provided overwhelming support for the joint product model over the pure public good model. Using time-series data for the 1956–87 period, Sandler and Murdoch (1990) examined a system of equations similar to equation 5.12 for ten NATO allies. The Nash joint product specification outperformed the pure public model for all sample allies. In another test of the two models, Khanna, Huffman, and Sandler (1990) investigated contributions to agricultural research in all forty-eight contiguous states of the United States during 1951–85. States were partitioned into six geoclimatic regions. Thus, multiple collective action groups were identified. For the majority of the states, the β_{i2} coefficient was significantly different from zero at the 5 percent significance level, thereby implying that the joint product model was the preferred representation of the demand for agricultural research. Private agricultural research benefits were judged to be playing a crucial role.

In the charity literature, neutrality has been indirectly tested by determining the influence of alternative contribution sources on the agents' demand for the public good.[7] If neutrality applies, then each dollar of tax-financed government expenditure would crowd out a dollar of private contributions—a -1

---

7. See, e.g., Weisbrod and Dominguez 1986; Posnett and Sandler 1989.

coefficient would characterize government contributions on the right-hand side of the agent's demand for contributions. These studies did not find evidence of complete crowding out and neutrality. In fact, the relevant coefficient was not near -1 (when negative) and, in some instances, was positive. Cross-sectional data were used in these tests. Other researchers found similar results.

In a seminal paper, Olson and Zeckhauser (1966) utilized distribution-free inferential or nonparametric methods to study the exploitation hypothesis for the NATO alliance in the mid-1960s. In particular, they used a Spearman rank correlation test in which each ally's gross domestic product (GDP) is rank ordered and then compared with the ally's rank order in terms of defense burdens. A positive and significant test statistic indicates that the large allies' defense shares are positively correlated with their economic sizes. Olson and Zeckhauser did uncover a positive and significant correlation, thus supporting the exploitation hypothesis. In a subsequent study, Sandler and Forbes (1980) applied nonparametric tests to a sample of NATO allies for the 1960–75 period and found that a positive and significant correlation between defense burdens (as measured by the ratio of defense expenditures to GDP) and GDP only characterized the alliance until 1966. Thereafter, the correlation was positive and insignificant, thus suggesting the absence of exploitation. A Kendall rank correlation test was used by Sandler and Forbes (1980). Moreover, other variables (e.g., exposed borders, per-capita GDP) were held constant in some of the tests. Based on these results, Sandler and Forbes argued that private, ally-specific benefits were more important for NATO after the mid-1960s. Nonparametric statistics are easy to apply and could be fruitfully used to examine burden-sharing behavior for a wide range of international organizations that provide collective goods.

5.2 Procedure 2: Distinguishing the Allocative Process

In an important contribution, McGuire and Groth (1985) formulated an econometric technique for testing between two allocative processes (i.e., Nash and Lindahl behavior) for a group that provides itself with a pure public good. Thus, the underlying game structure in a public good setting no longer has to be assumed, since reduced-form equations could be derived for various underlying games and then tested against one another.[8] In some tests, a specific utility function is needed to identify the competing models; in other tests, a general utility function is sufficient, as in section 5.1. When specific utility functions are used, typical forms are those of Cobb-Douglas and Stone-

---

8. A reduced-form equation expresses a dependent endogenous variable solely in terms of exogenous variables.

Geary.[9] Subsequent work by Sandler and Murdoch (1990) extended the McGuire-Groth framework to include joint products with private and pure public outputs. Moreover, Sandler and Murdoch (1990) operationalized the McGuire-Groth procedure by deriving reduced-form equation systems that can be compared with nonnested tests.

The purpose here is to discuss the test for distinguishing between Lindahl and Nash behavior when agents contribute to a collective activity yielding joint products. I focus on joint products because the test results cited previously provide strong support for the joint product model.

5.2.1 Lindahl Model

The Lindahl model corresponds to the outcome of a coordination game, in which agents are confronted with tax shares, t^i, and must choose their optimizing level of the collective activity. The tax shares indicate each agent's share of the cost of the collective activity and, as such, these shares must sum to one so that the activity is fully financed. A Lindahl equilibrium is reached when a set of tax shares is determined that is associated with the *same* optimizing level of the collective activity for the set of agents. That is, each agent calls out the same optimizing Q^i when a set of tax shares is assigned. At a disequilibrium, tax shares are raised for the high demanders and lowered for the low demanders. A Lindahl equilibrium is analogous to a competitive equilibrium inasmuch as the former abides by two fundamental welfare theorems: (1) every Lindahl equilibrium is Pareto optimal; and (2) any Pareto-optimal allocation may be sustained as a Lindahl equilibrium if preferences are convex (Cornes and Sandler 1986, 101). These two theorems have important normative implications. If the underlying allocation process for a collective action is statistically judged to abide by Lindahl behavior, then the equilibrium is not suboptimal, regardless of the number of participants.

For joint products, the ith agent's budget constraint is

$$p_y y^i + t^i p Q^i = I^i , \qquad (5.13)$$

where Q^i is the ith agent's choice of the collective good level and t^i is the agent's tax share. If, say, $t^i = 0.5$, then the individual pays 50 percent of the costs of the collective activity. As before, the collective good yields a private

---

9. For the pure public good model, a Stone-Geary utility function is

$$U^i = (Q^i - \phi^i)^\alpha (y^i - \theta^i)^\beta ,$$

where α and β are constant exponentials, and ϕ^i and θ^i are subsistence requirements for the public good and the private good, respectively.

and a public output. As shown in the appendix to this chapter, the demand functions for the collective good are

$$Q^i = Q^i(I^i, p_y, t^ip), \quad i = 1, \ldots, n.$$ (5.14)

A Lindahl equilibrium is obtained when there exists a set of tax shares such that the satisfaction of equation 5.14 corresponds to an identical choice level for the public good for each agent—$Q_L^e = Q_L^i = Q_L^i(I^i, p_y, t^ip)$ for each i, in which tax shares sum to one. The L subscript denotes Lindahl. As in the case of Nash behavior, equation 5.14 represents a system of demand equations. In log-linear form, equation 5.14 becomes

$$\ln Q^i = \gamma_{i0} + \gamma_{i1}\ln I^i + \gamma_{i2}\ln t^ip + \epsilon_i^L,$$ (5.15)

in which the γ_i's are unknown parameters, ϵ_i^L is an error term, and t^ip is the agent's share of the collective good's price. The p_y term has been normalized to have a value of one. In equation 5.15, the tax share or share term is correlated with the error term because Q^i is mathematically related to this tax share. Hence, the application of ordinary least squares to each equation is apt to lead to biased and inconsistent estimates of the unknown parameters. A two-stage least squares procedure is appropriate: the shares are first estimated in terms of a set of instruments that includes the constants and the set of incomes for the agents. In a time-series exercise, autocorrelation may have to be corrected.

5.2.2 Distinguishing between Models

To devise a test for discriminating between Nash and Lindahl behavior, we first compare equations 5.11 and 5.14, which represent the demand functions for the two allocation processes in a general functional form. These two sets of equations have the same left-hand side variable, Q^i, but contain different right-hand side variables, with the exception of p_y, which is typically normalized to have a value of one. Neither allocation specification can be nested within the other, since zero coefficients on either equation 5.11 or 5.14 would not give the other allocation process. This can be seen by comparing equations 5.12 and 5.15, the statistical representations for the general functional forms in log-linear terms. Thus, we employ a nonnested test methodology.[10]

---

10. Nonnested tests often require the equations to be compared to have the same dependent variables but different sets of independent variables that need not nest—e.g., $y = f(x)$ and $y = g(p, z)$.

An appropriate methodology for comparing estimates of equations 5.12 and 5.15 is a "*J*-test" as proposed by MacKinnon, White, and Davidson (1983). This test can be used when some of the independent variables are correlated with the error term, as is the case for both the Nash and Lindahl demand systems. The *J*-test requires both systems of equations to have the same dependent variables and the same set of instruments, and both conditions are fulfilled here (see Sandler and Murdoch 1990 for further details of the *J*-test).

The methodology of the *J*-test is straightforward. First, the estimates of equations 5.12 and 5.15 are employed to predict the values of $\ln Q$, assuming an equilibrium is realized. Second, we form a joint model, in which the Nash specification in equation 5.12 and the Lindahl *estimate*, $\hat{Q}_L$, of Q_L (using eq. 5.15) are combined in a linear fashion. Moreover, the Lindahl specification and the Nash *estimate* $\hat{Q}_N$, of Q_N using equation 5.12 are combined in a linear fashion. The parameters of the joint models are then estimated with two-stage least squares. The significance of the newly estimated parameters on $\hat{Q}_L$ and $\hat{Q}_N$ allows us to infer whether the Nash or Lindahl specification is adequate. If, for example, the coefficient on $\hat{Q}_L$ is insignificantly different from zero in the estimation of the first combined model, then the Nash model is appropriate. Four outcomes are possible: reject both models, reject Lindahl in favor of Nash, reject Nash in favor of Lindahl, or reject neither model. In the first and fourth cases, the tests are unable to distinguish between models.

A number of remarks are germane. First, the tests may be inconclusive, especially when both models are rejected. When this is the case, some as-of-yet unspecified model or underlying game structure is relevant. Second, the *J*-test appears likely to reject models, since only two of the many possible allocative processes are being tested. If both models are rejected, then other paradigms need to be judged. A more powerful test that can distinguish models along a continuum of model types is desirable. Third, an acceptance of the Lindahl (Nash) model over the Nash (Lindahl) model implies that the group has (has not) achieved Pareto optimality.

5.2.3 A Review of Recent Tests

The *J*-test methodology for discriminating between Lindahl and Nash equilibria was employed by Sandler and Murdoch (1990) on a sample of ten NATO allies for the 1956–87 period. Nonnested hypothesis tests supported the Nash specification for five of the smaller allies in the sample. Lindahl behavior was rejected for the entire sample. Hence, many of the large allies (i.e., the United States, the United Kingdom, France, West Germany, and Canada) did not appear to abide by either Nash or Lindahl behavior. A clear asymmetry of behavior based on wealth is apparent and may suggest examining a model such as leader-follower, with the small allies as followers. Clearly, some other allocative process is driving the large allies. Moreover, no evidence of Pareto optimality was found by this indirect test.

Khanna (1991) also used a J-test to discriminate between Nash and Lindahl behavior for geoclimatic groupings of U.S. states contributing to the collective good of agricultural research. Unlike other studies, Khanna (1991) distinguished between voluntary (state-level) contributions and nonvoluntary (federal-level) contributions. Khanna also used a price variable, unlike Sandler and Murdoch (1990). Her tests found support for the Nash behavior in just over half of the forty-eight sample states. Support for just the Lindahl model was only uncovered for two states. Four large states (i.e., Maryland, New Jersey, New York, and Texas) appeared to satisfy both models. The remainder of the forty-eight states displayed behavior that did not fit either model, thus suggesting an as-of-yet unspecified model.

Further work is required to identify these unspecified models. The non-nested test presented here is based on the attainment of equilibrium. If disequilibrium characterizes the allocation process, then the equilibrium test would be inadequate. To date, the tests for collective action have assumed a static framework; clearly, tests in a more dynamic setting are needed.

5.3 Procedure 3: A Test for Distinguishing Between Institutional Structures

Much of the work on the demand for collective goods has taken an approach based on the median voter theorem.[11] This theorem indicates that if an odd number of people cast their votes on a unidimensional issue, then the ideal choice of the median voter wins out with pairwise majority comparisons, in which two issues are compared sequentially until all alternatives have been considered. An issue is *unidimensional* if its basic characteristics can be measured along a single continuum. For example, the level of expenditures on defense is unidimensional, since spending levels can be measured from zero to some maximum (budget-constrained) amount. When voters must determine both expenditures and the composition of expenditures (e.g., deterrent versus conventional weaponry), more than one dimension is relevant and the issue is not unidimensional. Voters' preferences are assumed to be single peaked for the median voter theorem. Preferences are *single peaked* when there is an ideal point along a given dimension, and satisfaction declines on either side of this ideal point as distance increases (see Mueller 1989, 66–67, 189–93).

When the conditions of the median voter theorem are satisfied, the me-

---

11. See, for example, Borcherding and Deacon 1972; Bergstrom and Goodman 1973; Inman 1978; Denzau and Grier 1984; Pommerehne and Frey 1976.

dian voter's ideal choice beats everything else in a pairwise comparison, since $n/2 + 1$ voters prefer the median choice to any proposal to its right or left along the continuum. Thus, a winning majority chooses the median choice; a Condorcet winner exists and is the median proposal.[12]

If alienation occurs with distance and if voters whose ideal proposals are far from the median become sufficiently disenchanted that they do not vote, then the outcome is pulled toward the mode, not the median, for unimodal distributions. In most instances, the mode and median are sufficiently near one another that distinguishing between them does not make much difference. With multidimensional issues, a median in every direction may exist when circular indifference curves are used to characterize tastes. In such a case, the median voter theorem can be generalized.

When the median voter theorem applies, the demand for a collective good, such as defense, can be ascertained by estimating the median voter's (identified by median income) demand for the collective good.[13] In an interesting and important paper, Pommerehne (1978) argued that testing the median voter model against alternative paradigms can provide an empirical test of institutional form. If, for example, two political jurisdictions differ by governmental form (i.e., direct democracy versus representative democracy), then the median voter model should best characterize the direct democracy while the oligarchy model should best characterize the representative democracy. Moreover, the existence of referenda should limit the power of government bureaucracy and cause outcomes to be more in keeping with the median voter model (Pommerehne 1978, 270). The voting rule—plurality, simple majority, or two-thirds majority—may also have an effect on the outcome. A plurality voting rule may, for example, displace the outcome far from the median.

A statistical test is now presented for determining whether the median voter model, the decision-making oligarchy model, or neither best describes the demand for a collective good.[14] In the past, estimations for the median voter model have been compared with those for alternative models by merely presenting both results and judging the best on ad hoc grounds. Unless alternative models can be compared with a nested or nonnested hypothesis test, the performance of competing explanations of the collective action process cannot be assessed on rigorous statistical criteria. For this purpose, statistical tests are needed.

---

12. A Condorcet winner is an issue that beats all others in pairwise, majority rule comparisons.

13. On identifying the median voter with the median income holder, see Bergstrom and Goodman 1973; Inman 1978.

14. This work largely draws on Murdoch, Sandler, and Hansen 1991. The interested reader should consult that paper for details.

5.3.1 The Median Voter Model

Building on the work of Bergstrom and Goodman (1973), Borcherding and Deacon (1972), and, especially, Dudley and Montmarquette (1981), I first present a joint product, median voter model for an n-agent collective. In essence, the utility maximization problem of the median voter determines the group's level of the collective activity, q. The utility function of the median voter is

$$U = U(y, x, Z) ,\tag{5.16}$$

where superscripts are suppressed, y is the private numéraire, x is the private joint product, and Z is the aggregate amount of the pure public joint product. The joint product relationships are:

$$x = f(q) ,\tag{5.17}$$

and

$$z = g(q), \tilde{Z} = h(\tilde{Q}) .\tag{5.18}$$

If the pure public benefit is not perfectly substitutable, then the aggregate level of Z for the median voter is

$$Z = q + \Gamma \tilde{Q} ,\tag{5.19}$$

in which Γ is a nonnegative constant representing a weighting factor for spillins.[15]

The median voter chooses the level of the collective activity to

$$\underset{y, q}{\text{maximize}} \ \{U[y, f(q), q + \Gamma\tilde{Q}]|p_y y + \tau p q = I\} ,\tag{5.20}$$

in which τ is the tax share to the median voter and I is his or her income. From equation 5.20, the median voter's demand for the collective activity is [16]

$$q = q(I, \tau p, p_y, \Gamma\tilde{Q}) .\tag{5.21}$$

---

15. In eq. 5.19, $g(\bullet) = q$ and $h(\tilde{Q}) = \Gamma\tilde{Q}$. Other forms for these functions are also possible.

16. This follows from the FOCs of eq. 5.20 and an application of the implicit function theorem.

In equation 5.21, τp is the median voter's per-unit cost of the collective good and $\Gamma \tilde{Q}$ is the effective level of spillins, adjusted for spatial or other impurity considerations. If the collective good is normal, then the median voter's demand for q responds positively to income. Moreover, the demand for q should respond negatively to an increased tax share, since it acts like a price increase. A larger pool of taxpayers would increase q due to reduced tax shares. The reaction of q to changes in "effective" spillins depends on the consumption relationship of the jointly produced outputs and on income effects.

In practice, the median voter is difficult to identify. The common procedure is to use median income as a method for locating the median voter. If voters have the same tastes but different endowments, and if, moreover, the collective good is normal and varies positively with income, then the median income recipient will demand the median quantity of the collective good. When cross-sectional comparisons are made, a proportionality requirement on the distribution of voters across jurisdictions is required to ensure that median income and the median voter are related.[17] In numerous studies, mean income is used as a proxy for median income. This substitution is appropriate for time-series analysis provided that the mean and median incomes are highly correlated over time. This is *likely* to be the case. For cross-sectional studies, the use of mean income as a proxy is apt to lead to bias, since skewness in the distributions of income between different communities can cause the mean and the median to differ from one another. Pommerehne's 1978 cross-sectional study of Swiss municipalities demonstrated that the use of median, rather than mean, income improved the estimations. The identification of the tax share term is also fraught with difficulties. Often the reciprocal of the population, $1/N$, is used as a proxy.

5.3.2. Distinguishing Median Voter Models from Oligarchy Models

To devise the sought-after test, I must present a slightly different oligarchy model. In particular, I do not employ a full income approach so that the oligarchy's demand for its own subscription to the collective activity, q, is presented. This modification ensures that both models have identical left-hand side variables, which is needed for the comparison. The oligarchy now solves the following problem:

$$\text{maximize } \{U(y, q, \Gamma\tilde{Q})|p_y y + pq = I^0\} , \qquad (5.22)$$
$$y, q$$

---

17. See Bergstrom and Goodman 1973; Inman 1978.

where superscripts are suppressed and I^0 is the income of the oligarchy.[18] The associated demand function is

$$q = q(I^0, p, p_y, \Gamma\bar{Q}) . \tag{5.23}$$

In comparing equations 5.21 and 5.23, the identity of the decision maker responsible for the public sector allocation is seen to determine the manner in which income and other variables enter the demand function. The income variables in equations 5.21 and 5.23 are quite different. Other forms for the demand function would apply if the behavior of unelected bureaucrats were highlighted. To devise a test to discriminate between the median voter and oligarchy models, I invoke some additional assumptions by normalizing prices and setting $\Gamma = 1$.

Suppose that nations in a collective (say, a military alliance) share a collective good. The following econometric specification

$$q_{it} = \beta_{i0} + \beta_{i1}\text{TAU}_{it} + \beta_{i2}(\text{GDP}_{it}/L_{it}^{\lambda i}) + \beta_{i3}\text{SPILL}_{it} + \epsilon_{it} \tag{5.24}$$

can be used to represent both equations 5.21 and 5.23 under certain restrictions specified below (Murdoch, Sandler, and Hansen 1991). In equation 5.24, TAU is the tax share, GDP is gross domestic product, L is the number of employed people, SPILL is the level of spillins, and ϵ is an error term. The i subscript indicates the nation, and the t denotes the time period (relevant for time-series analysis). There are five unknown parameters to estimate: the β_{ij}'s and λ_i. If autocorrelation is corrected in a time-series analysis, then the autocorrelation coefficient would be a sixth parameter.

If $\lambda_i = 1$, then equation 5.24 would represent the median voter model with GDP/L as a proxy for median income;[19] if, however, $\lambda_i = \beta_{i1} = 0$, then equation 5.24 would denote the oligarchy model. Thus, alternative null hypotheses can be specified and tested with a standard nesting procedure. When both null hypotheses are rejected, an unspecified model applies. The importance of this exercise is to demonstrate that, with some ingenuity, the researcher can utilize the data to ascertain the appropriateness of different in-

---

18. By the joint product relationships of eqs. 5.6 through 5.7, the utility function $U = U(y, x, Z)$ becomes

$$U = U[y, f(q), g(q) + h(\bar{Q})] ,$$

from which utility is a function of y, q, and $\bar{Q}$ as in eqs. 5.22. The budget constraint is that of the oligarchy. If $g(\bullet)$ is the identity map and $h(\bullet)$ is $\Gamma\bar{Q}$, then eq. 5.22 follows.

19. Murdoch, Sandler, and Hansen (1991) showed that this mean approximation was highly correlated *over time* with median income for two sample nations where consistent median data were available.

stitutional behavior assumptions. Hence, the researcher does not have to fit the data to a single collective action paradigm. By engineering nested tests, alternative models can be evaluated with statistical criteria.

5.3.3 A Review of Recent Tests

Murdoch, Sandler, and Hansen (1991) applied this test to a sample of NATO allies using annual data from 1965–88. Equation 5.24 was estimated using a two-stage least squares approach, corrected for autocorrelation. Based on this test, Belgium, the United Kingdom, and the Netherlands appeared to abide by the median voter model, while France, West Germany, Italy, and the United States seemed to satisfy the oligarchy model. Neither model appeared appropriate for Denmark, Canada, and Norway.

Unlike the Murdoch, Sandler, and Hansen (1991) study, most tests of the median voter model have used cross-sectional data for local public goods such as police protection, parks, education, and fire suppression (see the references in n. 11). These tests have not considered alternative specifications, and many different estimating equations have been used. Most assume a constant elasticity of demand function and have a form similar to

$$\ln Q = \ln k + \alpha \ln y + (\alpha\beta + 1)\ln N + \beta \ln \tau + \epsilon , \qquad (5.25)$$

which is log linear. In equation 5.25, $\ln k$ is a constant, y is median income, N is population, τ is the tax share, and α and β are unknown parameters. This form is derived in the appendix to this chapter.

Tests of variants of equation 5.25 have estimated the income elasticity of the collective good to be positive and significant. This result is consistent with the normal good assumption. Moreover, the tax share elasticity is typically negative, as expected. Population is often a positive influence on collective good demand due to cost sharing. The only parameter whose estimate has posed problems is the crowding parameter, since its estimated value is often outside the unit interval. In some studies, a variant of equation 5.25 is derived by using a Stone-Geary utility function and a simultaneous equation approach to deal with the identification problem (see Dudley and Montmarquette 1981; McGuire, 1982).

5.4 Future Test Procedures

There are a number of alternative tests that should be devised to discriminate between different collective action scenarios. In the case of a military alliance, participants tend to be asymmetric with a dominant ally, such as the United States in the NATO alliance or the USSR in the now-defunct Warsaw

Pact. This asymmetry may be best captured with a leader-follower model, in which the dominant ally is the leader and the smaller allies are collectively the follower. The reduced-form demand functions would have to be derived from a leader-follower theoretical model, as presented in chapters 2 and 3. Thus, the leader would optimize with respect to the follower's Nash reaction path, and the follower would take the leader's response as given. In such a model, the follower's demand function would be like that of the Nash oligarchy model, whereas the leader's demand function would be dependent on the follower's anticipated response to the leader's expenditure. A specific utility function (e.g., Stone-Geary) might be required to distinguish the demand functions in a leader-follower model from those in the standard oligarchy model.

Another worthwhile test would allow different types of non-Nash behavior to be identified. What is needed is a statistical means for estimating the conjectural variations parameter along a continuum. With such a test, a zero value for the parameter is consistent with Nash-Cournot behavior. In its simplest form, the conjectural variation parameter could be estimated as a constant, thus implying a linear relationship between spillins and an agent's contribution. More complex relationships could be permitted and tested.

In a recent paper, McGuire (1990) derived a host of reduced-form demand equations to account for the mix of private and public aspects of a collective good. In particular, McGuire has used a Stone-Geary utility function to derive an econometric specification of Nash-Cournot and Lindahl behavior when spillins are partial—that is, γ is less than one. McGuire also examined partial spillins on the cost side that arise when participants have varying degrees of efficiency in providing the collective good. This surfaces as different price ratios for the agents. These impurity aspects are important because they can alter neutrality, suboptimality, and asymmetry.

Future empirical work must also consider intertemporal and dynamic aspects of the collective action problem. Thus far, much of the empirical work has been concerned with tests of equilibrium allocations. Disequilibrium is apt to characterize collectives and would pose difficult econometric problems. In earlier work on the NATO alliance,[20] the spillin variable performed well when it was lagged by one period and seemingly unrelated regression estimations were applied. Spillins had to be lagged in order to identify the equation. Although this lag structure is inconsistent with an equilibrium allocation,[21] the estimation performed better than some of the two-stage least squares estimations reported in subsequent studies. This suggests that a dynamic structure may be behind ally behavior. If such a dynamic structure could be

---

20. See, e.g., Murdoch and Sandler 1982 and 1984; Hansen, Murdoch and Sandler 1990.

21. In an equilibrium, the value of the dependent variable is unchanged from period to period. A lag structure implies a convergence to equilibrium.

identified, then the alliance model could be combined with an arms race model, thereby allowing interactions both within and between opposing alliances to be taken into account. The use of an intertemporal structure is also appropriate for a host of collective action problems, especially those concerning the environment, because acts in earlier periods influence the present and future. If collective action problems are long lived (e.g., the storage of nuclear wastes), a dynamic structure is needed.

Empirical methods must also be formulated to distinguish between diverse technologies of public supply. Throughout this book, the technology of public supply has been shown to be a crucial ingredient. For example, a test needs to be developed to ascertain whether a summation, best-shot, weakest-link, or other technology could have generated the expenditure data for a collective good. Within the class of summation technologies, such a test would identify the degree of substitutability or publicness along the lines being developed by McGuire (1990).

5.5 Concluding Remarks

To date, there have been numerous empirical analyses of the collective action problem. In this chapter, I have been selective in my presentation of the literature so as to concentrate on tests concerning some of the themes and developments presented in earlier chapters. In consequence, we have examined tests for discriminating between pure public goods and joint products, for identifying the underlying allocation process, and for distinguishing median voter from oligarchy behavior. Each of these tests can be further refined and extended to include more alternatives. Tests are still rather crude, because only two types of behavior are considered at a time. Hence, test results may indicate that an undetermined model underlies the estimations. If tests can identify a parameter value along a continuum, and if this parameter relates to a continuum of models (as in the case of the conjectural variations parameter), then a wide range of alternatives can be considered at the same time. For such a test in the case of non-Nash behavior, rich normative implications involving suboptimality would follow because the larger the negative conjecture is in absolute value, the greater the departure of provision levels from a Pareto-optimal ideal.

I have followed a basic philosophy in approaching the empirical analysis of collective action; that is, econometric models should have a clear antecedent theoretical paradigm. As such, the modeler must derive his or her econometric specification from an explicit theoretical framework. Examples that have followed this philosophy include Borcherding and Deacon 1972; Bergstrom and Goodman 1973; Inman 1978; Dudley and Montmarquette 1981; McGuire 1982; and Sandler and Murdoch 1990. In other cases, the antecedent model is not always easy to identify explicitly (see, e.g., Oneal and Elrod 1989; Palmer 1990). With agents adequately identified and an explicit theoretical paradigm specified, the independent variables (e.g., population, GDP, spillins) follow from the model. Changing the agents alters the constraints and tastes, and, with them, different variables become relevant. My philosophy is opposed to studies that add and subtract independent variables to manufacture the best statistical fit without caring whether any theoretical model exists that could produce the reduced-form equations.

Another important empirical paradigm for collective action is the experimental approach. I have not discussed specific experimental papers in this chapter, since this was done in chapters 2 and 3. The experimental paradigm has much to offer. First, it allows the researcher to examine hypothetical situations in a controlled environment. Data generated in the real world may have many intervening factors that cannot be sanitized or controlled. Second, experiments give researchers the latitude to vary the technology of supply and other aspects of the collective action problem in an identifiable manner. In empirical studies, changes in the technology of supply may be indistinguishable from other considerations when the reduced-form equations are the same. For example, the reduced-form equations for Lindahl behavior are identical for pure public goods and joint products (Sandler and Murdoch 1990) unless a specific utility function is used. Third, the experimental setting permits the researcher to generate data rapidly, rather than wait years for time-series data to be accumulated. Fourth, experimental data can be collected and coded in a consistent framework. In the case of cross-sectional and time-series data, the definition of variables and their coding may change from jurisdiction (nation) to jurisdiction (nation) and over time as coders and conventions are altered. Fifth, a wide range of scenarios can be manufactured in an experimental situation.

APPENDIX

5.A.1 Derivation of Joint Product Demand Equations

The level of spillins, $\tilde{Z}^i$, to agent i is assumed to be

$$\tilde{Z}^i = h(\tilde{Q}^i) , \tag{1}$$

where $\tilde{Q}^i = \sum_{j \neq i} q^j$. This function is monotonically increasing and strictly concave. By the joint product relationships in equations 5.6 and 5.7, and by equations 1 and 5.8, the utility function in equation 5.9 becomes

$$U^i = U^i[\,y^i, f_i(q^i),\ g_i(q^i) + h(\tilde{Q}^i)]\ , \tag{2}$$

in terms of the two purchased activities (y^i and q^i) and spillins. Since $q^i = Q^i - \tilde{Q}^i$, equation 2 can be rewritten in terms of its basic arguments as

$$U^i = U^i(y^i, Q^i, \tilde{Q}^i)\ . \tag{3}$$

If $p\tilde{Q}^i$ is added to both sides of the budget constraint in equation 5.10, then the agent faces the following "full income" problem:

$$\underset{y^i,\ Q^i}{\text{maximize}}\ \{U(y^i, Q^i, \tilde{Q}^i)|p_y y^i + pQ^i = I^i + p\tilde{Q}^i\}\ . \tag{4}$$

If the bordered Hessian is positive definite, then the associated FOCs imply, via the implicit function theorem, the demand functions in equation 5.11, since the exogenous variables are F^i, p_y, p, and $\tilde{Q}^i$.

5.A.2 Derivation of Lindahl Joint Product Demand Equations

The ith agent's utility function is

$$U^i = U^i(y^i, x^i, Z)\ , \tag{5}$$

where

$$Z = z^i + \tilde{Z}^i\ , \tag{6}$$

due to the pure publicness of this joint project. The joint product relationships are now

$$x^i = r_i(Q)\ , \tag{7}$$

and

$$Z = s(Q)\ , \tag{8}$$

where the *total level* of the collective activity, Q, produces both the private and public outputs experienced by each agent. The i index on r allows the private output relationships to be personalized. Since Lindahl behavior implies a cooperative game, the overall (equilibrating) level of the collective activity is important. Individuals do make personalized voluntary subscriptions, but are assigned individualized tax shares based on the aggregate provision level. Substituting equations 6 through 8 into equation 5 and then utilizing the budget constraint,

$$p_y y^i + t^i pQ = I^i \,, \tag{9}$$

yields the following optimization problem:

$$\underset{y^i,\, Q}{\text{maximize}} \; \{U^i(y^i, Q)|p_y y^i + t^i pQ = I^i\} \,. \tag{10}$$

For a nonzero bordered Hessian, the FOCs of equation 10 imply, via the implicit function theorem, the following Lindahl demand functions:

$$Q = Q(I^i, p_y, t^i p) \,, \quad i = 1, \ldots, n \,. \tag{11}$$

5.A.3 Derivation of Equation 5.25 for the Median Voter Model

The perceived or effective level of the collective good is

$$X = Q/N^\alpha \,, \tag{12}$$

where $0 \le \alpha \le 1$ denotes a crowding parameter, and Q is the amount of the collective good provided. If $\alpha = 0$, the good is purely public; if, however, $\alpha = 1$, the good is purely private. The constant elasticity demand function is

$$X = k y^\alpha t^\beta \,, \tag{13}$$

in which k is a constant, and t is the tax price of the collective good,

$$t = \tau p N^\alpha \,. \tag{14}$$

In equation 14, p is the per-unit price of the collective good, and τ is population. Substituting equations 12 and 14 into equation 13 gives

$$Q = k y^\alpha (\tau p N^\alpha)^\beta N^\alpha \,. \tag{15}$$

If $p = 1$ and logs are taken of both sides of equation 15, then equation 5.25 follows.

CHAPTER 6

Further Applications

In chapter 4, a host of traditional economic problems were analyzed with the principles of collective action that were developed in earlier chapters. This chapter concerns collective action issues that are more recent and, in some instances, more speculative in nature. A number of these problems are global, and may, in some instances, have profound effects on the future of human settlements and well-being. For each example, an identification of the participants' net benefits and their relationship to the pattern of payoffs in the collective assists in predicting the likely outcome of collective action. These payoff patterns can transcend considerations of group size when determining the likelihood of collective action. For example, both ozone depletion and global warming affect the entire global community; however, collective action on a global scale has been achieved for ozone depletion but not for global warming. The factors responsible for whether a group is privileged is behind these outcomes.

The remainder of the chapter contains five sections. Section 6.1 presents three problems of the global collective: (1) ozone depletion, (2) global warming, and (3) acid rain. Each implies vastly different patterns of payoffs for the community of nations and for current and future generations. In section 6.2, I examine the burden-sharing pledges and payoffs associated with Operation Desert Storm, which involved a military alliance of unprecedented size (including more than thirty nations) to free Kuwait from Iraqi occupying forces. Section 6.3 investigates some Star Wars scenarios. Section 6.4 studies the theory of revolutions, and concluding remarks are contained in section 6.5.

6.1 Global Collective Action: Three Cases

6.1.1 Space Invaders: Three Parables

At the risk of oversimplifying, I present three parables or imaginary stories in which a virus from outer space attacks the earth. Although none of the three space invader scenarios corresponds exactly to the three global problems presented subsequently, each scenario shares the more crucial features of these global contingencies.

In scenario 1, the space invader strikes all nations simultaneously and puts each earthling at equal risk. The viral invader poses a health risk to both current and future generations. The effects of the virus are irreversible; hence, inactivity means that once the virus gains a foothold there is no way to return to less-contaminated states. Collective action is required to forestall the further advance of the disease. Moreover, there is little or no uncertainty about the harmfulness of the attacker. To curb the spread of the disease, nations must act in concert, and arresting the disease depends on cumulative worldwide efforts; a summation technology of public supply applies. Finally, each nation's *current* generation reaps a benefit from its own nation's effort that exceeds the associated cost, regardless of the level of efforts elsewhere. From the current generation's viewpoint in each nation, the group is fully privileged because its net benefits from action are positive. The virus's irreversibility will spur immediate action. Since each nation faces equal per-person risks, all are likely to contribute to fighting the disease. If, moreover, all nations must act to remove fully the threat (so that an Assurance game applies with each nation in a pivotal role), then no nation will free ride. The first scenario is similar to the ozone depletion problem, where international agreements have been struck.

Scenario 2 involves a virus that strikes all nations, but to widely differing degrees. Some nations actually benefit from the infection, while others suffer. In many cases, there is uncertainty regarding those that will benefit and suffer. The disease advances slowly and its signs take years of observation to spot; hence, much of the perceived benefits of immediate action may be experienced by future generations, while the costs of the action must be borne by the present generation in each nation. For all practical purposes, the disease is irreversible. A weighted summation technology of public supply applies, so that some nations' efforts are more important than others. If, furthermore, the nations with the greatest impact or weight are those with the greatest costs from acting, then crucial contributors may not believe that there are sufficient gains from collective action. This problem is further complicated because much of the perceived gain is experienced by a future generation that is not able to contract with the current generation that decides the action. Moreover, the presence of uncertainty may motivate some nations to take a wait-and-see stance. Scenario 2 is similar to the global warming problem, which has, thus far, shown little international consensus and collective action.

From a collective action viewpoint, scenario 3 is the most troublesome. The space virus now disperses over the earth, and not all nations are infected. Those nations hosting the virus can take evasive actions to make it airborne and transfer it to some downwind neighbor, thereby removing the threat to its own population. Moreover, the harm is experienced by current and future generations. There is again uncertainty about the manner in which the virus causes harm. Knowledge concerning causation is further compounded, since the earth also produces an identical virus that is dispersed by the wind. Collective action is powerless against this naturally created production and dispersement. Finally, there is uncertainty about the irreversibility of the problem. Since the infection from the space virus is localized, no global action is likely. Furthermore, host nations are expected to transfer the virus to their neighbors, provided that the costs of doing so are cheaper than suffering the infection. The presence of the virus in the natural environment means that the transferring nation can engage others in debate over the source of the infection. Moreover, the uncertainty concerning the process of the disease adds to the debate and inactivity. Scenario 3 is similar to the acid rain problem. Any consummated international agreement is predicted to be bilateral or else among a few countries. In these instances, the downwind nations must possess some bargaining strength (e.g., the existence of a second externality with a reverse flow or mutually beneficial trade arrangements) over the generating nation to force it to cease its actions.

6.1.2 Ozone Depletion

In 1985, the British Antarctic Survey presented evidence that an alarming 40 percent drop in the springtime atmospheric concentration of ozone (O_3) took place over Halley Bay, Antarctica, between 1977 and 1984 (Stolarski 1988, 30). This so-called hole in the ozone layer of the stratosphere then drifts northward during the summer and mixes with other air masses, thus causing the depletion to be shared worldwide on a more or less equal basis. This unexpected 1985 finding supported earlier concerns that the production and release of chlorofluorocarbons (CFCs), used in air conditioners, refrigerators, aerosols, insulating foams, and the cleansing of circuit boards, may have had ozone-depleting effects far worse than at first thought possible. Despite the small concentrations of ozone in the earth's atmosphere, representing less than one part per million, ozone absorbs much of the ultraviolet radiation of the sun and, thus, shields humans and other organisms from the harmful effects of such radiation. An increase in ultraviolet radiation can enhance the risk of skin cancers to humans and slow the growth of phytoplankton at the base of the marine food chain.[1] Although the United States banned the use of CFCs in aerosols in 1978, the recent holes or low concentrations of ozone over the South Pole seemed to indicate that more far-reaching, global bans are needed.

There is little doubt concerning the harm to mankind if the earth's protec-

---

1. See Stolarski 1988 and Toon and Turco 1991 for an in-depth analysis of the ozone depletion problem. Further references can be found at the end of these articles. Much of my description of ozone depletion is drawn from these articles.

tive shield of ozone is depleted or diminished. The harmful effects of ultra-violet radiation are well documented and would be experienced by current and future generations alike. Less is known about the manner in which ozone is depleted and why holes have appeared in polar regions. After much specula-tion, a picture is beginning to emerge with CFCs as the culprit. At first, scientists thought that CFCs may not be a threat because once released into the atmosphere, sunlight breaks down the CFCs into chlorine, which reacts with ozone to form chlorine monoxide. This latter substance combines with nitro-gen dioxide and methane to form stable reservoirs of chlorine nitrate and hydrochloric acid (Toon and Turco 1991). In the stratosphere, neither of these reservoirs poses much of a problem. Throughout this conversion process, ozone depletion is small.

In recent years, scientists have shown that stratospheric nacreous and nitric acid trihydrate clouds, when cooled in the polar winter, trigger a reac-tion that causes the stable reservoirs of chlorine to release molecular chlorine. The resulting chlorine along with ozone are subsequently broken up by sun-light and, in the process, combine to form chlorine monoxide and oxygen.[2] During the chemical process, ozone is destroyed. Stable reservoirs do not form under these conditions, inasmuch as the nitrogen compound (needed for the reservoirs) precipitates due to stratospheric cloud formation. The frigid conditions are ideal for this ozone destruction. Since the South Pole is colder than the North, ozone holes are more of a problem in the south.

Ozone depletion has many of the features of the first space invader scenario. Since a uniform mixing of the stratosphere occurs within a few years, the potential risks imposed by ozone depletion are the same to each earthling, regardless of residency. Hence, worldwide concern is present. Moreover, risks are experienced by current and future generations because CFCs can survive from fifty to one hundred years, once released into the stratosphere. There is little uncertainty that ozone depletion causes harm, and the process of depletion is beginning to be understood. Since the ozone shield has taken a long time to develop, mankind could not expect to reverse a depletion quickly; hence, the problem is, in essence, irreversible.

Although the benefits from curbing the ozone depletion process and eventually eliminating it are spread worldwide, the costs of doing so are concentrated in the developed countries that are the primary producers and users of CFCs. Since environmental protection tends to have a high income elasticity (so that demand grows with wealth), the producers and users of CFCs are the very countries that place the greatest value on environmental preservation and reduced health risks. The income elasticity aspects can help overcome the skewed distribution of costs as substitutes for CFCs are devel-

---

2. See Toon and Turco 1991.

oped. Another factor that motivates developed nations to act is the *intra-national* distribution of the costs of banning CFCs. Since the earnings derived from CFCs affect a relatively small subset of industries, the overwhelming number of people in these nations favor the phasing out of CFCs once the health risks are understood. In summary, a fully privileged group is apt to characterize the global collective with respect to banning CFCs. Developing nations stand to gain from the action with little or no costs, while developed nations experience sizable costs but even greater benefits.

In 1990, a global collective agreed to phase out CFCs by 2000. This strong action followed the more modest 1987 Montreal Protocol on Substances that initially required a 50 percent reduction from 1986 CFC levels by 2000. The subsequent, more-stringent agreement came after scientific monitoring demonstrated that ozone depletion was occurring at an alarming pace. With chlorine reservoirs remaining for up to one hundred years, the depletion problem will worsen before it gets better, despite the phased-in ban. Nevertheless, the 1990 agreement indicates that a significant global threat can be met with collective action when the distribution of costs and benefits favors such action. The large number of concerned nations coupled with the relatively small number of nations needing to take significant actions assisted the passage of the agreement. The availability of substitute substances for CFCs also supported the global ban.

6.1.3 Global Warming

In recent years, the news media have given much attention to the problem of global warming that stems from a greenhouse effect as trapped gases in the earth's atmosphere let sunlight through but absorb and trap infrared radiation or radiant heat, thus raising the earth's mean temperature. Gases with this property include CFCs, methane (CH_4), nitrous oxide (N_2O) and carbon dioxide. The bulk of the atmosphere is, however, made up of oxygen and nitrogen, which do not act as greenhouse gases (GHGs). Unabated accumulation of GHGs can raise the mean temperature by as much as 2 to 5°C during the next century; estimates differ widely and thus add to the uncertainty.[3] Although carbon dioxide is the most-often mentioned GHG, the trace gases of methane and CFCs are more efficient absorbers of heat. Methane, for example, absorbs twenty-one times as much heat as an equal amount of carbon dioxide; hence, any comprehensive policy to curb global warming would have to examine the buildup of all GHGs. Evidence gathered by the National

---

3. On global warming, see Schneider 1989; Nordhaus 1991; Morrisette and Plantinga 1991; Morgenstern 1991; Houghton and Woodwell 1989; White 1990. Also see Repetto 1990 on deforestation.

Aeronautics and Space Administration's Goddard Institute of Space Studies suggests that the mean global temperature has risen by between 0.5° to 0.7°C since 1860.[4] Other estimates are between 0.3° and 0.8°C.[5] All estimates indicate a range consistent with the *lower* end of the computer simulation. This fact should be kept in mind when interpreting dire forecasts based on the upper end of these simulations. From 1880, scientists have ascertained that carbon dioxide, trapped in the earth's atmosphere, has increased by approximately 20 percent from 1880 to 1989.[6] Much recent concern can be traced to the finding that six of the warmest years on record include 1980, 1981, 1983, 1986, 1987, and 1988, with the most recent year being the warmest ever recorded. In interpreting this result, we must caution that many years of observations are required before concluding that recent years represent an important trend. Given the documented rise in atmospheric carbon dioxide and the more than doubling of methane (White 1990, 40), global warming is obviously a global collective action problem worthy of concern and analysis.

Can an international agreement along the lines of those for CFCs be expected? Is collective action likely—that is, is a privileged collective possible? What is current policy? These are the questions answered below. The global warming problem is most similar to the second space invader scenario and is unlikely, barring significant developments, to be met with much in the way of collective action. To explain why this is the case, we must first look closer at the underlying causes of global warming.

Unlike the ozone depletion process, global warming derives from a wide array of economic activities that includes the production of electricity by coal-fired power plants, the use of automobiles (carbon monoxide), the application of fertilizer (nitrous oxide), the manufacture of products, deforestation, and the decay of plants and animals (methane). I first focus on carbon dioxide, which is produced by both nature and mankind. In terms of nature, carbon dioxide is emitted by soil and plant respiration and is absorbed by plant photosynthesis; a net gain of zero atmospheric carbon dioxide is predicted by these exchanges. The oceans are also a source and sink or reservoir for carbon dioxide. Here the net gain is expected to be negative: physico-chemical diffusion emits about 100 billion metric tons per year and absorbs approximately 104 billion metric tons. Thus, the oceans can make room for additional carbon dioxide. The burning of fossil fuels adds about 5 billion metric tons per year, while deforestation may add 2–3 billion metric tons per year.[7] If these estimates are correct (and they are only rough), then atmospheric carbon dioxide emissions are increasing at about 3–5 billion metric tons per year. This figure

4. Houghton and Woodwell 1989.
5. See White 1990.
6. White 1990, 37.
7. The facts in this paragraph come from Houghton and Woodwell 1989, 38.

does not account for accelerating deforestation and other carbon dioxide emitting activities. The largest reservoirs of carbon dioxide are in the oceans, fossil fuel reserves, soil, and vegetation, in decreasing order of importance. Other GHGs have to be considered along with carbon dioxide if a full investigation of global warming is to be undertaken (Morgenstern 1991, 142). Global warming is also dependent on acid rain due to deforestation's role in producing methane and carbon dioxide, and on ozone depletion owing to CFCs' property as an efficient GHG. Hence, the interrelationship of these global collective problems would ideally have to be recognized in any general equilibrium treatment, thus complicating the analysis. These general equilibrium concerns are not addressed here, except in passing. The banning of CFCs by 2000 will, for example, mitigate global warming, especially since they are such efficient absorbers of heat radiation.

Global warming poses at least two problems. First, it is expected to alter climate and rainfall distribution, which can significantly influence food production. Some wet places may become semiarid, while some semiarid areas may become the world's bread baskets. There will be both gainers and losers. Even the temperature rise is not uniformly distributed: higher latitudes will experience most of the change. These effects are still highly speculative—some models, for example, predict a decrease in rainfall for the central farmbelt states of the United States and an increase for northern plains states (e.g., Minnesota) and Canada. Second, ocean levels are predicted to rise as polar ice melts, which will put coastal settlements in jeopardy. In consequence, infrastructure will have to accommodate the rising seas and populations will have to be relocated. The impact of global warming is very uncertain, and this reduces the incentives of nations to act and to form collective action groups. For example, nations do not want to invest heavily in emission-reducing technologies if dire forecasts later turn out to be overstated.

Table 6.1 presents two snapshots in time that indicate which regions

TABLE 6.1. Proportion of Worldwide Carbon Dioxide Emissions (in percentages)

Region/Countries	1950	1980
North America	45	27
USSR and Eastern Europe	18	24
Western Europe	23	17
Developing countries	6	12
Japan and Australia	3	6
Asia	1	9
Other	4	6

Source: White 1990, 41.
Note: Columns may not total 100 percent due to rounding.

contribute to the production of carbon dioxide. There are a number of note-worthy features shown in this table. First, the pattern has changed dramatically between 1950 and 1980. The contribution of North America and Western Europe fell from 68 percent to 44 percent of the total. Asia showed the largest percentage increase, followed by developing countries, Japan and Australia, and the USSR and Eastern Europe. This changing pattern indicates that the developing world is rapidly becoming a greater source of GHGs. Second, table 6.1 shows that North America, Western Europe, and the USSR and Eastern Europe are all important players. Third, the communist nations accounted for almost a quarter of all carbon dioxide emissions in 1980. Fourth, the table underestimates the true contributions of the developing countries, since the effects of deforestation are not included and most tropical forests facing destruction are located in these nations.

Like the second space invader scenario, the global warming problem effects nations differently. Nations with sizable population centers at or slightly above sea level face severe consequences, as do nations with potential rainfall shortages. Moreover, curbing GHG emissions will have vastly different economic effects on countries. If, for instance, developing countries curtail their deforestation programs, then this may cost them dearly in terms of short-term earnings.[8] Countries that burn massive quantities of fossil fuels for energy, such as the United States, confront significant costs from reducing carbon dioxide emissions. The same is true for the USSR and Eastern Europe. For these latter nations, the problem is especially acute because the switchover to a market economy is, in the short run, causing impovishment that limits their ability to deal with environmental concerns, which tend to be a luxury good. These countries are interested in a rapid transformation and are unwilling to put development programs on hold for the sake of limiting worldwide global warming.

Given this unequal pattern of costs and benefits from reducing global warming, it is easy to predict a partition of nations into four camps: activists, cautious, nations unable to act, and nations opposed to actions (Morrisette and Plantinga 1991). Nations facing great damage costs and small abatement costs from curtailing the emission of GHGs are activists. These nations would meet the sufficient conditions of being privileged. Australia is, for example, an activist because, with all but one of its major cities on the coast (Canberra), a rise in the sea level can spell disaster for much of its population and infrastructure. Few countries have such a large proportion of their population living on the coast. Nations that rely on nuclear energy and alternative fuels (e.g., Germany, France, Sweden) are also activists, since abatement costs are not so great.

---

8. Long-term earnings may, however, be enhanced. Hence, it is not clear that curtailing deforestation has such a high opportunity cost.

Cautious nations include the United States, which would experience significant abatement costs if carbon dioxide emissions were cut by 50 percent. Nordhaus (1991) calculated different levels of abatement costs and damage costs from meeting various levels of GHG emissions. His calculations indicate that much of the U.S. population is unaffected by even a $3°C$ increase in mean temperature. These calculations, however, ignore the loss of land value and other considerations associated with rising sea levels (Morgenstern 1991, 141). Even with these adjustments and additions, net discounted benefits for the United States from curtailing emissions of carbon dioxide do not appear, at this time, to justify the kinds of expenditure and investment really needed to make much impact on the problem. Thus, the United States remains cautious and is unwilling to agree to such bans or severe limits on GHGs as those approved for CFCs. Unlike the latter, carbon dioxide and other GHGs affect a wide range of economic activities, thus raising abatement costs.

Some nations appear unable to act either because of limited resources or a desire to push forward with economic development. Since many of these countries are poor, the income elasticity associated with environment preservation is likely to be low, thus keeping perceived damage costs (and action) low. The Eastern European countries and Russia fall into this category, as do many of the developing nations. Third world nations do not want others to tell them how to manage their natural resources; hence, they are opposed to agreements and conventions that limit their disposal of tropical forests. Although the collective to limit global warming is privileged due to the activists, little effective action is anticipated because, as shown in table 6.1, the bulk of the global warming problem is from emissions generated in the three inactive groups of nations. Furthermore, the emission of GHGs in this inactive set is growing over time, which serves to limit further the effectiveness of the activists.

Two additional aspects inhibit the possibility of an effective global collective to curb global warming. First, uncertainty about the distribution of costs and benefits from global warming encourages nations to hold off until more is known. Often, abatement costs are certain, but benefits are uncertain; hence, the latter must be discounted. Second, since much of the harm is imposed on future generations that are not represented, agreements are likely to ignore this harm.

This application highlights the important role played by heterogeneity when examining the feasibility and shape of a collective. If the dominant players are those with the most to gain from the collective action, then the action is feasible; otherwise, it is not. For the time being, collective action does not look promising for global warming. If, however, it does take place, then it will assume one of two forms: (1) the issuing of emission permits, or (2) the imposing of a tax on emissions. In the first system, emission rights or permits would be issued to countries so as to achieve some maximum allowable pollution level. If these permits can be traded, then they will be exchanged so that those who value them the most will purchase them. In the second system, taxes are imposed so as to internalize the externality. Costs imposed on both present and subsequent generations would have to be included in the calculation. Tax revenues can be used to mitigate the effects of global warming. Both control arrangements require an international authority to monitor and enforce the permits or taxes. The appendix to this chapter presents a model of stock externalities, analogous to the global warming problem, and derives an optimal time path for a tax instrument.

6.1.4 Acid Rain

A third collective action problem of global proportions is that of acid rain. The problem was first recognized in Europe and North America in the 1960s when decreasing pH levels (acidity) were measured in precipitation. The process leading to acid rain takes place in the part of the lower atmosphere known as the troposphere. Ozone in the troposphere is broken down by sunlight into oxygen (O_2) and a highly unstable molecular oxygen (0). These two constituent parts then combine with water to form hydrogen peroxide (H_2O_2) and a hydroxyl radical (HO). In either case, the resulting substance combines further with either nitrogen dioxide (NO_2) or sulfur dioxide (SO_2) to form nitrous acid or sulfuric acid, respectively.[9] The oxides of nitrogen come from motor vehicles, while the sulfur dioxide derives from the burning of fossil fuels and from nature. Nature produces sulfur dioxide in massive amounts during volcanic eruptions. As in the third space invader scenario, both man and nature are responsible for the problem. Even if mankind ceased all contributing pollutants, acid rain would still be present to some extent. Reducing manmade pollutants would, however, have a significant effect.

Acid rain poses a threat to lakes, rivers, forests, and manmade structures. As the acidity of lakes and rivers increases, fish populations are adversely affected. At sufficiently low pH levels, fish populations can disappear altogether and lakes die. Acid rain is also thought to be responsible for reduced forest growth. In severe cases, large-scale destruction of forests is believed caused by acid rain. The process by which acid rain destroys forests is not well understood. Some modelers believe that acid rain kills microorganisms in the soil, thus leading to nutrient stress (Mohnen 1988). Others think that acid rain harms evergreen trees' ability to withstand cold temperatures by adversely influencing certain natural processes in the trees. Thus, uncertainty concerning causality allows some polluting states to argue that

---

9. The information in this paragraph comes from Mohnen 1988.

there is insufficient proof to blame acid rain. This then serves as an excuse not to act. The presence of natural causes confounds the issue of culpability. Acid rain can also cause the deterioration of monuments and building facades as it eats away at surfaces.

The best method for dealing with acid rain is to burn low sulfur coal in power plants or to install desulfurization processes to clean out sulfur during the combustion process. Nitrous oxide emissions from automobiles also pose a problem; a means to reduce these emissions has not been found. In some instances, the pH levels of lakes can be raised with the use of limestone. New forests can also be planted. Hence, the destructive process of acid rain may be reversible, but it takes time.

To date, little progress has been achieved with respect to a global collective action for acid rain. This failure is easily understood, since the problem tends to be localized, affecting some countries and not others. Even among the nations experiencing damage, harm is not uniform. Forested countries downwind from power plants are adversely affected, as are nations with numerous lakes. Another cause of this collective failure concerns the ability of polluters to transfer the externality of acid rain from one region of a country to another, or from one nation to another by building smoke stacks on power plants and factories sufficiently high. Thus, the emissions from England are transported to Scotland and Scandinavia. Sulfur dioxide emissions from the United States are transported, in part, to Canada. Since the externality is transferable, polluters are expected to overprotect their own environments by transferring a *supraoptimal* amount abroad.[10] This solution is the Nash suboptimal provision turned on its head. Producer states have little or no reason to agree to international conventions that have *negative* net benefits for them. Moreover, receiving states have little power to force the producer states to cease or curb their harmful emissions. Uncertainty over causes and sources provides the polluting states grounds for stalling. Some progress can be expected in geographically large countries (e.g., the United States), since a recipient region (state) can resort to the courts to sue a producer region (state). If neighboring countries can form agreements on a number of issues, then a bargaining solution may yield a bilateral agreement. Global agreements are, however, unlikely due to the localized distribution of harmful effects.

6.2 Operation Desert Storm

The Iraqi invasion of Kuwait at the beginning of August, 1990, met with worldwide condemnation that isolated Iraq from many of its trading partners.

---

10. See Sandler and Lapan 1988 for an analogous model with respect to overprotecting against terrorist attacks. Also see the discussion in section 4.7.

The collective response was swift and surprising to Iraq's leadership. Fearing further aggression on the part of Iraq, Saudi Arabia agreed to the stationing of multinational forces on its soil. This deployment of troops to Saudi Arabia, its neighbors, and the Persian Gulf was known as Operation Desert Shield. The dominant contributor of forces and matériel was the United States. Over the ensuing months, the Bush administration cemented together an impressive alliance that would grow still further during the subsequent, warfare stage of Operation Desert Storm. Significant participants in the alliance included the United Kingdom, Egypt, Syria, France, the United Arab Emirates (UAE), Oman, Canada, Australia, the Netherlands, and Turkey. Some allies needed to be given significant selective incentives or private benefits for their participation—for example, the United States forgave billions of dollars of Egyptian debt.

Nearly $10 billion was pledged by six nations—Saudi Arabia, Kuwait, UAE, Germany, Japan, and South Korea—to support U.S. expenses during Operation Desert Shield. Table 6.2 shows that the largest first pledges came from Saudi Arabia and Kuwait—the two countries with the most to gain from the operation. Japan and Germany also made pledges but did not send troops to support the effort. Both of these countries depend on oil from the Persian Gulf.

TABLE 6.2. Contributions to the United States for Desert Shield and Desert Storm (in billions of dollars)

	Pledges of Cash and In-Kind Assistance (Estimates)			Contributions Received[a]		
	First Pledge	Second Pledge	Total	Cash	In Kind	Total
Saudi Arabia	3.3	13.5	16.8	4.54	3.06	7.60
Kuwait	2.5	13.5	16.0	7.00	0.02	7.02
United Arab Emirates	1.0	3.0	4.0	2.87	0.19	3.06
Japan[b]	1.7	7.8–9.0	9.6–10.7	8.70	0.66	9.35
Germany	1.1	5.5	6.6	5.77	0.78	6.55
Korea	0.1	0.3	0.4	0.11	0.04	0.15
Other[c]	—	—	—	0.00	0.01	0.02
Total	9.7	43.6–44.8	53.4–54.5	28.99	4.76	33.75

Sources: Pledge estimates from Office of Management and Budget (OMB), Department of Defense (DOD), and Embassy officials. Actual contributions from DOD and Daily Treasury Statements.

Note: This table was compiled by Kent R. Christensen of the U.S. Congressional Budget Office on April 16, 1991. His assistance is greatly appreciated.

[a] In-kind contributions received as of March 31, 1991; cash as of April 12, 1991. Totals may not add up due to rounding.

[b] The lower range is consistent with the Japanese estimate of their pledge; the upper with the U.S. administration's estimate of the Japanese pledge.

[c] These contributions are expected to be minimal.

Operation Desert Storm started on the morning of January 16, 1991, after last-minute efforts by the United Nations and the USSR failed to gain an Iraqi commitment to withdraw from Kuwait. Thus began an air campaign of unprecedented intensity. The air war was followed by a land war that required less than 100 hours to defeat Iraq. During Operation Desert Storm, the alliance eventually grew to include more than thirty nations. As shown in table 6.2, contributions during Operation Desert Storm (i.e., second pledges) topped $43 billion, thereby increasing total pledges to more than $53 billion.

Operation Desert Shield and Storm underscores the importance of joint products to the formation and maintenance of a collective. Each stage of the operation provided varies amounts of private (country-specific) and alliance-wide public benefits. Without these private benefits, the operation would have degenerated into a U.S. effort. During Operation Desert Shield, private benefits involved the forgiveness of debt, the protection of oil supplies, the forestalling of future aggression, and the desire to remain influential in the region. The protection of oil supplies concerned Japan, Germany, the Netherlands, and the United States; the fear of future aggression motivated Saudi Arabia, UAE, and Turkey; while the desire to remain influential in the Persian Gulf stimulated the United States, the United Kingdom, France, Syria, and Egypt.

After hostilities started, the alliance grew and, with this growth, pledges and troop commitments increased. Operation Desert Storm augmented the private benefits, and this motivated greater collective action. The possibility of future Iraqi aggression no longer appeared to be hypothetical, since Iraq showed no willingness to relinquish captured territory. Moreover, the Iraqi military was well entrenched and had deployed a sizable forward operation from which to launch possible attacks against neighboring nations. Oil prices had increased significantly by the start of the war, thus putting stress on countries heavily dependent on imported oil. Syria, Egypt, Turkey, and Iran had much to gain from an Iraqi defeat that would destroy some of its acquired arsenal. Such an attrition of troops and materiel would raise these nations' standing in the region. The shooting war also provided the prospect of future arms sales. Large arms traders, such as the United States, France, and the United Kingdom, had much to gain from a good showing of their technology. Daily briefings highlighted the capabilities of this technology. Kuwait promised to reward allies with construction contracts, thereby adding to the private benefits. Private benefits also rose from reputation considerations. The United States wanted to change its tarnished image after the Vietnam War and its failures in Beirut and Tehran.

These private benefits significantly fostered the alliance formation and stability by making many nations perceive large net benefits from participation. In consequence, the number of fully privileged members was large and increased after hostilities started. This collective action is especially noteworthy due to its membership, which included nations that are rarely on the same side of issues. The augmentation of private benefits is partly reflected by the quadrupling of pledges after the war's start.

If paid, the pledges would finance much of the incremental cost of the operation, which had been estimated by the U.S. Congressional Budget Office (1991a and 1991b) to range between $45 billion and $60 billion. As of April 16, 1991, approximately $34 billion, or about 63 percent of the pledges, had been collected. Both Saudi Arabia and Kuwait had paid less than half of their pledges by April, 1991. Once the Iraqi threat had been crushed, these nations had less incentive to reveal preferences through payments. By July 12, 1991, Saudi Arabia and Kuwait had paid $11.9 billion and $11.8 billion of their pledges, respectively, thus leaving $4.9 billion and $4.2 billion yet to be paid. The full pledges are likely to be paid, due to recent disclosures that Iraq still has some formidable weapons. In fact, the shipment of Patriot missiles to Saudi Arabia in September, 1991, underscores that nation's continued perception of an Iraqi threat. The rate of payment will surely depend on this threat perception.

Operation Desert Storm clearly demonstrates the importance of private benefits. Moreover, it shows that conventional protection can be provided by a set of allies that charges or collects fees from other interested nations. This club arrangement can be used for a wide range of collective action problems (e.g., disaster relief), in which excludability is feasible. The scheme works best when payment is made at the time that the service is rendered.

6.3 Strategic Defense Initiative

When examining burden-sharing behavior in an alliance, technology can play a major role because the publicness of the collective good may depend on technology. A good example of this influence concerns the different scenarios for the strategic defense initiative (SDI or "Star Wars") and its likely influence on burden sharing.[11] At least three scenarios have been considered. The most-comprehensive scenario involves the deployment of an impregnable, space- and earth-based defense system, capable of destroying 10,000 or more opposing nuclear warheads. Such a system would require various defense layers in space and on the ground to keep any missile from penetrating the shield. Most experts do not hold out much hope for this scenario. Ground-hugging cruise missiles pose a serious problem for any space-based defense. Moreover, technological breakthroughs are needed with respect to laser weapons, electromagnetic railguns, particle-beam accelerators, and other exotic weapons. The feasibility of targeting and destroying 10,000 objects, many of which

---

11. See Sandler 1988, 33.

would be launched from submerged submarines, within less that thirty minutes is a task of immense complexity.

A more likely SDI vision is one that defends U.S. intercontinental ballistic missiles (ICBMs) from attack. Unlike the comprehensive vision, the second SDI proposal enhances the need for nuclear missiles rather than making them obsolete. After the performance of the Patriot missile in the Gulf War, a third intermediate scenario for SDI has been envisioned, in which SDI provides protection for some key cities.

Before commenting on SDI's implications for publicness and burden sharing, I review the four stages of a ballistic missile flight path. A missile can be destroyed in any of four distinct stages of flight: (1) the boost phase, when a launch vehicle transports the payload out of the earth's atmosphere; (2) the postboost phase, when the "bus" sequentially releases the reentry vehicles and decoys; (3) the midcourse phase, when the reentry vehicle and its decoys travel the trajectory toward the target; and (4) the terminal phase, when the warheads in the reentry vehicle traverse the atmosphere to their targets. Not until the midcourse phase can there be complete assurance of the intended target.

A comprehensive SDI would probably have to destroy most of the missiles during the seven-minute boost stage, prior to the release of reentry vehicles and thousands of decoys. Such a shield would provide purely public benefits to allies, because at the boost stage and perhaps even beyond, there may be no way to know which allies' targets are at risk when destroying an enemy missile. An all-encompassing shield would probably eliminate any desire on the part of allies to contribute to the provider due to the pure publicness of benefits. Ironically, the Reagan vision would, if feasible, eliminate any incentive for the European allies to contribute to NATO's defense. Free riding would be widespread.

The more specific the shielding, the less public the benefits and the less free riding. The second scenario, counterforce protection of missiles, would yield the greatest share of country-specific private benefits and, with them, the greatest burden sharing. In this scenario, the incoming missiles must be well along on their flight path before the exact target can be identified. The third scenario, selective countervalue protection of major cities, would yield private benefits somewhere between the first two scenarios. When, for example, neighboring allies are closely clustered, SDI would provide public benefits as in the first scenario, and large allies would be exploited by the small. Greater spatial separation in the third scenario would imply a larger degree of privateness and reduced exploitation.

The willingness of such allies as the United Kingdom and Germany to join the United States in SDI research, development, and deployment perhaps underscores their expectations that the most-likely scenario for SDI is to provide country-specific protection to their defense systems. This version of SDI distributes defense burdens according to benefits received. Ground-based countervalue protection, in the form of an advanced Patriot system, can be sold across markets to interested allies—no international collective action is required.

6.4 Political Revolution: Toward a Collective Action Explanation

In a recent opinion editorial, Mancur Olson asked why the people of Iraq had not assassinated Saddam Hussein. To answer this question, Olson offered a collective action explanation.

> The gains from the removal of a calamitous leader go to the population as a whole, including those who have done nothing to get rid of him. But the terrible costs of opposing a dictator—which can include life itself— are borne entirely by those who take action against him. Thus everyone could gain if a totalitarian leader were overthrown, yet each individual could at the same time lose from acting to get rid of him. (Olson, *Wall Street Journal*, February 22, 1991)

Olson is surely correct that the overthrowing of a repressive regime represents a collective good with the potential for inactivity due to free riding. The real puzzle is why assassinations and political revolutions ever occur. In Iraq, the Kurds tried to throw Saddam Hussein from power and may have succeeded with some outside help. In May, 1991, a woman, believed to be a Tamil revolutionary, assassinated Rajiv Gandhi in a suicide bombing. People power brought down the Marcos government. Other examples include the American Revolution, the French Revolution in 1789, the Russian Revolution of 1917, the Iranian Revolution of 1978–79, the Czechoslovakian Velvet Revolution of 1989, the Romanian Revolution of 1989, and other recent revolutions in Eastern Europe.

This section reviews two important attempts to model political revolutions. Rather than develop an internally consistent theory of revolutions, I instead try to pave the way toward the formulation of such a theory by showing the important ingredients missing in previous collective choice explanations. Any theory of revolution would require much modeling ingenuity to capture the discrete threshold aspects as well as the general equilibrium nature of a very complex social phenomenon. A definition of revolution is needed at the outset. A political revolution occurs when there is a sudden change in the government or collective choice that is not brought about through legitimate, institutionalized channels such as election, natural succession, or retirement.

Any theory of revolution must incorporate a number of important features. First, private (person-specific) benefits must be included along with collective benefits if the motivation of participants in a revolution is to be understood. If individuals were to derive no person-specific satisfaction from participating, but were, if captured, to experience severe penalties, then a classic free-rider problem is likely to exist and the revolutionary collective would remain latent. As in other collective action cases, these private benefits can help overcome the free-rider problem and motivate people to unite. Second, the heterogeneity of participants needs to be taken into account so that leaders are distinguished from followers. Leaders are expected to receive a larger amount of person-specific benefits, since they are likely to become the government of the future if the revolution succeeds. Third, a general equilibrium analysis must consider the interaction of agents among the revolutionaries as well as between the revolutionaries and the government. Neither side can be analyzed in insolation. Fourth, the actions and reactions within each collective must be internally consistent. Fifth, the model must allow for threshold effects and bandwagon phenomenon as the number of participants increases. No model, to date, captures all of these features.

*6.4.1 Tullock's Model of Revolution Participation

Tullock (1974) examined participation in a revolution from the viewpoint of a representative agent who gains satisfaction from both a successful outcome and his or her participation. The former results from collective benefits, while the latter is the private or person-specific benefit. Each participant contributes q^i units of effort, which can be measured in terms of time devoted to the revolution. A self-protection problem is hypothesized in which the individual efforts and those, $\tilde{Q}$, of the other revolutionaries increase the perceived probability, θ^i, of success. The probability of success is

$$\theta^i = \theta^i(q^i, \tilde{Q}) , \tag{6.1}$$

with $\theta^i_1 > 0$ and $\theta^i_2 > 0$, where subscripts denote partial derivatives. Increases in one's own efforts or those of the rest of the collective raise the success likelihood. In equation 6.1, specific technologies of public supply could allow for complex interactions between q^i and $\tilde{Q}$. The number of participants could be added as another determinant. If the revolution succeeds, the ith agent receives a fixed benefit of B^i. Regardless of the outcome, the agent receives a private benefit of u^i, which also depends on his or her own efforts and those of the collective. Presumably, individual benefits increase as more effort is expended by the rest of the collective.

On the cost side, each agent can be penalized F^i if caught in revolutionary activities. The probability of apprehension, ϕ^i, is dependent on one's own level of effort, the efforts of others, and the policing expenditures of the government:

$$\phi^i = \phi^i(q^i, \tilde{Q}, R) , \tag{6.2}$$

with $\phi^i_1 > 0$, $\phi^i_2 < 0$, and $\phi^i_3 > 0$. Since there is safety in numbers, an increase in group activity (or size) reduces the possibility of apprehension. If the government expends more resources to repress and police, the likelihood of capture increases. The revolutionaries also expend resources in terms of opportunity cost when participating in antigovernment activities. This cost is equal to wq^i where w is the wage per unit of time or effort. The model could be expanded to allow for a variety of different protest activities, including both violent and nonviolent acts (Lichbach 1987). Each activity would then have its own price and payoff so that substitution efforts would arise as these prices change. Ironically, a government that increases repression of non-violent acts may induce revolutionaries to switch into more destabilizing, violent acts.

With a single kind of revolutionary act, the agent chooses q^i to

$$\text{maximize } \{\theta^i(q^i, \tilde{Q})B^i + u^i(q^i, \tilde{Q}) - \phi^i(q^i, \tilde{Q}, R)F^i - wq^i\} , \tag{6.3}$$

where $\tilde{Q}$, B^i, F^i, and w are exogenous. For an interior solution, the FOC is

$$\theta^i_1 B^i + u^i_1 = \phi^i_1 F^i + w , \tag{6.4}$$

so that the *sum* of the individual's marginal expected collective benefit and the marginal participation benefit must equal the *sum* of the marginal expected penalty cost and marginal participation costs.

Given the simple form of the FOC, the comparative statics follow from differentiating equation 6.4. An increase in policing cost or the wage rate will reduce the ith agent's optimizing level of revolutionary activities, whereas an increase in the collective's efforts will increase the ith agent's optimizing level of revolutionary effort. If an agent is a leader, then his or her marginal expected benefits from participation are larger than those for followers, since θ^i_1 and u^i_1 are apt to be larger. In consequence, leaders are predicted to be more active than the average member. If government repression were allowed to increase private participation benefits as greater personal satisfaction is perceived when opposing a more regressive regime, then increases in enforcement expenditure may raise or lower revolutionary activities. It all depends on how such expenditure increases shift the u^i and ϕ^i functions. Many alternative variations of the basic model are possible.

Even though the Tullock (1974) model gives some insights, it does not go sufficiently far, since the government side of the interaction is not presented and integrated with the revolutionaries' choice. Moreover, the true Nash equilibrium is not really displayed, because the analysis is partial from the viewpoint of an agent. Membership size of the revolutionary group is not addressed, but should be. At some levels of $\tilde{Q}$, some individuals might be unwilling to participate ($q^i = 0$) so that a corner solution applies, while, at higher levels of $\tilde{Q}$, these individuals and others will participate so that $q^i > 0$. To capture these discrete changes, inequality constraints are required and Kuhn-Tucker nonlinear programming methods are appropriate. The size of the revolutionary group must be incorporated as an additional factor influencing participation so that bandwagon effects can be studied. With this modification, both the cumulative efforts of the other revolutionaries and their numbers will influence action thresholds and the efforts of revolutionaries. Once the size of the revolutionary group is introduced, a club analysis can determine the optimal size.

A fuller investigation would use optimal control to examine the growth of the revolutionary group over time by using a transition equation. The latter would relate the changes in group membership size to recruitment and attrition. Recruitment would depend on the time profile of successful protests. A successful revolution could be likened to the attainment of a certain threshold of support. In such a model, government deterrence would need to be integrated.

6.4.2 The Kuran Theory

Timur Kuran (1989 and 1991) has offered a model that nicely captures the bandwagon effect by focusing on the threshold choices for participating in a revolution. Kuran demonstrated that small oppositions can grow large overnight and sweep governments from power, as in the case of Eastern Europe during 1989. In the Kuran (1991) model, the benefits from revolutionary involvement (B^i and u^i) are positively related to the size, n, of the revolutionary collective. For each potential participant, the size of n corresponds to when the threshold of participation is first ascertained; that is, the smallest n for which $q^i > 0$. Individuals are then ordered according to these thresholds; agents whose thresholds are the smallest are first in the ordering. Suppose that the threshold sequence is $S^1 = (0, 2, 2, 3, 4, 5, 6, 7, 8, 10)$ for a population of ten people in which each number denotes the threshold size of the revolutionary group before the relevant individual opposes the government. That is,

individual 1 has a threshold n of 0 so that he or she participates in revolutionary activities regardless, while individual 10 never participates. Individual
2 and 3 become revolutionaries provided that the revolution includes at least
two people; individual 4 joins provided that three or more people are involved;
and so on.

With S^1, an equilibrium exists with just one revolutionary, since individual 2 onward will not join unless more than just one individual is involved. If,
however, an exogenous change occurs (e.g., lower wages or more repression)
that were to reduce individual 2's threshold to 1, then S^1 would imply a
bandwagon effect that stops with 9 revolutionaries (Kuran 1991, 122). This
follows because once individual 2 joins, individual 3's threshold is then met.
With three revolutionaries, individual 4's threshold is obtained. And so it goes
until individual 9 joins and a new equilibrium is reached. If little separates the
numbers in the sequence, as in S^1, then revolutions may attain large size with
small precipitating causes. Revolutions then become difficult to predict, especially when individuals falsify or hide their true preferences prior to meeting
their thresholds. With sequence $S^2 = (0, 1, 5, 7, 8, 8, 8, 8, 8, 10)$, the society
is insulated from large-scale revolutions but may face persistent terrorism due
to 20 percent of the population with low thresholds. When populations are
large and diverse, a number of different discrete plateaus must be surpassed
before a revolutionary fervor is generated. The distribution of preferences
over the population becomes a crucial consideration when considering the
bandwagon phenomenon.

The Kuran (1991) model needs to be expanded to include greater interaction with the government collective. Resource constraints for the opposing
collectives must be introduced. Moreover, the information structure of the
revolutionary environment must be addressed. Who is better informed? In
most cases, the government may not know the true strength of the revolutionary forces and may have to rely on these forces' actions to judge strength. A
Bayesian learning function can then permit the government to update its
belief. In some instances, a signaling equilibrium may exist in which the
government is best off capitulating to a revolutionary movement whose actions exceed a given threshold.

6.4.3 Eastern Europe in 1989 and beyond

In Poland, East Germany, Hungary, Czechoslovakia, Yugoslavia, and Ro-
mania, revolutionary thresholds were surpassed with lightening speed and
governments fell one after another. These revolutionary successes took the
experts by surprise. Clearly, a self-generating bandwagon effect occurred.
Moreover, a signaling equilibrium's threshold appeared to be surpassed in
country after country, so that the government perceived the opposition as

sufficiently strong to bring about the government's eventual downfall. These recent examples underscore the inability of traditional models to predict revolutionary outcomes. This inability motivated Kuran's (1989 and 1991) innovative work.

The formation and dissolution of nations is a little-understood collective action problem of immense interest to the study of political science. With each passing year, nations appear to be splitting apart, thereby giving rise to new nations. Any theory capable of explaining this devolutionary process must also be able to explain why larger nations are sometimes forged from smaller ones.

With freedom regained, Eastern Europe now confronts a host of collective action problems, as market economies are constructed from the failed command systems. There is no blueprint for making this transition. If the invisible hand is to guide the allocation of resources, markets and their price signals are needed. Markets are, themselves, indivisible collective goods. To provide the proper incentives for market exchange, property rights to profits must be allowed and this, in turn, requires privatization as ownership of firms is assigned to individuals. Obstacles are many. For example, numerous state enterprises are monopolies with outmoded equipment. If competitive forces are not introduced through the breakup of monopolies (when warranted), monopoly rents will distort prices and impede the invisible hand. For natural monopolies with significant scale economies, laws must be enacted to regulate prices. These laws also represent collective goods. Furthermore, emerging market economies must devise tax systems to finance such collective goods as public inputs, enforcement of property rights, defense, and education.

If these emerging market economies fail to recognize market failures and to institutionalize some form of collective action, their economic performance will be suboptimal. Eastern European economies must not only institute the proper preconditions to sustain and to support markets, but also establish means for correcting market failures. This second aspect is particularly troublesome to some reformers who find any government interference anathema after living for over forty years in a command system. The pendulum of reform is apt to swing too far toward markets before an optimal balance between markets and controls is struck. In communist nations (e.g., the USSR, China), vested interests will exercise every means available to maintain control. Reforms will be sabotaged. The dissolution of these pockets of resistance also represents a collective good of a purely public character.

As reforms progress, the Eastern European nations must be considered for membership in international collectives such as the International Monetary Fund (IMF), the World Health Organization (WHO), and the European Community (EC). Since currency convertibility is nearly a purely public good in terms of rivalry, the IMF is likely to be an inclusive club that should take in all willing nations. Other international organizations have crowding aspects that restrict membership to an exclusive subset.

6.5 Concluding Remarks

This chapter is intended to demonstrate that many exigencies confronting mankind today and in the years to come are collective action problems. Some collective problems, such as ozone depletion, may automatically be dealt with by collective action, while others, such as acid rain, will not. The issues mentioned in this chapter are only representative, since space does not permit an analysis of all such issues. An important example, not discussed above, is species preservation. The loss of a species is forever and has consequences for both present and future generations in the global collective. Failure to act to preserve species has led to extinction in the case of the passenger pigeon, the Tasmanian tiger, and the dodo bird, and to the near extinction of the blue whale and the California condor. In many ways, species preservation has all of the earmarks of a particularly difficult collective action problem, because the uneven distribution of species implies that the host nation may have the highest opportunity cost, in terms of foregone revenues, from preservation, while other nations receiving net benefits may have no power over the host country. The problem is compounded by the existence of future generations, whose net benefits from preservation cannot be represented in the bargaining process.

Developing nations, such as Brazil, probably contain half of the world's species in their teeming jungles. Yet Brazil's push toward development means that short-run gains from slash-and-burn destruction of the Amazon rain forest appears difficult to resist. Unless the rest of the world can compensate Brazil for foregone gains from its current destruction of the Amazon jungles, the heritage of mankind will be severely depleted.

Other collective exigencies include the use of the oceans as a dumping ground for nuclear and other contaminants. Many of the most dangerous substances are being deliberately placed in an ecosystem whose circulatory property spreads the pollutants worldwide. The parking of spy satellites with nuclear reactors in low orbits is another collective action problem. When these orbits deteriorate, dangerous debris reenters the earth's atmosphere and then plunges earthward in a game of Russian roulette.

Mankind has tremendous opportunities to raise worldwide well-being if proper attention is paid to collective action problems. Unfortunately, inactivity and/or noncooperative behavior can spell disasters of unprecedented proportions.

APPENDIX

6.A.1 Controlling Stock Externalities with a Pigouvian Tax

This appendix presents the first-best control of a stock externality using a Pigouvian tax that charges polluters the external costs of their activities. Only a first-best path for the price control is presented (the interested reader should consult Ko, Lapan, and Sandler 1992 for second-best policies). Initially, we examine everything from a single polluter's viewpoint.[12]

Equation 1 is the law of motion governing the change of the state of an externality stock:

$$\dot{q}_t = \alpha X_t - \delta q_t , \tag{1}$$

where q_t denotes the level of the externality-generating stock at time t, α and δ depict positive fractions, and X_t represents the rate of emissions. The stock q_t may correspond to the level of carbon dioxide in the atmosphere. This equation allows a fixed portion, α, of the emission to accumulate as a contaminant when discharged, while the remainder, $(1 - \alpha)X_t$, is assimilated by the environment's carrying capacity through photosynthesis or some other process. In equation 1, the stock of contaminants deteriorates by δq_t per period.

I follow standard practice and assume a strictly concave net benefit function $B(X_t)$, where $dB/dX_t = B' > 0$ up to some maximizing level, $\bar{X}$, for emissions and then $B' < 0$ thereafter. In the absence of an emission tax, the polluter maximizes net benefits, say profits, when $B'(\bar{X}) = 0$. Profits or net benefits are maximized for a competitive industry when the inverse market demand equals the marginal private cost.

The accumulation of the stock externality implies a strictly convex damage function, $D(q_t)$. The objective functional of the controlling authority is to maximize the stream of discounted future benefits net of damage:

$$V(q_0) = \max_{X_t} \int_0^\infty e^{-rt} [B(X_t) - D(q_t)] \, dt \tag{2}$$

subject to $\dot{q}_t = \alpha X_t - \delta q_t$, where r denotes the social rate of discount. An infinite time-horizon is invoked. The current value Hamiltonian is

---

12. This appendix is partially based on Ko, Lapan, and Sandler 1992. The kind permission of Elsevier Science Publishers is acknowledged.

$$H_t = B(X_t) - D(q_t) + \lambda_t[\alpha X_t - \delta q_t] , \tag{3}$$

with costate variable λ_t. Corner solutions are ruled out by assuming

$$\lim_{X \to 0} B'(X) = \infty.$$

The FOCs that are both necessary and sufficient for an interior solution are

$$\partial H_t / \partial X_t = B'(X_t) + \alpha \lambda_t = 0 , \tag{4}$$

$$\partial H_t / \partial q_t = -(\dot{\lambda}_t - r\lambda_t) = -D'(q_t) - \delta\lambda_t , \tag{5}$$

and

$$\partial H_t / \partial \lambda_t = \dot{q}_t = \alpha X_t - \delta q_t . \tag{6}$$

With an infinite horizon, the transversality conditions are given as

$$\lim_{t \to \infty} \lambda_t e^{-rt} = 0 , \tag{7}$$

and

$$\lim_{t \to \infty} \lambda_t[\alpha X_t - \delta q_t] = 0 , \tag{8}$$

for which $\lambda_t > 0$ implies the convergence to a steady state.

I assume that the initial state of the environment, q_0, is sufficiently close to the steady state level q^* and investigate the movement of the variables around the steady state. Equations 5 and 6 can be rearranged to yield

$$\dot{\lambda}_t = (r + \delta)\lambda_t + D'(q_t) , \tag{9}$$

and

$$\dot{q}_t = \alpha X(\lambda_t) + \delta q_t , \tag{10}$$

where the dependency of emission activities on the costate variable, as implied by equation 4, is recognized in equation 10.

Let (q_s^*, λ_s^*) denote the unique optimal steady state values that simultaneously solve equations 9 and 10 and are independent of q_0. By equation 4, λ_s^* implies a steady state solution X_s^* for activities producing emissions. Equation

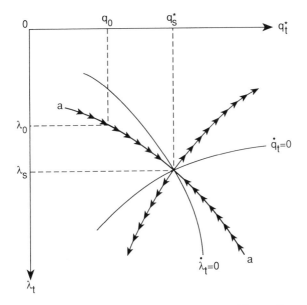

Fig. 6.1. Dynamic path of the first-best pricing policy

4 indicates that assigning a specific negative value to the costate is equivalent to a Pigouvian tax on emissions. With this tax at the rate p_t, the polluter's profit maximization occurs when $B'(X_t) = p_t$. To follow the optimal dynamic path under such a Pigouvian tax, an emission charge of $-\alpha\lambda_t$ is required at time t.

The solution is displayed in the phase plane diagram in figure 6.1. The fourth quadrant is relevant, since q_t is positive when λ_t is negative. The $\dot{\lambda}_t = 0$ locus is negatively sloped since $d\lambda_t/dq_t = -D''(q_t)/(r + \delta) < 0$ by the implicit function rule. The $\dot{q}_t = 0$ locus is positively sloped since $d\lambda_t/dq_t = -\delta B''(X_t)/\alpha^2 > 0$. The convexity of the two loci requires the marginal damage and marginal benefit functions to be convex. The optimal saddle path in figure 6.1 is aa. If the initial state is q_0, then to approach the steady state along the saddle path, the costate variable must start at λ_0 and be varied continuously along aa. Proposition 1 follows from an inspection of figure 6.1.

Proposition 1. If the initial state of the environment is less contaminated than the optimal steady state, then the optimal emission level at the start of the control is greater than the steady state emission level, and the optimal level of emissions continues to decrease over time, but the state of the environment will continuously deteriorate, approaching the steady state level asymptotically. If, however, the initial state is more deteriorated than the steady state, then the reverse results apply.

6.A.2 An Extension

A logical extension would be to include a number of nations, where each nation's emissions add to the total stock externality Q, where $Q = q + \bar{Q}$. Damage now depends on Q. The equation of motion is now

$$\dot{Q}_t = \alpha \sum_i X_{it} - \delta Q_t \, . \tag{11}$$

The Nash solution will regulate q_t in each country, taking $\bar{Q}_t$ and $\dot{\bar{Q}}_t$ as given. Too little collective action will result.

CHAPTER 7

Conclusions

Although more than a quarter-century has passed since the publication of
Logic, the questions raised by Olson's pathbreaking book remain just as
relevant today as they were in 1965. In fact, advances in technology and the
growth of population will increase the importance of collective action in the
1990s and the century to come. Collective action is concerned with the formation of groups and the behavior of these groups in allocating resources to
collective goods that provide benefits to a clearly defined set of individuals.
Because collective goods include a wide range of activities with a varying
degree of appropriability, indivisibility of benefits, and mix of private and
public joint benefits, an understanding of collective action is a key ingredient
for uncovering the principles of public expenditure theory. Inasmuch as collective goods represent an important class of market failures, the theory of
collective action has much to say about the study of such failures. Applications of collective action abound and involve every field of economic analysis.
Collective action is also germane to a number of social sciences. Since collective action is associated with lobbying activities, interest group formation,
and the behavior of parties, it has relevance for political science. The organization of groups with common interests makes collective action of interest to
sociology. Collective action is also relevant to anthropology, since any study
of mankind must explain such issues as the formation of cities and communities, the development of languages, and the preservation of cultures.

In many ways, *Logic* was a synthesis of thoughts on the collective action
problem dating back to Smith, Ricardo, Malthus, Senior, and Mill. Olson's
book has been so influential because it provided a unifying framework in the
form of easy-to-understand principles and themes. His message was a radical
departure from the way in which groups were then examined in economics
and related disciplines, since groups had been viewed as fostering the collective interest. According to Olson, collectives may fail to form, or, when
formed, may fail to achieve an optimal level of action. Although groups are
intended to pursue the collective well-being, the pursuit of private gains by
constituent agents may lead to outcomes that spell disaster for collective
benefits. Olsonian themes tied these failures to the size and composition of the
collective.

The primary purpose of my study has been to reexamine these themes in light of the vast literature generated by *Logic*. In the process, I identified the technology of collective supply, the form of the utility function, the strategic assumption, and the constraints of the problem as the essential ingredients behind the validity of the Olsonian propositions. A number of qualifications were shown to be needed to transform these propositions into valid theorems. A second purpose has been to present wide-ranging applications that demonstrate the current importance and general applicability of collective action. A third purpose has been to relate recent developments in public economics (e.g., the neutrality theorem and the theory of clubs) to the theory of collective action. A final purpose has been to present means for testing the principles of collective action with econometric procedures.

7.1 Olsonian Themes Revisited

Theme 1 involves a number of propositions concerning the influence of group size on collective action. Based on the work of McGuire (1974) and Chamberlin (1974), the aggregate provision level is no longer believed to be inversely related to group size when goods are normal with positive income elasticities. In fact, provision approaches a finite limit, based upon the marginal propensity to spend on the collective good, as group size increases without bounds. This increase in aggregate provision is accompanied by a decrease in average or per-person contributions.

Even though provision is not inversely related to group size as first hypothesized, suboptimality and collective failure may, under reasonable scenarios, still worsen with group size in the manner proposed by Olson. An apt example was illustrated in chapter 4 with the commons, where each exploiter accounts for one nth of the industry profit. Another example corresponds to pure public goods with a summation technology (see section 2.3.3). An updated version of Olson's proposition concerning group size and suboptimality might be: *With identical individuals and symmetric equilibria, an increase in group size worsens suboptimality when a summation technology applies.* Simple direct relationships between group size and inefficiency require stylized, but important, special model structures with numerous real-world analogues. Since so many possible combinations of ingredients concerning model structure are available, it is surely impossible to formulate general propositions that apply to a wide range of technologies, distributions of tastes, strategic assumptions, and sets of constraints. Given these difficulties, researchers in experimental economics must be particularly cautious not to generalize their experimental results too much. Moreover, the essential ingredients of the underlying model must be specified, especially since seemingly slight alterations in the technology of public supply may make for opposite predictions (e.g., the weakest-link versus best-shot technologies).

Group size may or may not influence whether a collective is privileged. The willingness of nations to deal collectively with the ozone depletion problem indicates that even global collectives are feasible, provided the pattern of payoffs is sufficiently favorable for collective action. Thus, group size is not a sufficient condition for latency. Charities, for example, collect billions of dollars from large-scale collectives every year. As shown in chapter 2, the underlying game structure, implied by the net benefits to the agents for various participation scenarios, is a crucial determinant of whether the group is privileged. If each potential participant is better off from contributing regardless of the extent of spillovers, then the group is fully privileged up to any size. If, on the other hand, the net benefits derived from a collective action imply a Prisoner's Dilemma, then any size group is unlikely to be privileged when agents do not interact repeatedly. In consequence, the underlying game structure and its temporal nature must be addressed in bringing Olson's proposition for privileged groups up to date. Coordination and Chicken game structures attenuate the importance of the size of the collective. Since the underlying game structure is itself determined by the technology of public supply, strategic assumptions, and tastes, we again see that simple, general relationships are not possible.

Olson's second theme involves the composition of the collective in terms of the asymmetry of tastes and endowments. Over the course of this book, the influence of group asymmetry has been shown (by way of different cases) to depend on the strategic assumption, the technology of publicness, and the distribution of tastes and endowments. If, for instance, leader-follower behavior applies and the leader is the larger agent, the exploitation hypothesis can be turned on its head with the small exploited by the large. With a weakest-link technology, no exploitation may result even when great disparity in endowments is present; with best shot, however, exploitation may follow even when a small disparity is prevalent. For the standard Nash case of a *summation technology,* the updated exploitation hypothesis might be: *If all goods are normal and tastes are identical, then the rich (large) will be exploited by the poor (small). Income asymmetry is apt to lead to a privileged group.*

Perhaps the least updating is required for Olson's third theme, concerning the use of selective incentives and institutional design to promote more effective collective action. Developments since the early 1970s have investigated the influence of joint products, which can include all types of selective incentives, in promoting collective action. These joint products are prevalent in successful instances of collective action, including charities, labor unions, military alliances, police protection, education, recreation facilities, and parks. Joint products, or selective incentives, can promote collective action in a number of ways. First, joint products can motivate preference revelation, especially when private outputs are complementary in consumption to public outputs. Second, joint products can forestall neutrality and crowding out, thus paving the way for corrective tax policies. Third, joint products can imply game structures more conducive to collective action.

By altering the technology of public supply, institutional design can foster collective action. In chapter 2, a simple example demonstrated that, with an Assurance game, the inhibiting effect of group size can be lessened by sharing risks in a nonrefundable contribution scenario. Simple changes in institutional design can have profound effects on the viability and feasibility of a collective. Design principles that minimize both fixed and variable transaction costs should also support collective action. Surely, transaction costs are a crucial, but little studied, aspect of collective action. This is, indeed, surprising since *Logic* clearly raised the importance of transaction costs in group formation.

7.2 Means for Promoting Collective Action: Taking Stock

Collective action abounds in the real world. Some types of collective action materialize on their own, while others require a nudge. In still other cases, collective action is resistant and requires a great deal of outside support to be feasible. Successful instances of collective action appear to share one or more of the following features: (*a*) private or excludable joint products, (*b*) a pattern of payoffs favorable to dominant players, (*c*) an exclusion mechanism coupled with a toll scheme, or (*d*) repeated interactions among players. I have already mentioned that joint products can support collective action by privatizing some of the benefits derived from collective action. This privatizing role is not unlike the establishment of property rights, since the individual cannot receive the private output(s) unless he or she contributes to the collective activity. We should, therefore, expect that many successful collective action cases are associated with the presence of joint products. Empirical results seem to support this hypothesis.

The underlying game structure is also a crucial feature. This is most evident in an assurance-type game in which *each* individual is in a pivotal role, so that the success (and higher payoffs to all) of collective action hinges on each individual doing his or her part. The failure of even one individual to cooperate causes the higher payoffs for all to be lost. Contracts and pledges then become self-enforcing. In essence, such an arrangement is analogous to the design of a preference-revelation mechanism that places each individual in a pivotal role through the use of sidepayments. These mechanisms put the individual in a position in which his or her objective function corresponds to that of the collective. A supporting game structure, if not inherent in the problem, can be promoted through institutional design.

If collective action is to amount to much, then the net payoffs from participation must be positive for those agents who are in a position to have the greatest impact. Such agents need not be the largest or best endowed. A privileged group may not accomplish much when the active members are least able to promote the desired action. The global warming problem discussed in chapter 6 is an apt example. Since the activist nations are not the primary generators of greenhouse gases, their willingness to curtail emissions is not expected to have much impact. Being privileged is a necessary condition for successful collective action, but it is not sufficient. To foster collective action when some assistance is needed, institutional design may have to engineer a sufficient skewness of benefits to promote participation among those agents who are best positioned to make a difference. In the literature, the impact of the distribution of payoffs is often forgotten, since many theoretical treatments focus on identical players and symmetric equilibria. The required skewness may be easily achieved if institutions are designed to promote a supportive technology. If, for example, the distribution of benefits are more-or-less equal among potential participants, then an institutional design that emphasizes a weakest-link technology of public supply would work best.

The implementation of an exclusion mechanism, when economically feasible, is also conducive to efficient collective action. With an exclusion mechanism, tolls can be assigned on a per-utilization basis (e.g., visits or percentage of use) so as to internalize any crowding externality. The revenues from the tolls can be used to finance the collective good, with shortfalls made up by membership fees. Such an arrangement is called a club and can serve as a nongovernmental means for providing collective goods. The "Chunnel" linking England and France will operate as a club. Other large-scale infrastructure needs (e.g., satellite networks or airfields for NATO) can be provided in a club arrangement. The 70,000-man rapid deployment force for the European NATO allies, announced on May 28, 1991, has the makings of a club arrangement. The U.S. solicitation of burden shares from its allies for Operation Desert Storm is analogous to charging tolls for a club good. If exclusion is feasible and tolls can be charged on a user basis, then club arrangements can foster collective action.

A final means for promoting collective action is to establish institutions in which participants must interact on a repeated basis. Repeated interactions foster participants' concern for reputation. Short-run gains from reneging on pledges must then be compared with long-run gains from not reneging. Agents who deal with one another on a repeated basis are apt to place more weight on cooperation.

7.3 Directions For Future Research

Important theoretical and empirical questions concerning collective action still need to be answered, and finding their answers will provide a research agenda for many years to come. Much more work is required to investigate collectives whose members are heterogeneous. A recent paper by Dasgupta and Itaya (1991) has made a start in this direction by examining comparative statics in a conjectural variations framework when agents are heterogeneous. Their work is noteworthy because it demonstrates that some symmetric equilibria results may not hold when heterogeneity applies.

The easiest type of agent heterogeneity to model concerns different income levels arranged along a continuum, but with identical tastes for the agents. If, however, tastes differ, then a means for expressing and ordering these differences needs to be discovered, and this poses a problem. Often a one-parameter taste term that lies along a continuum is used, but the meaning of such a parameter is elusive. More creative ways for accounting for taste differences must be devised.

Heterogeneity also requires further analysis in the theory of clubs. For tractability, most modelers have assumed homogeneous memberships when studying clubs. A notable, and important, exception is Scotchmer and Wooders 1987. Their means for identifying heterogeneous members can prove fruitful in other applications. Toll schemes and membership determination must allow for heterogeneous participants.

For dynamic analyses of collective action, more attention to heterogeneity is needed in terms of differing discount rates, alternative learning functions, and varying adjustment rates. The introduction of a temporal structure adds a whole new set of heterogeneity concerns. When nations are the members of a collective, heterogeneity may include differences in population growth, income growth, or technology adoption.

Most studies of collective action have focused on a single collective good. In the global collective problems discussed in chapter 6, we saw that global warming, ozone depletion, and acid rain are interrelated; hence, collective action concerning each problem should not be considered in isolation. In many instances, multiple public goods or collective activities with multiple public outputs are considered. To capture the essence of multiple public goods in an interesting fashion, the researcher must consider taste interrelationships (e.g., substitutability and complementarity) in consumption *and* interrelationships in production. The latter is typically overlooked and includes such concerns as economies of scope and cost subadditivity. Moreover, the notion of transaction costs becomes relevant, since multiple public goods can share administrative and other transaction expenses. Much additional work in this area is needed, especially since most collectives allocate resources to multiple goods. Extension to a multiple public good framework is only useful when the model explicitly addresses such issues as the optimal number of jointly supplied goods, the cross-subsidization of activities, and the composition of members. If standard models are merely extended to include more public goods with no thought to these issues, then little additional insights are gained.

More work is also needed in terms of dynamic analysis. The repeated game framework of supergames must be extended to allow the game itself to evolve with time. In the standard analysis, supergames involve the same game being played a large number of times. With learning endogenized, the game structure itself might evolve with time. Also, the number of participants may vary from period to period. Control modeling is needed to study the optimal time path for provision and financing. Some collective action problems, particularly those concerning the environment, must be investigated in an optimal control paradigm.

Further work on institutional structures is also desirable. The architecture of these structures must consider the technology of publicness and the conjectural variations or strategic assumptions that the structures' designs elicit. An analysis of institutions is needed, and this requires the discrete comparison of alternative forms, each with its own set of net benefits for the agents and total benefits. Often, researchers settle for a comparison between a few prototypes.

At the end of chapter 5, we saw that much also needs to be done in terms of empirical studies. Further tests must be engineered to distinguish between such strategic assumptions as leader-follower and Nash behavior, or between various underlying game structures. When devising a test to differentiate the former, the researcher must be careful not to rely on neutrality as a criterion, since, as shown in chapter 3, both leader-follower and Nash behavior imply neutrality. In practice, a specific utility function (e.g., Stone-Geary) may have to be attributed to the agents in order to identify each strategic assumption by its reduced-form equations. A test for other kinds of conjectural variations also should be formulated. The next logical extension is to develop a test for a constant conjectural variation along a continuum. If more general conjectural variations, such as $\sigma = \sigma(q, Q)$, are to be tested, then specific utility functions must be imposed. This follows because the reduced-form demand equation for the collective action is, when utility is expressed in general functional form, indistinguishable from such other model variations as joint products (see Dasgupta and Itaya 1991). This means that nonneutrality and other features have multiple sources.

Another worthwhile empirical extension is to introduce an explicit dynamic or intertemporal framework for the reduced-form equations, so that diverse lag structures can be investigated. Reactions to spillins are unlikely to be timeless, as implied by the standard Nash (simultaneous-move) equilibrium model. Disequilibrium may require time to work itself out. If the researcher were to move in this direction, then an explicit dynamic model with an allowance for discrete adjustments and adaptation, is needed. No such model exists for collective action.

A final empirical extension would consider both the demand and supply sides of the collective action problem. To date, most empirical studies have been demand based, with the supply aspects playing a passive, accommodating role. In the future, the supply side must be given more considerations in constructing the reduced-form equations. For some analyses, an equilibrium demand-supply, simultaneous-equation system is appropriate.

7.4 Concluding Remarks

One message is clear: collective action is as important today as it was in 1965 when Mancur Olson first wrote *Logic*. Each additional development in the theory has paved the way for new insights, applications, and the need for still further refinements. As technology, population growth, and resource needs draw the nations of the world closer together, the relevance of collective action increases. An understanding of collective action and its supporting processes and environment will allow policymakers to foster the required preconditions to achieve effective collective action. With current fiscal crises confronting cities, counties, states, and nations, the ability to promote collective action without resorting to government intervention increases in importance. Collective action is achievable when the configuration of incentives to participants is supportive. This formula for successful collective action can be designed into emerging institutions.

The study of collective action involves numerous scenarios and model structures. A wide range of cases can be illuminated with the theory. Given the subject's complexity and richness, general (and simple) propositions are nearly impossible to develop. Many facets of the problem are relevant and can affect the outcome. The next quarter-century should witness further exciting developments and insights.

Appendix: A Review of Basic Economic Concepts

This appendix is intended for those readers who have a knowledge of economics at the principles level. Because space is limited, the review is highly selective and rather brief, and concepts used throughout the book are given the most emphasis. For a more in-depth presentation, the reader should consult a standard text in intermediate microeconomics.

1. Indifference Curves

In the modern treatment of consumer behavior, indifference curves are used to depict consumer tastes or preferences for goods. Indifference analysis depends on the ability to rank order available market baskets or bundles from best to worst. When ranking any two bundles, say bundle a and b, a consumer must compare the two bundles in one of three mutually exclusive ways: (1) bundle a is preferred to bundle b; (2) bundle b is preferred to bundle a; or (3) bundles a and b are equal in satisfaction. If bundles are viewed as equal in satisfaction, then the consumer is said to be indifferent between them. This modern treatment is an ordinal analysis inasmuch as consumers are only required to rank order alternative bundles. Consumers need not indicate a utility value or level.

To keep the presentation simple, I assume the existence of only two goods: good x and good y. At least three assumptions concerning consumer preferences are invoked at the outset. First, consumers are assumed to prefer more of a good to less. If, for example, bundle a has more of good x and no less of good y than that of bundle b, then the consumer must prefer bundle a to bundle b. This assumption is known as *monotonicity*. Second, preferences are assumed consistent in the sense that if the consumer is indifferent between bundle a and bundle b and is also indifferent between bundle b and bundle c, then the consumer is indifferent between bundle a and bundle c. This property is known as *transitivity*. Finally, a technical assumption of *continuity* is imposed so that all bundles can be ranked in one of the three ways; there do not exist bundles that cannot be compared. Continuity ensures that rankings change in a smooth fashion. This assumption is responsible for indifference curves being continuous, with no holes or points missing. Since every bundle is either judged as preferred, inferior, or indifferent to any other, the consumer's rank ordering is *complete*.

With these three assumptions, a consumer's tastes or utility function can be depicted with an indifference map made up of indifference curves. Each indifference curve indicates all combinations of two goods (i.e., bundles) that yield a constant level of satisfaction. Consider the left-hand side of table A.1, which displays five bundles or combinations of goods x and y that give a constant utility level, U_1, to a particular consumer. In table A.1, 12 units of y and 1 of x yield the same satisfaction as 9 of y and 2 of x, or as 7 of y and 3 of x. As the consumer acquires more x, he or she must relinquish some y in order to maintain constant utility. This trade-off is needed to fulfill monotonicity.

In figure A.1, the five bundles on indifference curve U_1 (corresponding to the bundles in table A.1) are depicted, in which good y is measured on the vertical axis and good x on the horizontal axis. Bundle a has 12 units of y and 1 unit of x, while bundle b has 9 of y and 2 of x, and so on. The indifference curve U_1 is drawn smooth and unbroken by connecting all points between and beyond the five bundles with a continuous curve called an indifference curve. Moving up or down curve U_1 maintains constant utility. Indifference curve U_2 in figure A.1 corresponds to the right-hand side of table A.1 and denotes a higher level of utility than curve U_1. This follows because curve U_2 contains bundles that have more of at least one good and no less of the other good. In fact, some bundles along U_2 have more of both goods; bundle d on U_2 has 7 units of each good, while bundle d on U_1 has only 5 of each good.

Indifference curves have a number of crucial properties. First, they are downward sloping due to the assumption of monotonicity. If an indifference curve were positively or upward sloping, then two bundles would be judged indifferent even though one contains more of both goods. Montonicity rules out this possibility. Second, indifference curves (such as U_2) that lie above and to the right of another (such as U_1) represent a higher level of satisfaction. Third, indifference curves are continuous by assumption. Fourth, they do not intersect. If intersection were permitted, then transitivity would be violated

TABLE A.1. Preferences for Good x and Good y

Bundle	U_1			U_2		
	Good y	Good x	$\text{MRS}_{xy} = -\Delta y/\Delta x$	Good y	Good x	MRS_{xy}
a	12	1	—	18	2	—
b	9	2	3/1	14	3	4/1
c	7	3	2/1	10	5	2/1
d	5	5	1/1	7	7	3/2
e	3	8	2/3	4	10	1/1

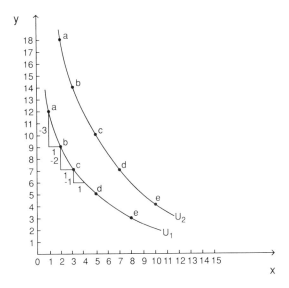

Fig. A.1. Indifference curves

because one bundle would be in two different indifference classes. Each indifference class contains all bundles with the same utility level. If some bundle, say *b*, were in two different indifference classes simultaneously, then the bundles in one class would have to be indifferent to those in the other class vis-à-vis a comparison with common bundle *b*. But then the two classes could not be distinct. By completeness, every bundle lies on some indifference curve. The entire set of indifference curves is the indifference map and corresponds to the consumer's utility function.

The slope of the indifference curves relates to the willingness of a consumer to trade between the two goods while maintaining the same level of utility. This slope is indicated by the ratio $\Delta y/\Delta x$ along the curve. In figure A.1, this ratio on U_1 is $-3/1$ between bundles *a* and *b*, $-2/1$ between bundles *b* and *c*, and $-1/1$ between bundles *c* and *d*. The *negative* of this slope is called the marginal rate of substitution between good *x* and good *y* (denoted by MRS_{xy}) and is equal to $-\Delta y/\Delta x$. In table A.1, MRS_{xy} is computed when changing between bundles along the indifference curve. The MRS indicates a consumer's willingness to trade one good for another while maintaining a constant utility level. A large MRS_{xy} implies that the consumer favors good *x*, since he or she is willing to trade a lot of *y* for an additional unit of *x*. Furthermore, MRS_{xy} equals the ratio of marginal utilities of the two goods—that is, $MRS_{xy} = MU_x/MU_y(= -\Delta y/\Delta x)$.

A final property of indifference curves corresponds to how the MRS changes as more of, say, good x is acquired relative to good y. In figure A.1, the indifference curves are convex to the origin, since MRS_{xy} declines as more x is obtained. This decline indicates that the consumer becomes less willing to trade y for x as more x is acquired and less y remains in his or her possession. A convex-to-the-origin indifference curve occurs when the MRS diminishes as more x is obtained relative to y. A diminishing MRS implies that the willingness to trade goods depends on a consumer's *relative* holdings; the more of good y that the person has relative to good x, the more willing he or she is to trade y for more of x. At bundle a in figure A.1, the consumer is relatively well supplied with good y and, hence, is willing to trade 3 units of y for 1 of x. At bundle c, the consumer has less y and more x than at bundle a and, consequently, is less willing to trade y for more x. The trade-off ratio is now one to one. A diminishing MRS means that a consumer prefers "interior positions," where some of both goods are consumed, rather than corner positions, where only a single commodity is enjoyed. Empirical studies find support for a diminishing MRS in most cases.

2. Consumer Budget Constraint

Consumer preferences, as depicted by indifference curves, denote the consumer's desires or wishes. Before an equilibrium can be found, the budget constraint of the consumer must be brought into the analysis. The budget constraint limits the consumer's choices to affordable or feasible bundles by considering the consumer's income, I, and commodity prices.

The general form for the budget constraint is

$$p_x x + p_y y = I ,\tag{1}$$

in which p_x is the per-unit price of x and p_y is the per-unit price of y. In its general form, the budget line is a straight line with slope $-p_x/p_y$. Moreover, the budget line has an x-intercept of I/p_x and a y-intercept of I/p_y. Consider the following specific budget constraint,

$$\$5x + \$2y = \$60 ,\tag{2}$$

in which p_x is \$5, p_y is \$2, and I is \$60. In figure A.2a, the middle budget line corresponds to equation 2 with the x-intercept at 12 ($= 60/5$) and the y-intercept at 30 ($= 60/2$). The slope ($-p_x/p_y$) equals $-5/2$. If the price of x rises to \$10 so that $\$10x + \$2y = \$60$ denotes the new constraint, then the budget line pivots in toward the origin from the y-intercept. The x-intercept is now 6, but the y-intercept remains at 30. If, instead, the price of x falls to \$3, then the

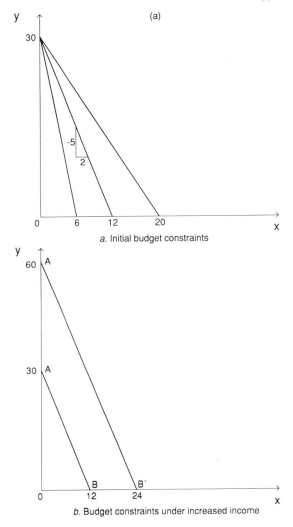

Fig. A.2. Budget line shifts

budget line pivots outward as the *x*-intercept becomes 20. For the price rise in *x*, the slope of the budget line is −5/1 in figure A.2a, while for the price fall in *x*, the slope is −3/2. Changes in the price of good *y* result in the budget line pivoting around the *x*-intercept if p_x remains fixed.

Again consider the middle budget line in figure A.2a. All points on or between the budget constraint and the two axes are affordable with the given income and prices. Points along the budget line require expenditures to exhaust income, while points inside the budget line do not exhaust income. Points beyond the budget line are not affordable unless income rises or prices fall. Bundles on the budget line are termed feasible *allocations* of the consumer's income.

A rise in income is depicted next. Suppose that income doubles so that the budget line is

$$\$5x + \$2y = \$120 . \tag{3}$$

In figure A.2b, the budget line shifts outward from AB to $A'B'$ when income doubles. As shown, an income change gives a parallel outward shift to the budget constraint. Both of the intercepts double due to the income change, but the slope, showing the consumer's ability to trade one good for another, remains unchanged.

3. Consumer Equilibrium

A consumer equilibrium is shown in figure A.3 at point E. The budget line AB denotes feasible allocations that exhaust income. An equilibrium occurs when the *desire* of the consumer to trade off (or substitute) the two goods matches the *ability* of the consumer to do so. Suppose that the consumer is at point C, where indifference curve U_1 intersects budget line AB. At point C, the consumer's ability to trade off the goods is $-p_x/p_y$, while the consumer's willingness to trade off the goods is minus the marginal rate of substitution. Since the indifference curve is steeper than the budget line at point C, the following inequality holds:

$$-\text{MRS}_{xy} < -p_x/p_y . \tag{5}$$

By removing the minus signs and cross-multiplying, we have

$$MU_x/p_x > MU_y/p_y , \tag{6}$$

or that the marginal utility per dollar spent on good x exceeds that of good y. If, therefore, the consumer reallocates expenditures between the two goods so as to buy more x and less y by moving toward point E, then utility increases as a higher indifference curve is reached.

In figure A.3, the highest feasible indifference curve is reached at the consumer's equilibrium at point E, where market basket (x_e, y_e) is purchased. If the consumer were at point D, then utility could be improved by buying more y and less x. At point E, the consumer is maximized with respect to his or her budget constraint and the following condition,

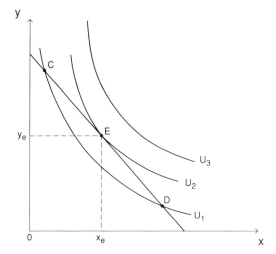

Fig. A.3.   Consumer equilibrium

$$\text{MRS}_{xy} = p_x/p_y \,, \tag{7}$$

holds as the indifference curve is tangent to the budget constraint. Equation 7 is the FOC associated with the consumer problem,

maximize $U(x, y)$

subject to $p_x x + p_y y = I$.

An FOC is a necessary condition for a maximum and identifies places where the rate of change of the objective function (here utility), when constrained, is zero. Condition 7 follows by using standard mathematical techniques. One procedure is to set up a Lagrangian expression,

$$L = U(x, y) + \lambda[I - p_x x - p_y y] \,, \tag{8}$$

in which the objective function is augmented by the constraint and λ is a Lagrangian multiplier (see Chiang 1984). Condition 7 is derived by setting the first derivatives of equation 8 with respect to x, y, and λ equal to zero and then taking ratios to eliminate λ. A second technique is to solve for x (or y) using the budget constraint, and then to substitute this solution for x (or y) in the utility function. The first derivative of this "constrained" utility function gives equation 7.

4. Derivation of Consumer Demand

The demand curve displays the relationship between the quantity demanded per unit time by the consumer and the price per unit, while holding other influences constant. These other influences include money income, the price of other goods, tastes, and expectations. To derive the demand curve, we must investigate a series of price changes for good x in an indifference diagram. In figure A.4a, the price of x is allowed to vary so that $p_x^1 > p_x^2 > p_x^3$. As the price of x falls, the budget line becomes flatter, since its slope is $-p_x/p_y$ and p_y is held constant. At each price of x, the equilibrium occurs where an indifference curve is tangent to the budget constraint. In figure A.4a, point E_1 is the equilibrium for p_x^1, E_2 for p_x^2, and E_3 for p_x^3. A price consumption curve, PC, connects these points of tangency.

At equilibrium E_i, the quantity demanded of good x is x_i. The price-consumption curve indicates an inverse relationship between the quantity demanded and the price per unit so that a decrease in the price of x is associated with an increase in the quantity demanded. The information shown in figure A.4a on the price-consumption curve can be translated to figure A.4b so as to derive the downward-sloping demand curve. In the figure, the equilibrium quantities can be translated directly to figure A.4b as shown by the dashed lines. The price levels shown in figure A.4b are related to the x-intercepts shown in figure A.4a. By way of illustration, consider the x-intercept associated with budget line TA for p_x^1. This intercept is at A so that distance $0A$ equals I/p_x^1. Consequently, p_x^1 in figure A.4a equals $I/0A$, where income is divided by distance $0A$. Similarly, $I/0B$ is the price level for p_x^2, and $I/0C$ is the price level for p_x^3. Since $0C > 0B > 0A$ and I is constant, the prices accordingly decline on the vertical axis in figure A.4b. At each point on the demand curve, the MRS equals the respective price ratio. Since the MRS is a measure of the marginal benefit of good x in terms of good y, this marginal (or marginal utility) benefit ratio equals the price ratio at every point along a demand curve.

If competitive forces are at play so that every consumer faces the same price ratio, then, in equilibrium, each equates his or her MRS to this price ratio and, in consequence, satisfies

$$\text{MRS}_{xy}^i = \text{MRS}_{xy}^j, \quad i \neq j, \tag{9}$$

which is the Pareto-optimal condition of exchange efficiency. Condition 9 corresponds to an allocation of goods between traders so that person i maximizes his or her utility subject to a constant level of utility (and, hence, an indifference curve) for individual j. In essence, a tangency between indifference curves in an Edgeworth-Bowley box relates to this exchange efficiency condition. If condition 9 were not satisfied, it would be possible to

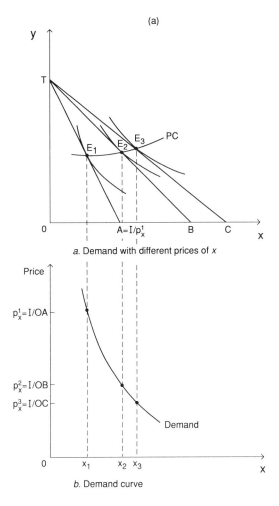

(a)

a. Demand with different prices of *x*

b. Demand curve

Fig. A.4.   Derivation of demand

redistribute goods between the two traders to increase the utility of one person without decreasing the utility of the other.

5. Income and Substitution Effects for a Price Change

For pedagogical purposes, the effects of a change in price on the quantity demanded is often separated into a substitution effect and an income effect. The substitution effect isolates the influence of the change in relative prices on the quantity demanded, while the income effect focuses on the effect of the change in purchasing power on the quantity demanded. These effects are

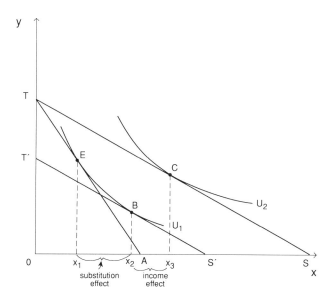

Fig. A.5.   Income and substitution effects

displayed in figure A.5 for a fall in the price of good x. Prior to this fall, the equilibrium is at point E. After the price change, the new equilibrium is at point C where x_3 is demanded. To illustrate the substitution effect, we draw price line $T'S'$ parallel to the postprice-change budget line TS. Moreover, line $T'S'$ is drawn tangent to the original indifference curve U_1. This construction removes the real income increase, as reflected by the movement to the higher indifference curve U_2. The movement from point E to B results in an increase in the quantity demanded of $x_2 - x_1$, which is the substitution effect. This change in the quantity demanded is solely the result of the relative price change as embodied in the different slopes of line TA and line $T'S'$. The movement from point B on $T'S'$ to point C on TS is the income effect, and isolates the change in the quantity demanded of $x_3 - x_2$, resulting from the increase in purchasing power. The slopes of $T'S'$ and TS are both equal to the new relative price ratio; hence, the change in the quantity demanded associated with the income effect keeps relative prices constant. The parallel shift of the two budget lines acts as an income increase.

In figure A.5, the increase in purchases of x associated with the income effect is positive, thus indicating that good x is *normal*. For a normal good, the quantity demanded increases with income. If good x is inferior, then the income effect is in the opposite direction to the substitution effect. The latter is always positive owing to the convexity of the indifference curves.

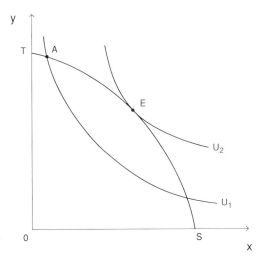

Fig. A.6.   Robinson Crusoe economy

6. A Robinson Crusoe Economy

The technique of constrained optimization can be further illustrated for a Robinson Crusoe economy in which a single person is both the sole producer and consumer of two goods—goods x and y. The constraint for the individual is his or her production possibility frontier, which depicts all combinations of the two goods that can be produced with a fixed set of resources. In figure A.6, the concave-to-the-origin production possibility frontier is displayed. This standard shape for the production possibility frontier derives, in part, from resources being more specialized or useful for the production of some goods and not others. The concave-to-the-origin shape implies increasing relative costs as production is increasingly specialized in one good. The negative of the slope of the production possibility frontier is the marginal rate of transformation of good x for good y (MRT_{xy}) and corresponds to the ratio of marginal costs in producing the two goods. For the shape displayed, the MRT increases as the production of x increases. This, in turn, implies that the marginal cost of x increases in relation to that of y as more x and less y is produced.

The nonlinear production possibility frontier serves as the constraint; points along and inside the frontier are feasible. A constrained optimum is attained at point E in figure A.6, where indifference curve U_2 is just tangent to the transformation frontier. No higher indifference curve can be reached among the feasible allocations. Other points, such as A, can be ruled out as in the budget line case. At the optimum, the consumer satisfies

$$MRS_{xy} = MRT_{xy} , \tag{10}$$

since the slopes of the two curves are equal.

Next consider an economy made up of many individuals. Once again, a production possibility frontier represents the relevant constraint, and demarcates feasible and infeasible production baskets, given technology and the fixed set of resources. In figure A.6, the indifference map is now that of a social aggregator and indicates the combinations of the two goods that hold the welfare level of this social aggregator constant. The welfare function of the social aggregator, who trades off the utilities of the individual agents, is known as a social welfare function. An optimum is again reached at the point of tangency where the economy's MRT now equals the social MRS. This equality is known as the top-level Pareto optimum and corresponds to the best assignment of resources when both exchange and production are considered.

The economy's production possibility frontier indicates all output combinations that are production efficient. *Production efficiency,* from a Pareto-optimal viewpoint, requires resources to be used in such a fashion that it is not possible to increase the output of one industry without lowering that of another. Mathematically, production efficiency requires the maximization of output of one industry subject to a given level of output in the other industries. Output is fixed along an *isoquant,* which displays all combinations of inputs that yield a constant level of output. Isoquants are analogous to indifference curves and relate to a production function,

$$Q = Q(K, L) , \tag{11}$$

which relates output, Q, to efficient combinations of capital, K, and labor, L. The slope of the isoquant is the marginal rate of technical substitution ($MRTS_{KL}$). In the two-output case, production efficiency is reached when isoquants are tangent to one another in an Edgeworth-Bowley production box with the two inputs on the axes. At production efficient points, the following equality is satisfied:

$$MRTS_{KL}^{x} = MRTS_{KL}^{y} , \tag{12}$$

where superscripts denote the industry. Since the production possibility frontier is made up of production efficient points, equation 12 is fulfilled implicitly along the frontier.

7. Essential Economic Concepts: Margin, Average, and Elasticity

Some basic economic concepts, used throughout the book, are now reviewed. Consider a function,

$$y = f(x) \ , \tag{13}$$

that relates a dependent variable, y, to an independent variable, x. Such a function gives a total value of the relationship; at any x value, the resulting y value is determined. An average function can be computed by dividing the function by the units of the independent variable:

$$y/x = f(x)/x \ . \tag{14}$$

The marginal function is derived by taking the derivative of $f(x)$ with respect to x; that is, $dy/dx = f'(x)$. The margin is the slope and is used when optimizing a function because the top of a hill (for a maximum) or the bottom of a valley (for a minimum) occurs where the slope or marginal function is zero. Since both hill tops and valley bottoms have zero slopes, so-called second-order conditions are needed to distinguish the two. These second-order conditions examine the shape of the function by analyzing how the slope itself is changing on either side of the zero-sloped maximum or minimum. If the slope is decreasing (i.e., the second derivative is negative), then a maximum has been attained; if, however, the slope is increasing, then a minimum has been reached.

The elasticity, η, of a function is a unit-free measure of responsiveness that equals the *proportional* change in the dependent variable divided by the proportional change in the independent variable:

$$\eta = \frac{dy/y}{dx/x} \ , \tag{15}$$

where d denotes a differential or change in the variable. Since both dy and y are in the same units of measurement, units cancel in the numerator. The same is true in the denominator, thus giving a unit-free measure. The elasticity can be rewritten as

$$\eta = \frac{dy/dx}{y/x} \ , \tag{16}$$

or the ratio of the margin to the average.

To illustrate, we consider a specific example—a demand function for good x,

$$x = f(p_x, I) ,$$ (17)

that depends on the good's price and on the consumer's income. The price elasticity of demand is

$$\eta_p = \frac{dx/x}{dp_x/p_x} .$$ (18)

If the proportional change in the quantity demanded exceeds (is less than) that of price, then the good's elasticity is greater (less) than one in absolute value. When the two proportional changes are equal, the good is unit elastic. The demand curve is elastic (inelastic) at those points where the price elasticity is greater (less) than one.

The ratio of the proportional change in the quantity demanded to the proportional change in income is the income elasticity. If an increase in income is associated with a positive proportional change in the quantity demanded, then the good is a normal good. Otherwise, it is inferior. In the latter case, an increase in income causes the demand curve to shift leftward and down (i.e., an increase in income leads to a decrease in the quantity demanded at each price) when graphed against price.

8. Optimization Illustrated: Profit Maximization

In microeconomics, the two key agents are the consumer and the firm. The latter combines inputs to produce an output that is then sold to maximize profit. To illustrate the simple notion of optimization, we briefly review profit maximization in the simplest of cases, where markets are competitive so that prices are beyond the control of the firm. To maximize profits, π, the competitive firm must maximize the difference between revenues or sales and the cost of production. Since sales equal price times quantity, a firm must choose quantity, q, to

$$\text{maximize } [pq - C(q)] ,$$ (19)

in which $C(q)$ denotes the firm's cost of production.

The optimization is easily conceptualized with a diagram. In figure A.7a, the firm's revenue and cost functions are displayed; q is measured on the horizontal axis, while cost and revenue are measured on the vertical axis. The revenue function is linear with a slope equal to price due to the assumption of perfect competition. The cost function starts at a height of fixed cost, which

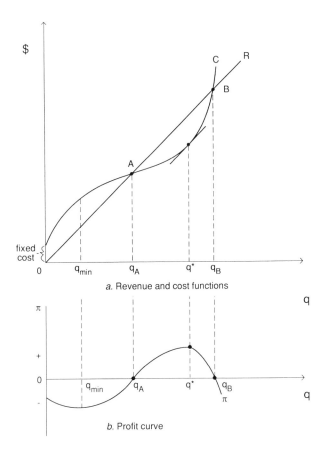

a. Revenue and cost functions

b. Profit curve

Fig. A.7. Profit maximization

has to be paid even if output is zero. Cost first rises at a decreasing rate and then rises at an increasing rate. Profit is shown in figure A.7b and corresponds to the vertical distance between the revenue and cost schedules. Profit is zero at breakeven points A and B, where revenue equals cost. To the left of A and to the right of B, profit is negative. Between q_A and q_B, profit is positive since revenue exceeds cost. Profit is maximized at q^* where the gap between the revenue and cost curves is the greatest and positive. The maximum output also corresponds to the place at which the slope of the cost curve, marginal cost (MC), equals the slope of the revenue curve. Thus, $p = $ MC at the profit maximum. Since p is also marginal revenue (MR), MR $=$ MC also identifies a possible point of profit maximization.

In figure A.7, q_{min} is the output at which profit is minimized or loss is maximized. This output also corresponds to a place where the slopes of the cost and revenue curves are equal. Consequently, the p = MC condition is not a sufficient requirement for profit maximization, since *both* profit maximums and minimums fulfill this condition. The two can be distinguished by examining whether the slope of the profit function in figure A.7b is decreasing in the vicinity of the optimum. To the left of q^*, the slope is positive, and to the right, it is negative; hence, the slope of the profit curve is, indeed, decreasing at q^*. The reader should confirm that the slope of profit is increasing in the vicinity of q_{min}.

Mathematically, the necessary condition for a profit maximum is identified by taking the first derivative of profit in equation 19 with respect to q. In doing so, we get p = MC as suggested by the diagram. This procedure identifies points where marginal profit is zero. To examine second-order conditions, we must take a second derivative of equation 19 and ensure that it is negative for a maximum. For equation 19, this requires the marginal cost curve to be rising.

References

Abrams, Burton A., and Schmitz, Mark D. "The 'Crowding-Out' Effect of Government Transfers on Private Charitable Contributions." *Public Choice* 33, no. 1 (1978): 29–41.

Akerlof, George A. "A Theory of Social Custom of Which Unemployment May Be One Consequence." *Quarterly Journal of Economics* 94 (June, 1980): 749–75.

Alchian, Armen A., and Allen, William R. *University Economics: Elements of Inquiry.* 3d ed. Belmont, CA: Wadsworth Publishing, 1972.

Andreoni, James. "Private Charity, Public Goods, and the Crowding Out Hypothesis." Manuscript. Madison: University of Wisconsin, 1987.

Andreoni, James. "Privately Provided Public Goods in a Large Economy: The Limits of Altruism." *Journal of Public Economics* 35 (February, 1988a): 57–73.

Andreoni, James. "Why Free Ride? Strategies and Learning in Public Goods Experiments." *Journal of Public Economics* 37 (December, 1988b): 291–304.

Andreoni, James. "Giving with Impure Altruism: Applications to Charity and Ricardian Equivalence." *Journal of Political Economy* 97 (December, 1989): 1447–58.

Andreoni, James. "Impure Altruism and Donations to Public Goods: A Theory of Warm-Glow Giving." *Economic Journal* 100 (June, 1990): 464–77.

Appelbaum, Elie, and Katz, Eliakim. "Transfer Seeking and Avoidance: On the Full Social Costs of Rent Seeking." *Public Choice* 48, no. 2 (1986): 175–81.

Austen-Smith, David. "Voluntary Pressure Groups." *Economica* 48 (May, 1981): 143–53.

Axelrod, Robert. *The Evolution of Cooperation.* New York: Basic Books, 1984.

Bagnoli, Mark, and Lipman, Barton L. "Provision of Public Goods: Fully Implementing the Core through Private Contributions." *Review of Economic Studies* 56 (October, 1989): 583–601.

Bagnoli, Mark, and McKee, Michael. "Voluntary Contribution Games: Efficient Private Provision of Public Goods." *Economic Inquiry* 29 (April, 1991): 351–66.

Baumol, William J.; Panzar, John C.; and Willig, Robert D. *Contestable Markets and the Theory of Industry Structure.* Revised ed. San Diego: Harcourt Brace Jovanovich, 1988.

Becker, Gary S. "A Theory of Social Interactions." *Journal of Political Economy* 82 (November/December, 1974): 1063–93.

Berglas, Eitan. "On the Theory of Clubs." *American Economic Review,* 66 (May, 1976): 116–21.

Berglas, Eitan. "The Market Provision of Club Goods Once Again." *Journal of Public Economics* 15 (June, 1981): 389–93.

Bergstrom, Theodore C.; Blume, Lawrence; and Varian, Hal. "On the Private Provision of Public Goods." *Journal of Public Economics* 29 (February, 1986): 25–49.

Bergstrom, Theodore C., and Goodman, Robert P. "Private Demands for Public Goods." *American Economic Review* 63 (June, 1973): 280–96.

Bernheim, B. Douglas. "On the Voluntary and Involuntary Provision of Public Goods." *American Economic Review* 76 (September, 1986): 789–93.

Bianco, William T., and Bates, Robert H. "Cooperation by Design: Leadership, Structure, and Collective Dilemmas." *American Political Science Review* 84 (March, 1990): 133–47.

Blümel, Wolfgang; Pethig, Rüdiger; and von dem Hagen, Oskar. "The Theory of Public Goods: A Survey of Recent Issues." *Zeitschrift für die Gesamte Staatwissenschaft* 142 (June, 1986): 241–309.

Booth, Alison L. "A Public Choice Model of Trade Union Behavior and Membership." *Economic Journal* 94 (December, 1984): 883–98.

Booth, Alison L. "The Free Rider Problem and a Social Custom Model of Trade Union Membership." *Quarterly Journal of Economics* 100 (February, 1985): 253–61.

Borcherding, Thomas E., and Deacon, Robert T. "The Demand for the Services of Non-Federal Governments." *American Economic Review* 62 (December, 1972): 891–901.

Boyer, Mark. "Trading Public Goods in the Western Alliance System." *Journal of Conflict Resolution* 33 (December, 1989): 700–727.

Bruce, Neil. "Defense Expenditures by Countries in Allied and Adversarial Relationships." *Defence Economics* 1 (May, 1990): 179–95.

Buchanan, James M. "An Economic Theory of Clubs." *Economica* 32 (February, 1965): 1–14.

Cauley, Jon, and Sandler, Todd. "Agency Theory and the Chinese Enterprise under Reform." Manuscript. Hilo, HI: University of Hawaii at Hilo, 1991.

Cauley, Jon; Sandler, Todd; and Cornes, Richard. "Nonmarket Institutional Structures: Conjectures, Distribution, and Efficiency." *Public Finance* 41, no. 2 (1986): 153–72.

Chamberlin, John. "Provision of Collective Goods as a Function of Group Size." *American Political Science Review* 68 (June, 1974): 707–16.

Chiang, Alpha C. *Fundamental Methods of Mathematical Economics.* 3d ed. New York: McGraw-Hill, 1984.

Choi, Kwang. "A Statistical Test of Olson's Model." In Dennis Mueller, ed., *The Political Economy of Growth,* 57–58. New Haven: Yale University Press, 1983.

Clarke, Edward. "Multipart Pricing of Public Goods." *Public Choice* 11 (Fall, 1971): 17–33.

Clarke, Edward. "Multipart Pricing of Public Goods: An Example." In S. Mushkin, ed., *Public Prices for Public Products,* 125–30. Washington, DC: Urban Institute, 1972.

Clotfelter, Charles T. *Tax Incentives and Charitable Giving.* Chicago: University of Chicago Press, 1985.

Conybeare, John, and Sandler, Todd. "The Triple Entente and the Triple Alliance, 1880–1914: A Collective Goods Approach." Manuscript. Ames, IA: Iowa State University, 1989.

Conybeare, John, and Sandler, Todd. "The Triple Entente and the Triple Alliance, 1880–1914: A Collective Goods Approach." *American Political Science Review* 84 (December, 1990): 1197–1206.

Cornes, Richard; Mason, Charles; and Sandler, Todd. "The Commons and the Optimal Number of Firms." *Quarterly Journal of Economics* 101 (August, 1986): 641–46.

Cornes, Richard, and Sandler, Todd. "Easy Riders, Joint Production, and Collective Action." Working Paper no. 060 in Economics and Econometrics. Canberra: Australian National University, 1981.

Cornes, Richard, and Sandler, Todd. "On Commons and Tragedies." *American Economic Review* 73 (September, 1983): 787–92.

Cornes, Richard, and Sandler, Todd. "Easy Riders, Joint Production, and Public Goods." *Economic Journal* 94 (September, 1984a): 580–98.

Cornes, Richard, and Sandler, Todd. "The Theory of Public Goods: Non-Nash Behaviour." *Journal of Public Economics* 23 (April, 1984b): 367–79.

Cornes, Richard, and Sandler, Todd. "The Simple Analytics of Pure Public Good Provision." *Economica* 52 (February, 1985): 103–16.

Cornes, Richard, and Sandler, Todd. *The Theory of Externalities, Public Goods, and Club Goods.* New York: Cambridge University Press, 1986.

Dasgupta, Dipankar, and Itaya, Jun-ichi. "Comparative Statics for the Private Provision of Public Goods in a Conjectural Variations Model with Heterogeneous Agents." Manuscript. Otaru, Japan: Otaru University of Commerce, 1991.

Deacon, Robert. "A Demand Model for the Local Public Sector." *Review of Economics and Statistics* 60 (May, 1978): 184–92.

Deaton, Angus, and Muellbauer, John. *Economics and Consumer Behavior.* New York: Cambridge University Press, 1980.

de Gorter, Harry, and Zilberman, David. "On the Political Economy of Public Good Inputs in Agriculture." *American Journal of Agricultural Economics* 72 (February, 1990): 131–37.

de Jasay, Anthony. *Social Contract, Free Ride: A Study of the Public Goods Problem.* Oxford: Oxford University Press, 1989.

Denzau, Arthur, and Grier, Kevin. "Determinants of Local School Spending: Some Consistent Estimates." *Public Choice* 44, no. 2 (1984): 375–83.

Dixit, Avinash K. *Optimization in Economic Theory.* 2d ed. Oxford: Oxford University Press, 1990.

Dudley, Leonard, and Montmarquette, Claude. "The Demand for Military Expenditures: An International Comparison." *Public Choice* 37, no. 1 (1981): 5–31.

Farrell, Joseph. "Cheap Talk, Coordination, and Entry." *Rand Journal of Economics* 18 (Spring, 1987): 34–39.

Fershtman, Chaim, and Nitzan, Shmuel. "Dynamic Voluntary Provision of Public Goods." *European Economic Review* 35 (July, 1991): 1057–67.

Forbes, John. "International Cooperation in Public Health and the World Health Organization." In Todd Sandler, ed., *The Theory and Structures of International Political Economy,* 115–31. Boulder, CO: Westview, 1980.

Frohlich, Norman, and Oppenheimer, Joe A. *Modern Political Economy.* Englewood Cliffs, NJ: Prentice-Hall, 1978.

Gardner, Roy, and Ostrom, Elinor. "Rules and Games." *Public Choice* 70 (May, 1991): 121–49.

Gardner, Roy; Ostrom, Elinor; and Walker, James. "The Nature of Common-Pool Resource Problems." *Rationality and Society* 2 (July, 1990): 335–58.

Goff, Brian L., and Tollison, Robert D. "Is National Defense a Pure Public Good?" *Defence Economics* 1 (February, 1990): 141–47.

Gonzales, Rodolfo A., and Mehay, Stephen L. "Publicness, Scale, and Spillover Effects in Defense Spending." *Public Finance Quarterly* 18 (July, 1990): 273–90.

Gonzales, Rodolfo A., and Mehay, Stephen L. "Burden Sharing in the NATO Alliance: An Empirical Test of Alternative Views." *Public Choice* 68 (January, 1991): 107–16.

Gradstein, Mark; Nitzan, Shmuel; and Slutsky, Steven. "Private Provision of Public Goods under Price Uncertainty." Manuscript. 1988a.

Gradstein, Mark; Nitzan, Shmuel; and Slutsky, Steven. "Neutrality and the Private Provision of Public Goods with Incomplete Information." Manuscript. 1988b.

Groves, Theodore. "Incentives in Teams." *Econometrica* 41 (July, 1973): 617–31.

Groves, Theodore, and Loeb, Martin. "Incentives and Public Inputs." *Journal of Public Economics* 4 (August, 1975): 211–26.

Guttman, Joel M. "Understanding Collective Action: Matching Behavior." *American Economic Review* 68 (May, 1978): 251–55.

Guttman, Joel M. "A Non-Cournot Model of Voluntary Collective Action." *Economica* 54 (February, 1987): 1–19.

Hansen, Laurna; Murdoch, James C.; and Sandler, Todd. "On Distinguishing the Behavior of Nuclear and Non-Nuclear Allies in NATO." *Defence Economics* 1 (January, 1990): 37–55.

Hansmann, Henry. "The Role of Nonprofit Enterprise." *Yale Law Journal* 89 (April, 1980): 835–901.

Hardin, Garrett. "The Tragedy of the Commons." *Science* 162 (1968): 1243–48.

Hardin, Russell. *Collective Action.* Baltimore: Johns Hopkins University Press, 1982.

Harrison, Glenn W., and Hirshleifer, Jack. "An Experimental Evaluation of Weakest Link/Best Shot Models of Public Goods." *Journal of Political Economy* 97 (February, 1989): 201–23.

Henderson, J. V. "A Note on the Economics of Intermediate Inputs." *Economica* 41 (August, 1974): 322–27.

Hillman, Arye L. "Symmetries and Asymmetries between Public Input and Public Good Equilibria." *Public Finance* 33, no. 3 (1978): 269–79.

Hirshleifer, Jack. "From Weakest-Link to Best Shot: The Voluntary Provision of Public Goods." *Public Choice* 41, no. 3 (1983): 371–86.

Hoel, Michael. "Global Environmental Problems: The Effects of Unilateral Actions Taken by One Country." *Journal of Environmental Economics and Management.* 20 (January, 1991): 55–70.

Holmstrom, Bengt. "Moral Hazard in Teams." *Bell Journal of Economics* 13 (Autumn, 1982): 324–40.

Houghton, Richard A., and Woodwell, George M. "Global Climate Change." *Scientific American* 260 (April, 1989): 36–44.

Inman, Robert P. "Testing Political Economy's 'As If' Proposition: Is the Median Income Voter Really Decisive?" *Public Choice* 33, no. 4 (1978): 45–65.

International Monetary Fund. *International Financial Statistics Yearbook*. Washington, DC: International Monetary Fund, various years.

Isaac, R. Mark, and Walker, James M. "Group Size Effects in Public Goods Provision: The Voluntary Contribution Mechanism." *Quarterly Journal of Economics* 103 (February, 1988a): 179–99.

Isaac, R. Mark, and Walker, James M. "Communication and Free-Riding Behavior: The Voluntary Contribution Mechanism." *Economic Inquiry* 24 (October, 1988b): 585–608.

Isaac, R. Mark; Walker, James M.; and Thomas, Susan H. "Divergent Evidence on Free Riding: An Experimental Examination of Possible Explanations." *Public Choice* 43, no. 2 (1984): 113–49.

Jack, Bryan, and Olson, Mancur. "War Neutrality and the Natural Egalitarianism of Voluntary Public Good Provision." Manuscript. College Park, MD: University of Maryland, 1991.

Johnson, Ronald N., and Libecap, Gary D. "Contracting Problems and Regulation: The Case of the Fishery." *American Economic Review* 72 (December, 1982): 1005–22.

Kaizuku, Keimei. "Public Goods and Decentralization of Production." *Review of Economics and Statistics* 47 (February, 1965): 118–20.

Katz, Eliakim; Nitzam, Shmuel; and Rosenberg, Jacob. "Rent-Seeking for Pure Public Goods." *Public Choice* 65, no. 1 (1990): 49–60.

Khanna, Jyoti. "Cooperative Versus Noncooperative Behavior: The Case of Agricultural Research." Manuscript. Cleveland, OH: Cleveland State University, 1991.

Khanna, Jyoti; Huffman, Wallace E.; and Sandler, Todd. "State Government Decisions on Goods Having Joint Public-Private Characteristics: An Econometric Examination of Agricultural Research." Manuscript. Ames, IA: Iowa State University, 1990.

Kim, Iltae. "The Effects of Uncertainty on the Public Good: The Case of Nash and Non-Nash Behavior." Manuscript. Kwangju, South Korea: Chonnam National University, 1991.

Kim, Oliver, and Walker, Mark. "The Free Rider Problem: Experimental Evidence." *Public Choice* 43, no. 1 (1984): 3–24.

Ko, Il-Dong; Lapan, Harvey E.; and Sandler, Todd. "Controlling Stock Externalities: Flexible Versus Inflexible Pigouvian Corrections." *European Economic Review* 36 (1992). In press.

Kohli, Ulrich. "Technology and Public Goods." *Journal of Public Economics* 26 (April, 1985): 379–400.

Kreps, David, and Wilson, Robert. "Sequential Equilibria." *Econometrica* 50 (July, 1982): 863–94.

Krueger, Anne O. "The Political Economy of Rent-Seeking Society." *American Economic Review* 64 (June, 1974): 291–303.

Krugman, Paul R. "Is Free Trade Passé?" *Journal of Economic Perspectives* 1 (Fall, 1987): 131–44.

Kuran, Timur. "Sparks and Prairie Fires: A Theory of Unanticipated Political Revolution." *Public Choice* 61, no. 1 (1989): 41–74.

Kuran, Timur. "The East European Revolution of 1989: Is It Surprising That We Were Surprised?" *American Economic Review* 81 (May, 1991): 121–25.

Lee, Dwight R. "Free Riding and Paid Riding in the Fight Against Terrorism." *American Economic Review* 78 (May, 1988): 22–26.

Libecap, Gary D. *Contracting for Property Rights.* New York: Cambridge University Press, 1990.

Libecap, Gary D., and Wiggins, Steven N. "Contracting Responses to the Common Pool: Prorationing of Crude Oil Production." *American Economic Review* 74 (March, 1984): 87–98.

Lichbach, Mark I. "Deterrence or Escalation? The Puzzle of Aggregate Studies of Repression and Dissent." *Journal of Conflict Resolution* 31 (June, 1987): 266–97.

Lipnowski, Irwin, and Maital, Shlomo. "Voluntary Provision of a Pure Public Good as the Game of Chicken." *Journal of Public Economics* 20 (April, 1983): 381–86.

Luce, R. Duncan, and Raiffa, Howard. *Games and Decisions.* New York: Wiley, 1957.

MacDonald, Glenn. "New Directions in the Economic Theory of Agency." *Canadian Journal of Economics* 17 (August, 1984): 415–40.

McGuire, Martin C. "Group Size, Group Homogeneity, and the Aggregate Provision of a Pure Public Good Under Cournot Behavior." *Public Choice* 18 (Summer, 1974): 107–26.

McGuire, Martin C. "U.S. Assistance, Israeli Allocation, and the Arms Race in the Middle East." *Journal of Conflict Resolution* 26 (June, 1982): 199–235.

McGuire, Martin C. "Mixed Public-Private Benefit and Public-Good Supply with Application to the NATO Alliance." *Defence Economics* 1 (January, 1990): 17–35.

McGuire, Martin C., and Groth, Carl H. "A Method for Identifying the Public Good Allocation Process Within a Group." *Quarterly Journal of Economics* 100, supplement (1985): 915–34.

MacKinnon, James G.; White, Halbert; and Davidson, Russell. "Test for Model Specification in the Presence of Alternative Hypotheses: Some Further Results." *Journal of Econometrics* 21 (January, 1983): 53–70.

McMillan, John. "The Free-Rider Problem: A Survey." *Economic Record* 55 (June, 1979a): 95–107.

McMillan, John. "Individual Incentives in the Supply of Public Inputs." *Journal of Public Economics* 12 (August, 1979b): 87–98.

McMillan, John. *Game Theory in International Economics.* Chur, Switzerland: Harwood Academic Publishers, 1986.

Manning, Richard; Markusen, James R.; and McMillan, John. "Paying for Public Inputs." *American Economic Review* 75 (March, 1985): 235–38.

Martin, Robert E.; Zacharias, Thomas P.; and Lange, Mark D. "Public Inputs in Agriculture." Manuscript. Baton Rouge: Louisiana Agricultural Experiment Station, 1990.

Marwell, Gerald, and Ames, Ruth F. "Economists Free Ride, Does Anyone Else? Experiments on the Provision of Public Goods." *Journal of Public Economics* 15 (June, 1981): 295–310.

Mickolus, Edward F. *Transnational Terrorism: A Chronology of Events, 1968–1979.* Westport, CT: Greenwood, 1980.

Mishan, Erza J. "The Relationship Between Joint Products, Collective Goods, and External Effects." *Journal of Political Economy* 77 (May/June, 1969): 329–48.

Mohnen, Volker A. "The Challenge of Acid Rain." *Scientific American* 259 (August, 1988): 30–38.

Mohring, Herbert. "The Peak Load Problem with Increasing Returns and Pricing Constraints." *American Economic Review* 60 (September, 1970): 693–705.

Mohring, Herbert, and Boyd, J. Hayden. "Analyzing 'Externalities': 'Direct Interaction' vs. 'Asset Utilization' Framework." *Economica* 38 (November, 1971): 347–61.

Morgenstern, Richard D. "Towards a Comprehensive Approach to Global Climate Change Mitigation." *American Economic Review* 81 (May, 1991): 140–45.

Morrisette, Peter M., and Plantinga, Andrew J. "The Global Warming Issue: Viewpoints of Different Countries." *Resources*, no. 103 (Spring, 1991): 2–6.

Mueller, Dennis C. *Public Choice II.* New York: Cambridge University Press, 1989.

Murdoch, James C., and Sandler, Todd. "A Theoretical and Empirical Analysis of NATO." *Journal of Conflict Resolution* 26 (June, 1982): 237–63.

Murdoch, James C., and Sandler, Todd. "Complementarity, Free Riding, and the Military Expenditures of NATO Allies." *Journal of Public Economics* 25 (November, 1984): 83–101.

Murdoch, James C.; Sandler, Todd; and Hansen, Laurna. "An Econometric Technique for Comparing Median Voter and Oligarchy Choice Models of Collective Action: The Case of the NATO Alliance." *Review of Economics and Statistics* 73 (November, 1991): 624–31.

Murrell, Peter. "The Comparative Structure of the Growth of the West German and British Manufacturing Industries." In Dennis Mueller, ed., *The Political Economy of Growth*, 109–31. New Haven: Yale University Press, 1983.

Negishi, Takashi. "The Excess of Public Expenditures on Industries." *Journal of Public Economics* 2 (July, 1973): 231–40.

Nitzan, Shmuel, and Romano, Richard E. "Private Provision of a Discrete Public Good with Uncertain Cost." *Journal of Public Economics* 42 (August, 1990): 357–70.

Nordhaus, William D. "A Sketch of the Economics of the Greenhouse Effect." *American Economic Review* 81 (May, 1991): 146–50.

Olson, Mancur. *The Logic of Collective Action.* Cambridge, MA: Harvard University Press, 1965.

Olson, Mancur. *The Rise and Decline of Nations.* New Haven: Yale University Press, 1982.

Olson, Mancur, and Zeckhauser, Richard. "An Economic Theory of Alliances." *Review of Economics and Statistics* 48 (August, 1966): 266–79.

Olson, Mancur, and Zeckhauser, Richard. "Collective Goods, Comparative Advantage, and Alliance Efficiency." In Roland McKean, ed., *Issues of Defense Economics*, 25–48. New York: National Bureau of Economic Research, 1967.

Oneal, John R., and Elrod, Mark A. "NATO Burden Sharing and the Forces of Change." *International Studies Quarterly* 33 (December, 1989): 435–56.

Ordeshook, Peter C. *Game Theory and Political Theory*. New York: Cambridge University Press, 1986.

Ostrom, Elinor. "The Implications of the Logic of Collective Inaction for Administrative Theory." Manuscript. Bloomington: Indiana University, 1987.

Ostrom, Elinor. *Governing the Commons: The Evolution of Institutions for Collective Action*. New York: Cambridge University Press, 1990.

Ostrom, Elinor, and Nitzan, Shmuel. "The Nature and Severity of Collective Action Problems—The Voluntary Provision of Mixed Public Goods Approach." Manuscript. Bloomington: Workshop in Political Theory and Policy Analysis, 1990.

Ostrom, Elinor; Walker, James; and Gardner, Roy. "Covenants with and without a Sword: Self-Enforcement is Possible." Manuscript. Bloomington: Indiana University, 1991.

Palfrey, Thomas R., and Rosenthal, Howard. "Participation and the Provision of Discrete Public Goods: A Strategic Analysis." *Journal of Public Economics* 24 (July, 1984): 171–93.

Palmer, Glenn. "Alliance Politics and Issue Areas: Determinants of Defense Spending." *American Journal of Political Science* 34 (February, 1990): 190–211.

Pauly, Mark V. "Clubs, Commonality, and the Core: An Integration of Game Theory and the Theory of Public Goods." *Economica* 34 (August, 1967): 314–24.

Pauly, Mark V. "Optimality, 'Public' Goods, and Local Governments: A General Theoretical Analysis." *Journal of Political Economy* 78 (May/June, 1970): 572–85.

Pethig, Rüdiger, ed. *Public Goods and Public Allocation Policy*. Frankfurt am Main: Verlag Peter Lang, 1985.

Pommerehne, Werner W. "Institutional Approaches to Public Expenditures: Empirical Evidence from Swiss Municipalities." *Journal of Public Economics* 9 (April, 1978): 163–201.

Pommerehne, Werner W., and Frey, Bruno S. "Two Approaches to Estimating Public Expenditures." *Public Finance Quarterly* 4 (October, 1976): 395–407.

Posner, Richard A. "The Social Costs of Monopoly and Regulation." *Journal of Political Economy* 83 (August, 1975): 807–27.

Posnett, John. "Trends in the Income of Registered Charities, 1980–1985." In *Charity Trends 1986/87*, 6–8. Tonbridge: Charities Aid Foundations, 1987.

Posnett, John, and Sandler, Todd. "Joint Supply and the Finance of Charitable Activity." *Public Finance Quarterly* 14 (April, 1986): 209–22.

Posnett, John, and Sandler, Todd. "Transfers, Transaction Costs and Charitable Intermediaries." *International Review of Law and Economics* 8 (December, 1988): 145–60.

Posnett, John, and Sandler, Todd. "Demand for Charity Donations in Private Non-Profit Markets: The Case of the U.K." *Journal of Public Economics* 40 (November, 1989): 187–200.

Rasmusen, Eric. "Moral Hazard in Risk-Averse Teams." *Rand Journal of Economics* 18 (Autumn, 1987): 428–35.

Repetto, Robert. "Deforestation in the Tropics." *Scientific American* 262 (April, 1990): 36–42.

Roberts, Russell D. "A Positive Model of Private Charity and Public Transfers." *Journal of Political Economy* 92 (February, 1984): 136–48.

Ross, Stephen A. "The Economic Theory of Agency: The Principal's Problem." *American Economic Review* 63 (May, 1973): 134–39.

Runge, C. Ford. "Institutions and the Free Rider: The Assurance Problem in Collective Action." *Journal of Politics* 46 (February, 1984): 154–81.

Samuelson, Paul A. "A Diagrammatic Exposition of a Theory of Public Expenditure." *Review of Economics and Statistics* 37 (November, 1955): 350–56.

Sandler, Todd. "Impurity of Defense: An Application to the Economics of Alliances." *Kyklos* 30, no. 3 (1977): 443–60.

Sandler, Todd. "Club Optimality: Further Clarifications." *Economics Letters* 14, no. 1 (1984): 61–65.

Sandler, Todd. "Sharing Burdens in NATO." *Challenge* 31 (March/April, 1988): 29–35.

Sandler, Todd, and Cauley, Jon. "On the Economic Theory of Alliances." *Journal of Conflict Resolution* 19 (June, 1975): 330–48.

Sandler, Todd, and Forbes, John F. "Burden Sharing, Strategy, and the Design of NATO." *Economic Inquiry* 18 (July, 1980): 425–44.

Sandler, Todd, and Lapan, Harvey E. "The Calculus of Dissent: An Analysis of Terrorists' Choice of Targets." *Synthese* 76 (August, 1988): 245–61.

Sandler, Todd, and Murdoch, James C. "Nash-Cournot or Lindahl Behavior?: An Empirical Test for the NATO Allies." *Quarterly Journal of Economics* 105 (November, 1990): 875–94.

Sandler, Todd, and Posnett, John. "The Private Provision of Public Goods: A Perspective on Neutrality." *Public Finance Quarterly* 19 (January, 1991): 22–42.

Sandler, Todd, and Sterbenz, Frederic P. "Harvest Uncertainty and the Tragedy of the Commons." *Journal of Environmental Economics and Management* 18 (March, 1990): 155–67.

Sandler, Todd; Sterbenz, Frederic P.; and Posnett, John. "Free Riding and Uncertainty." *European Economic Review* 31 (December, 1987): 1605–17.

Sandler, Todd, and Tschirhart, John. "The Economic Theory of Clubs: An Evaluative Survey." *Journal of Economic Literature* 18 (December, 1980): 1481–1521.

Sandler, Todd, and Tschirhart, John. "Mixed Clubs: Further Observations." *Journal of Public Economics* 23 (April, 1984): 381–89.

Sandler, Todd, and Tschirhart, John. "Multiproduct Clubs: Membership and Sustainability." Manuscript. Ames, IA: Iowa State University, 1991.

Sandmo, Agnar. "Optimality Rules for the Provision of Collective Factors of Production." *Journal of Public Economics* 1 (April, 1972): 149–57.

Sandmo, Agnar. "Public Goods and the Technology of Consumption." *Review of Economic Studies* 40 (October, 1973): 517–28.

Schelling, Thomas C. *The Strategy of Conflict.* Cambridge, MA: Harvard University Press, 1960.

Schelling, Thomas C. "Hockey Helmets, Concealed Weapons, and Daylight Saving: A Study of Binary Choices with Externalities." *Journal of Conflict Resolution* 17 (September, 1973): 381–428.

Schneider, Stephen H. "The Changing Climate." *Scientific American* 261 (September, 1989): 70–79.

Schotter, Andrew. *The Economic Theory of Social Institutions.* New York: Cambridge University Press, 1980.

Scotchmer, Suzanne. "Profit-Maximizing Clubs." *Journal of Public Economics* 27 (June, 1985): 25–45.

Scotchmer, Suzanne. "Public Goods and the Invisible Hand." Manuscript. Berkeley: University of California, 1991.

Scotchmer, Suzanne, and Wooders, Myrna H. "Competitive Equilibrium and the Core in Club Economies with Anonymous Crowding." *Journal of Public Economics* 34 (November, 1987): 159–73.

Selten, Reinhardt. "Reexamination of the Perfectness Concept for Equilibrium Points in Extensive Games." *International Journal of Game Theory* 4, no. 1 (1975): 25–55.

Sen, Amartya K. "Isolation, Assurance, and the Social Rate of Discount." *Quarterly Journal of Economics* 81 (February, 1967): 112–24.

Shibata, Hirofumi. "A Bargaining Model of Pure Theory of Public Expenditure." *Journal of Political Economy* 79 (February, 1971): 1–29.

Shogren, Jason F. "Negative Conjectures and Increased Public Good Provision." *Economics Letters* 23, no. 2, (1987): 181–84.

Shogren, Jason F. "On Increased Risk and the Voluntary Provision of Public Goods." *Social Choice and Welfare* 7 (July, 1990): 221–29.

Smith, Adam. *The Wealth of Nations.* Edited by Edwin Cannan. Chicago: University of Chicago Press, 1976.

Smith, Ron P. "The Demand for Military Expenditures." *Economic Journal* 90 (December, 1980): 811–20.

Stegeman, Mark. "Advertising in Competitive Markets." *American Economic Review* 81 (March, 1991): 210–23.

Steinberg, Richard. "Charitable Giving As a Mixed Public/Private Good: Implications for Tax Policy." *Public Finance Quarterly* 14 (October, 1986): 415–31.

Steinberg, Richard. "Voluntary Donations and Public Expenditures in a Federalist System." *American Economic Review* 77 (March, 1987): 24–36.

Sterbenz, Frederic P., and Sandler, Todd. "Sharing Among Clubs: A Club of Clubs Theory." *Oxford Economic Papers* 44 (January, 1992): 1–19.

Stiglitz, Joseph A. "Risk Sharing and Incentives in Sharecropping." *Review of Economic Studies* 61 (April, 1974): 219–56.

Stockholm International Peace Research Institute. *World Armaments and Disarmament: SIPRI Yearbook.* New York: Crane, Russak and Co., various years.

Stolarski, Richard S. "The Antarctic Ozone Hole." *Scientific American* 258 (January, 1988): 30–36.

Sugden, Robert. "On the Economics of Philanthropy." *Economic Journal* 92 (June, 1982): 341–50.

Sugden, Robert. "Reciprocity: The Supply of Public Goods Through Voluntary Contributions." *Economic Journal* 94 (December, 1984): 772–87.

Taylor, Michael. *The Possibility of Cooperation.* New York: Cambridge University Press, 1987.

Thies, Wallace J. "Alliances and Collective Goods: A Reappraisal." *Journal of Conflict Resolution* 31 (June, 1987): 298–332.

Thucydides. *The Peloponnesian War.* Translated by Rex Warner. Baltimore: Penguin, 1970.

Tiebout, Charles M. "A Pure Theory of Local Expenditures." *Journal of Political Economy* 64 (October, 1956): 416–24.

Tollison, Robert D. "Rent Seeking: A Survey." *Kyklos* 35, no. 4, (1982): 35, 575–602.

Toon, Owen R., and Turco, Richard P. "Polar Stratospheric Clouds and Ozone Depletion." *Scientific American* 264 (June, 1991): 68–74.

Tullock, Gordon. "The Welfare Costs of Tariffs, Monopolies, and Theft." *Western Economic Journal* 5 (June, 1967): 224–32.

Tullock, Gordon. *The Social Dilemma: The Economics of War and Revolution.* Blacksburg, VA: University Publications, 1974.

Tullock, Gordon. "Efficient Rent Seeking." In James Buchanan, Robert Tollison, and Gordon Tullock, eds., *Toward a Theory of the Rent-Seeking Society,* 3–15. College Station: Texas A&M University Press, 1980.

U.S. Congressional Budget Office. "Costs of Operation Desert Shield." Congressional Budget Office Staff Memorandum. Washington, DC: Congressional Budget Office, 1991a.

U.S. Congressional Budget Office. "Statement of Robert D. Reischauer, Director, Congressional Budget Office." Congressional Budget Office Testimony. Washington, DC: Congressional Budget Office, 1991b.

U.S. Department of State. *Patterns of Global Terrorism.* Washington, DC: U.S. Department of State, 1990.

van de Kragt, Alphons J. C.; Orbell, John M.; and Dawes, Robyn M. "The Minimal Contribution Set as a Solution to Public Goods Problems." *American Political Science Review* 77 (March, 1983): 112–22.

Vedder, Richard, and Gallaway, Lowell. "Rent-Seeking, Distributional Coalitions, Taxes, Relative Prices and Economic Growth." *Public Choice* 51, no. 1 (1986): 93–100.

Vicary, Simon. "Transfers and the Weakest Link: An Extension of Hirshleifer's Analysis." *Journal of Public Economics* 43 (December, 1990): 375–94.

Walker, James M.; Gardner, Roy; and Ostrom, Elinor. "Rent Dissipation in Limited-Access Common-Pool Resources: Experimental Evidence." *Journal of Environmental Economics and Management* 19 (November, 1990): 203–11.

Warr, Peter G. "Pareto Optimal Redistribution and Private Charity." *Journal of Public Economics* 19 (October, 1982): 131–38.

Warr, Peter G. "The Private Provision of a Public Good Is Independent of the Distribution of Income." *Economics Letters* 13 (1983): 207–11.

Weisbrod, Burton. *The Nonprofit Economy.* Cambridge, MA: Harvard University Press, 1988.

Weisbrod, Burton, and Dominguez, Nestor D. "Demand for Collective Goods in Private Nonprofit Markets: Can Fundraising Expenditures Help Overcome Free-Riding Behavior?" *Journal of Public Economics* 30 (June, 1986): 83–95.

White, Robert M. "The Great Climate Debate." *Scientific American* 263 (July, 1990): 36–43.

Williamson, Oliver. *Markets and Hierarchies: Analysis and Antitrust Implications.* New York: Free Press, 1975.

Author Index

Subject Index